CompTIA Se

Get Certified Get Ahead

SY0-401 Practice Test Questions

By Darril Gibson

CompTIA Security+: Get Certified Get Ahead SY0-401 Practice Test Questions

YCDA, LLC,
1124 Knights Bridge Lane,
Virginia Beach, VA, 23455

YCDA, LLC books may be purchased for educational, business, or sales promotional use. For information, please contact Darril Gibson at darril@darrilgibson.com.

Technical editor: Steve Johnson
Book cover: Denise Kelly
ISBN-10: 1-939136-03-2
ISBN-13: 978-1-939136-03-9

Dedication

To all the readers that have sent me notes indicating one or more of my books or resources have helped them pass an exam. I'm very grateful I am able to help others get certified and get ahead, and I treasure these emails.

Acknowledgements

Books of this size and depth can't be done by a single person, and I'm grateful for the many people who helped me put this book together. First, thanks to my wife. She has provided me immeasurable support throughout this project.

These questions were derived from the full study guide and I had some great help from several people on that book. The technical editor, Steve Johnson, provided some good feedback throughout the project.

I'm extremely grateful for all the skills and expertise of Karen Annett. She's an awesome copy editor and proofer and even though she didn't edit this book directly, she did edit all the questions in this book.

While I certainly appreciate all the feedback everyone gave me, I want to stress that any technical errors that may have snuck into this book are entirely my fault and no reflection on anyone who helped. I always strive to identify and remove every error, but they still seem to sneak in.

About the Author

Darril Gibson is the CEO of YCDA, LLC (short for You Can Do Anything). He has contributed to more than 35 books as the sole author, a coauthor, or a technical editor. Darril regularly writes, consults, and teaches on a wide variety of technical and security topics and holds several certifications, including CompTIA A+, Network+, Security+, and CASP; (ISC)2 SSCP and CISSP; Microsoft MCSE and MCITP, and ITIL Foundations.

In response to repeated requests, Darril created the **http://gcgapremium.com/** site where he provides study materials for several certification exams, including the Security+ exam. Darril regularly posts blog articles at **http://blogs.getcertifiedgetahead.com/**, and uses this site to help people stay abreast of changes in certification exams. You can contact him through either of these sites.

Darril lives in Virginia Beach with his wife and two dogs. Whenever possible, they escape to a small cabin in the country on over twenty acres of land that continue to provide them with peace, tranquility, and balance.

Table of Contents

Introduction

Congratulations on your purchase of this CompTIA Security+: Get Certified Get Ahead Practice Test Questions. You are one step closer to becoming CompTIA Security+ certified. This certification has helped many individuals get ahead in their jobs and their careers, and it can help you get ahead, too.

It is a popular certification within the IT field. One IT hiring manager told me that if a résumé doesn't include the Security+ certification, or a higher-level security certification, he simply sets it aside. He won't even talk to applicants. That's not the same with all IT hiring managers, but it does help illustrate how important security is within the IT field.

Who This Book Is For

This book isn't a full study guide, but is instead a set of practice test questions derived from the full CompTIA Security+ Get Certified Get Ahead SY0-401 Study Guide. The Study Guide has a lot more content explaining all of the concepts and the content. However, if you've used other resources to study, this set of practice test questions can help you test your knowledge and readiness for the live exam. Some people have also told me they found it helpful as a supplement to the Study Guide because it has helped them focus on individual domains

It's organized into six chapters with each chapter covering one of the Security+ Domains. The chapters have different numbers of questions, based on the percent of examination content and the topics covered. The six Security+ domains are:

- **Chapter 1 Network Security.** 20 percent.
- **Chapter 2 Compliance and Operational Security.** 18 percent.

- **Chapter 3 Threats and Vulnerabilities.** 20 percent.
- **Chapter 4 Application, Data and Host Security.** 15 percent.
- **Chapter 5 Access Control and Identity Management.** 15 percent.
- **Chapter 6 Cryptography.** 12 percent.

Each chapter includes a list of the objectives for the relevant domain. At this writing, these objectives accurately match the objectives listed on the CompTIA website, but CompTIA includes the following disclaimers:

- *"The lists of examples provided in bulleted format below each objective are not exhaustive lists. Other examples of technologies, processes or tasks pertaining to each objective may also be included on the exam although not listed or covered in this objectives document."*

- *"The CompTIA Security+ Certification Exam Objectives are subject to change without notice."*

You can verify that the objectives haven't changed by checking on **http://www.comptia.org**.

How to Use This Book

Each chapter has two sections. The first section includes the questions without any answers and the second section includes the same questions with the correct answer and an explanation.

If you want to test your comprehension without seeing the answer right away, use the first section. Ideally, you should be able look at any question and know why the correct answer is correct, and why the incorrect answers are incorrect. Take notes on the ones that aren't clear to you and look at the answers and explanations later. The second section allows you to see the correct answer right away. This allows you to read the questions and answers together. There's no right way or wrong way to use the sections. Use the method that helps you learn.

Some chapters have a third section with some extras. For example, chapter 1 includes a table listing relevant protocols and their matching ports that you should know for the exam.

How to Pass a Certification Exam

When practicing for any certification exam, the following steps are a good recipe for success:

- **Review the objectives.** The domain objectives for the SY0-401 exam are listed at the beginning of each chapter.

- **Learn the material related to the objectives.** The full study guide covers all the objectives and this book provides a sampling of practice test questions to test your comprehension of the objectives.

- **Take practice questions.** A key step when preparing for any certification exam is to make sure you can answer the exam questions. Yes, you need the knowledge, but you also must be able to read a question and select the correct answer. This simply takes practice. When using practice test questions, ensure they have explanations. Questions without explanations often give you the wrong answers.

- **Read and understand the explanations.** When preparing, you should make sure you know why the correct answers are correct and why the incorrect answers are incorrect. The explanations provide this information and are worded to help you answer similar questions correctly.

This book has over 300 practice test questions you can use to test your knowledge and your ability to answer them correctly. Every question has a detailed explanation to help you understand why the correct answers are correct and why the incorrect answers are incorrect.

Vendor Neutral

CompTIA certifications are vendor neutral. In other words, certifications are not centered on any single vendor, such as Microsoft, Apple, or Linux. With that in mind, you don't need significantly deep knowledge of any of the operating systems, but don't be surprised if you see more questions about one OS over another simply because of market share.

In August 2014, Windows had about 91 percent market share of desktop and laptop computer operating systems. Apple MACs were next with about 6 percent, and Linux had about 1 percent. Looking at mobile operating systems such as tablets and smartphones, it's close to a tie with Android devices having 44.6 percent market share and Apple iOS systems having 44.19 percent.

Because over 90 percent of the systems you'll touch in a corporate environment are Microsoft based, don't be surprised to see some Microsoft-specific questions.

Web Resources

Check out **http://GetCertifiedGetAhead.com** for up-to-date details on the CompTIA Security+ exam. This site includes additional information related to the CompTIA Security+ exam and this book.

Although many people have spent a lot of time and energy trying to ensure that there are no errors in this book, occasionally they slip through. This site includes an errata page listing any errors we've discovered.

If you discover any errors, please let me know through the links on the web site. I'd also love to hear about your success when you pass the exam. I'm constantly getting good news from readers and students who are successfully earning their certifications.

In response to all the requests I've received for additional materials, such as online practice test questions, flash cards, and audio files, I created this site: **http://gcgapremium.com/**. It includes access to various study materials.

Last, I've found that many people find cryptography topics challenging, so I've posted some videos on YouTube (**http://www.youtube.com/**). As time allows, I'll post additional videos, and you can get a listing of all of them by searching YouTube with "Darril Gibson."

Assumptions

The CompTIA Security+ exam assumes you have at least two years of experience working with computers in a network. It also assumes you earned the CompTIA Network+ certification, or at least have the equivalent knowledge. While writing this book, I have largely assumed the same thing.

However, I'm well aware that two years of experience in a network could mean many different things. Your two years of experience may expose you to different technologies than someone else's two years of experience.

When it's critical that you understand an underlying network concept in order to master the relevant exam material, I have often included the concept within the background information in the full study guide.

About the Exam

CompTIA first released the Security+ exam in 2002, and it has quickly grown in popularity. They revised the exam objectives in 2008, 2011, and again in 2014. The 2014 exam is numbered as SY0-401 (or JK0-022 for the academic version of the exam). SY0-201 retired on December 31, 2011, and SY0-301 is scheduled to retire on December 31, 2014.

The SY0-401 exam is the same as the JK0-022 exam. CompTIA uses the JK0-022 code for CompTIA Academy Partners. If you attend a Security+

course at a CompTIA Academy partner, they might give you a JK0-022 voucher. Everyone else uses the SY0-401 code.

A summary of the details of the exam includes:

- **Number of questions:** Maximum of 90 questions
- **Time to complete questions:** 90 minutes (does not include time to complete pretest and posttest surveys)
- **Passing score:** 750
- **Grading criteria:** Scale of 100 to 900 (about 83 percent)
- **Question types:** Multiple choice and performance-based
- **Exam format:** Traditional—can move back and forth to view previous questions
- **Exam prerequisites:** None required but Network+ is recommended
- **Exam test provider:** Pearson Vue

Number of Questions and Duration

You have 90 minutes to complete up to 90 questions. This gives you about one minute per question. Don't let this scare you; it's actually a good thing. With only about a minute to read and answer a question, you know the questions can't be very long. The exception is the performance-based questions, but you'll only see a few of those.

Passing Score

A score of 750 is required to pass. This is on a scale of 100 to 900. If the exam is paid for and you don't get a single question correct, you still get a score of 100. If you get every testable question correct, you get a score of 900.

If all questions are weighted equally, then you need to get 75 questions correct—a passing score of 750 divided by 900 equals .8333 or 83.33 percent.

CompTIA doesn't say if all questions are scored equally or whether harder questions are weighted and worth more. However, most people believe that the performance-based questions are worth more than a typical multiple-choice question.

Also, a score of 83 percent is higher than many other certification exams, so you shouldn't underestimate the difficulty of this exam. However, many people regularly pass it and you can pass it, too. With this book, you will be well prepared.

Exam Prerequisites

All that is required for you to take the exam is money. Other than that, there are no enforced prerequisites. However, to successfully pass the exam, you're expected to have at least two years of experience working with computers in a networking environment. If you have more than that, the exam materials will likely come easier to you. If you have less, the exam may be more difficult.

Exam Format

Questions are multiple-choice types where you select one answer or multiple answers. When you need to select multiple answers, the question may direct you to select two, select three, or select all that apply.

You start at question 1 and go to the last question. During the process, you can mark any questions you want to review when you're done. Additionally, you can view previous questions if desired. For example, if you get to question 10 and then remember something that helps you answer question 5, you can go back and redo question 5.

Beta Questions

Your exam may have some beta questions. They aren't graded but instead are used to test the validity of the questions. If everyone gets a beta question correct, it's probably too easy. If everyone gets it incorrect, there's probably something wrong with the question. After enough people have tested a beta question, CompTIA personnel analyze it and decide if they want to add it to the test bank, or rewrite and test it as a new beta question.

The good news is that CompTIA doesn't grade the beta questions. However, you don't know which questions are ungraded beta questions and which questions are live questions, so you need to treat every question equally.

Question Types

Expect many of the questions on the exam to be straightforward. For example, what's 5 × 5? Either you know the answer is 25 or you don't. The exam questions test your knowledge of the material, not necessarily your ability to dissect the question so that you can figure out what the question is really trying to ask.

I'm not saying the knowledge is simplistic, only that the questions will be worded so that you can easily understand what they are asking.

As a comparative example, Microsoft certification questions can be quite complex. Microsoft questions often aren't just testing your knowledge of the topic, but your ability to analyze the material and logically come to the right conclusion.

Here are two examples of questions—the first shows how Microsoft may word the question on a Microsoft certification exam, and the second shows how CompTIA may word it for the CompTIA Security+ exam.

- **Microsoft.** You are driving a bus from Chicago to Atlanta at 55 mph with 22 passengers. The bus is painted blue. At the same time, a train is traveling from Miami to Atlanta at 40 mph. The train has a yellow caboose. What color are the bus driver's eyes?

- **CompTIA Security+.** What color are your eyes?

Notice the first question adds a lot of superfluous information. Two pieces are critical to answering the first question. It starts by saying, "You are driving a bus..." and then ends by asking, "What color are the bus driver's eyes?" You're required to put the two together and weed through the irrelevant information to come to the correct answer.

The second question is straightforward. "What color are your eyes?" There's very little analysis required. Either you know it or you don't. This is what you can expect from many of the CompTIA Security+ questions.

Some of the CompTIA exam questions may have a little more detail than just a single sentence, but overall, expect them to be one- to three-sentence questions. They are only giving you about one minute for each question, and it's not intended to be a reading comprehension exam.

As a simple example, you may see a question like: "What port does SSH use?" In this case, you'd need to know that Secure Shell (SSH) uses Transmission Control Protocol (TCP) port 22.

However, CompTIA can reword the question to test your depth of comprehension. For example, you might see a question like this: "You need to configure a firewall to block Telnet traffic and allow traffic used by a more secure replacement of Telnet. What port needs to be opened on the firewall?" In this case, you'd need to know that Secure Shell (SSH) is a secure replacement for Telnet and SSH uses TCP port 22.

You may also see questions that use phrases such as "BEST choice," "BEST description," or "MOST secure." In these examples, don't be surprised if you see two answers that could answer the question, while only one is the best choice. For example, which one of the following numbers is between 1 and 10 and is the HIGHEST: 2, 8, 14, 23.

Clearly, 2 and 8 are between 1 and 10, but 14 and 23 are not. However, only 8 is both between 1 and 10 and the highest.

Here is a more realistic, security-related question that shows this: Question: You need to send several large files containing proprietary data to a business partner. Which of the following is the BEST choice for this task?

A. FTP

B. SNMP

C. SFTP

D. SSH

File Transfer Protocol (FTP) is a good choice to send large files. However, the question also says that the files include proprietary data, indicating they should be protected with encryption. Secure File Transfer Protocol (SFTP) is the best choice because it can send large files in an encrypted format. When you see key words like BEST or MOST, be careful not to jump on the first answer. There may be a more correct answer.

Multiple Choice

Most questions are multiple-choice types where you select one answer or multiple answers. When you need to select multiple answers, the question will include a phrase such as "Select TWO" or "Select THREE."

Performance-Based Questions

You can expect as many as 10 non-multiple choice questions. CompTIA refers to these as performance-based questions and instead of picking from a multiple-choice answer, you're often required to perform a task. CompTIA's goal is to provide more accurate testing to verify people have a full understanding of a topic.

A question people often ask about these questions is if they get partial credit. People at CompTIA know, but I haven't seen anywhere they've clarified this. It's entirely possible that you get partial credit on some of these types of questions while others require you to answer them completely. It's best to do the best you can with each question.

The following sections cover the different types of questions you can expect. You can also check out some of the blogs on performance-based questions that I've written here:

http://blogs.getcertifiedgetahead.com/security-blog-links/.

Matching

In a matching performance-based question, you will see two lists and need to match them. As a simple example, one list might include several protocols and the other list might include several protocol numbers. You would need to match the correct protocol numbers with each protocol.

If you know the protocols and ports listed in Table 1.1 (at the end of Chapter 1), this becomes trivial. Then again, if you don't know which ports go with which protocols, this can be quite difficult.

Drag and Drop

In some questions, you might need to drag items from one location on the screen to another location to answer a question. You can think of these as multiple-choice questions with multiple answers that are correct. However, instead of selecting the check boxes to indicate a correct answer, you drag it to somewhere else on the screen.

Chapter 2 of the full study guide (CompTIA Security+ Get Certified Get Ahead: SY0-401 Study Guide) has an example of a potential drag-and-drop question in the practice test questions section. It provides a scenario with several locations and devices, and lists several security controls used to secure the locations. You're asked to drag and drop the appropriate controls to the appropriate location or device.

Another example is in Chapter 11 of the full study guide. The question presents a scenario related to forensics, and then asks you to arrange an out-of-order list of data based on volatility.

Data Entry

Some performance-based questions might ask you to analyze a scenario and then enter appropriate data. For example, Chapter 4 of the full study guide discusses the configuration of wireless access points and wireless routers. A related question might ask you to configure an access point to work with WPA2 Enterprise mode. The Configuring a Wireless Router Lab mentioned in Chapter 4 of the full study guide and available online (**http://gcgapremium.com/labs/**) shows you the steps to do this.

Similarly, I wrote a series of blog articles on creating rules for routers and firewalls. The second post shows an example of a performance-based question and the last post provides the solution. You can read the posts here:

- **ACLs and Security+.**
  http://blogs.getcertifiedgetahead.com/acls-and-security/

- **Firewall Rules and Security+.**
  http://blogs.getcertifiedgetahead.com/firewall-rules-and-security/

- **Firewall Rules Solution.**
  http://blogs.getcertifiedgetahead.com/firewall-rules-solution/

Performance-Based Questions Strategy

You'll see the performance-based questions first and they take much longer than typical multiple-choice questions. If the answer is clear to you, then by all means, take the time to answer it. However, if the question isn't clear, mark the question and skip it. You can come back to it later. It's entirely possible that the question is a poorly worded beta question that doesn't even count. However, if you spend 45 minutes on it, you might run out of time before you finish the multiple-choice questions.

Performance-based questions have occasionally caused problems for the test systems. A common problem is that instead of displaying the question, the screen is mostly blank. If this happens, you can often just use the reset button for the question. This allows you to move past the problem and continue with the test. However, resetting the question erases any answer you've entered.

It's common for people to be nervous when thinking about these performance-based test questions. However, the majority of people who take the test say that these questions really aren't that difficult. As long as you understand the concepts from the exam objectives, you won't have any problem. I do recommend you check out the posts on performance-based questions that I've posted here: **http://blogs.getcertifiedgetahead.com/security-blog-links/**.

Exam Test Provider

You can take the exam at a Pearson Vue testing site. Some testing sites provide testing and nothing else. However, most testing sites are part of another company, such as a training company, college, or university. You can take an exam at the training company's testing site even if you haven't taken a course with them.

The Pearson Vue web site includes search tools you can use to find a testing site close to you. Check them out at **http://www.pearsonvue.com**.

Voucher Code for 10 Percent Off

As of this writing, the CompTIA Security+ exam is $293 in the United States if you purchase it at full price. However, you can get a 10 percent discount using a discount code. This code changes periodically, so you'll need to go to this page to access the current code:

http://gcgapremium.com/discounted-comptia-vouchers/.

When you purchase a voucher, you'll get a voucher number that you can use to register at a testing site. A word of caution: Some criminals sell bogus vouchers on Internet sites such as eBay. You won't know you've been ripped off until you try to use it and by that time, the criminal will probably have disappeared. In contrast, if you use the discount code, you buy the voucher directly from CompTIA.

About the Study Guide

This book is only practice test questions with answers. However, if you're looking for more than just practice test questions for the CompTIA Security+ SY0-401 exam, check out the CompTIA Security+: Get Certified Get Ahead: SY0-401 Study Guide (ISBN 1939136024). That book is an update to the top selling SY0-201 and SY0-301 study guides, which have helped thousands of readers pass the exam the first time they took them.

It covers every aspect of the SY0-401 exam, and includes the same elements readers raved about in the previous versions. Each of the eleven chapters presents topics in an easy to understand manner and includes real-world examples of security principles in action. I used many of the same analogies and explanations I honed in the classroom that have helped hundreds of students master the Security+ content. You'll understand the important and relevant security topics for the Security+ exam, without being overloaded with unnecessary details. Additionally, each chapter includes a comprehensive review section to help you focus on what's important.

With over 400 realistic practice test questions with in-depth explanations, the book also includes a 100 question pre-test, a 100 question post-test, and practice test questions at the end of every chapter to help you test your comprehension and readiness for the exam. Each practice test question includes a detailed explanation to help you understand the content and the reasoning behind the question. You'll be ready to take and pass the exam the first time you take it.

If you plan to pursue any of the advanced security certifications, the SY0-401 Security+ Study Guide will also help you lay a solid foundation of security knowledge. Learn the material, and you'll be a step ahead for other exams. The CompTIA Security+: Get Certified Get Ahead: SY0-401 Study Guide is for any IT or security professional interested in advancing in their field, and a must read for anyone striving to master the basics of IT systems security.

√ **Get Certified**

√ **Get Ahead**

Chapter 1 Network Security

Network Security topics are **20 percent** of the CompTIA Security+ exam. The objectives in this domain are listed on the following pages:

1.1 Implement security configuration parameters on network devices and other technologies.

- Firewalls
- Routers
- Switches
- Load Balancers
- Proxies
- Web security gateways
- VPN concentrators
- NIDS and NIPS
  - Behavior based
  - Signature based
  - Anomaly based
  - Heuristic
- Protocol analyzers
- Spam filter
- UTM security appliances
  - URL filter
  - Content inspection
  - Malware inspection
- Web application firewall vs. network firewall
- Application aware devices
  - Firewalls
  - IPS
  - IDS
  - Proxies

1.2 Given a scenario, use secure network administration principles.

- Rule-based management
- Firewall rules
- VLAN management
- Secure router configuration
- Access control lists
- Port Security
- 802.1x

- Flood guards
- Loop protection
- Implicit deny
- Network separation
- Log analysis
- Unified Threat Management

1.3 Explain network design elements and components.

- DMZ
- Subnetting
- VLAN
- NAT
- Remote Access
- Telephony
- NAC
- Virtualization
- Cloud Computing
  - Platform as a Service
  - Software as a Service
  - Infrastructure as a Service
  - Private
  - Public
  - Hybrid
  - Community
- Layered security / Defense in depth

1.4 Given a scenario, implement common protocols and services.

- Protocols
  - IPSec
  - SNMP
  - SSH
  - DNS
  - TLS
  - SSL
  - TCP/IP
  - FTPS
  - HTTPS
  - SCP
  - ICMP
  - IPv4
  - IPv6
  - iSCSI
  - Fibre Channel
  - FCoE

- o FTP
- o SFTP
- o TFTP
- o TELNET
- o HTTP
- o NetBIOS
- Ports
  - o 21
  - o 22
  - o 25
  - o 53
  - o 80
  - o 110
  - o 139
  - o 143
  - o 443
  - o 3389
- OSI relevance

1.5 Given a scenario, troubleshoot security issues related to wireless networking.
- WPA
- WPA2
- WEP
- EAP
- PEAP
- LEAP
- MAC filter
- Disable SSID broadcast
- TKIP
- CCMP
- Antenna Placement
- Power level controls
- Captive portals
- Antenna types
- Site surveys
- VPN (over open wireless)

The CompTIA Security+: Get Certified Get Ahead SY0-401 Study Guide (ISBN 1939136024) discusses these topics in much more depth.

√ **Get Certified**

√ **Get Ahead**

Practice Test Questions
for Network Security Domain

1. Your organization wants to prevent users from accessing file sharing web sites. Which of the following choices will meet this need?

    A. Content inspection

    B. Malware inspection

    C. URL filter

    D. Web application firewall

2. Your organization wants to combine some of the security controls used on the network. What could your organization implement to meet this goal?

    A. SSO

    B. UTM

    C. VPN

    D. VLAN

3. Which of the following operates on the HIGHEST layer of the OSI model, and is the most effective at blocking application attacks?

    A. IDS

    B. Router

    C. WAF

    D. Stateless firewall

4. Which of the following network tools includes sniffing capabilities?

    A. IDS

    B. WAP

    C. VPN

    D. NAC

5. A HIDS reported a vulnerability on a system using an assigned vulnerability identification number. After researching the number on the vendor's web site, you identify the recommended solution and begin applying it. What type of HIDS is in use?

 A. Network-based

 B. Signature-based

 C. Heuristic-based

 D. Anomaly-based

6. Management is concerned about malicious activity on your network and wants to implement a security control that will detect unusual traffic on the network. Which of the following is the BEST choice to meet this goal?

 A. Network firewall

 B. Signature-based IDS

 C. Anomaly-based IDS

 D. Honeypot

7. You need to configure a UTM security appliance to restrict access to peer-to-peer file sharing web sites. What are you MOST likely to configure?

 A. Content inspection

 B. Malware inspection

 C. URL filter

 D. Stateless inspection

8. Your organization wants to protect its web server from cross-site scripting attacks. Which of the following choices provides the BEST protection?

 A. WAF

 B. Network-based firewall

 C. Host-based firewall

 D. IDS

9. Management recently learned that several employees are using the company network to visit gambling and gaming web sites. They want to implement a security control to prevent this in the future. Which of the following choices would meet this need?

    A. WAF

    B. UTM

    C. DMZ

    D. NIDS

10. Which of the following protocols operates on Layer 7 of the OSI model?

    A. IPv6

    B. TCP

    C. ARP

    D. SCP

11. A network technician incorrectly wired switch connections in your organization's network. It effectively disabled the switch as though it was a victim of a denial-of-service attack. What should be done to prevent this in the future?

    A. Install an IDS.

    B. Only use Layer 2 switches.

    C. Install SNMP on the switches.

    D. Implement STP or RSTP.

12. Your organization frequently has guests visiting in various conference rooms throughout the building. These guests need access to the Internet via wall jacks, but should not be able to access internal network resources. Employees need access to both the internal network and the Internet. What would BEST meet this need?

A. PAT and NAT

B. DMZ and VPN

C. VLANs and 802.1x

D. Routers and Layer 3 switches

13. Your network currently has a dedicated firewall protecting access to a web server. It is currently configured with the following two rules in the ACL along with an implicit allow rule at the end:

PERMIT TCP ANY ANY 443

PERMIT TCP ANY ANY 80

You have detected DNS requests and zone transfer requests coming through the firewall and you need to block them. Which of the following would meet this goal? (Select TWO. Each answer is a full solution.)

A. Add the following rule to the firewall: DENY TCP ALL ALL 53.

B. Add the following rule to the firewall: DENY UDP ALL ALL 53.

C. Add the following rule to the firewall: DENY TCP ALL ALL 25.

D. Add the following rule to the firewall: DENY IP ALL ALL 53.

E. Change the implicit allow rule to implicit deny.

14. What would you configure on a Layer 3 device to allow FTP traffic to pass through?

A. Router

B. Implicit deny

C. Port security

D. Access control list

15. What type of device would have the following entries used to define its operation?

permit IP any any eq 80

permit IP any any eq 443

deny IP any any

A. Layer 2 switch

B. Proxy server

C. Web server

D. Firewall

16. Your organization is hosting a wireless network with an 802.1x server using PEAP. On Thursday, users report they can no longer access the wireless network. Administrators verified the network configuration matches the baseline, there aren't any hardware outages, and the wired network is operational. Which of the following is the MOST likely cause for this problem?

A. The RADIUS server certificate expired.

B. DNS is providing incorrect host names.

C. DHCP is issuing duplicate IP addresses.

D. MAC filtering is enabled.

17. What would administrators typically place at the end of an ACL of a firewall?

A. Allow all all

B. Timestamp

C. Password

D. Implicit deny

18. A network administrator needs to open a port on a firewall to support a VPN using PPTP. What ports should the administrator open?

A. UDP 47

B. TCP 50

C. TCP 1723

D. UDP 1721

19. You need to divide a single Class B IP address range into several ranges. What would you do?

    A. Subnet the Class B IP address range.

    B. Create a virtual LAN.

    C. Create a DMZ.

    D. Implement STP.

20. Your organization hosts a web server and wants to increase its security. You need to separate all web-facing traffic from internal network traffic. Which of the following provides the BEST solution?

    A. VLAN

    B. Firewall

    C. DMZ

    D. WAF

21. An automated process isolated a computer in a restricted VLAN because the process noticed the computer's antivirus definitions were not up to date. What is the name of this process?

    A. NFC

    B. NIPS

    C. NIDS

    D. NAC

22. Of the following choices, which one is a cloud computing option that allows customers to apply patches to the operating system?

    A. Hybrid cloud

    B. Software as a Service

    C. Infrastructure as a Service

    D. Private

23. An organization wants to provide protection against malware attacks. Administrators have installed antivirus software on all computers. Additionally, they implemented a firewall and an IDS on the network. Which of the following BEST identifies this principle?

A. Implicit deny

B. Layered security

C. Least privilege

D. Flood guard

24. Your organization has implemented a network design that allows internal computers to share one public IP address. Of the following choices, what did they MOST likely implement?

A. PAT

B. STP

C. DNAT

D. TLS

25. A company is implementing a feature that allows multiple servers to operate on a single physical server. What is this?

A. Virtualization

B. IaaS

C. Cloud computing

D. DLP

26. Management within your organization wants some users to be able to access internal network resources from remote locations. Which of the following is the BEST choice to meet this need?

A. WAF

B. VPN

C. IDS

D. IPS

27. What protocol does IPv6 use for hardware address resolution?

    A. ARP

    B. NDP

    C. RDP

    D. SNMP

28. What is the default port for SSH?

    A. 22

    B. 23

    C. 25

    D. 80

29. You are configuring a host-based firewall so that it will allow SFTP connections. Which of the following is required?

    A. Allow UDP 21

    B. Allow TCP 21

    C. Allow TCP 22

    D. Allow UDP 22

30. You need to send several large files containing proprietary data to a business partner. Which of the following is the BEST choice for this task?

    A. FTP

    B. SNMP

    C. SFTP

    D. SSH

31. Your organization is planning to establish a secure link between one of your mail servers and a business partner's mail server. The connection will use the Internet. What protocol is the BEST choice?

A. TLS

B. SMTP

C. HTTP

D. SSH

32. You need to prevent the use of TFTP through your firewall. Which port would you block?

A. TCP 69

B. UDP 69

C. TCP 21

D. UDP 21

33. You need to enable the use of NetBIOS through a firewall. Which ports should you open?

A. 137 through 139

B. 20 and 21

C. 80 and 443

D. 22 and 3389

34. Lisa wants to manage and monitor the switches and routers in her network. Which of the following protocols would she use?

A. Telnet

B. SSH

C. SNMP

D. DNS

35. You need to reboot your DNS server. Of the following choices, which type of server are you MOST likely to reboot?

A. Unix server

B. Apache server

C. BIND server

D. Web server

36. Your organization is increasing security and wants to prevent attackers from mapping out the IP addresses used on your internal network. Which of the following choices is the BEST option?

A. Implement subnetting.

B. Implement secure zone transfers.

C. Block outgoing traffic on UDP port 53.

D. Add a WAF.

37. Network administrators connect to a legacy server using Telnet. They want to secure these transmissions using encryption at a lower layer of the OSI model. What could they use?

A. IPv4

B. IPv6

C. SSH

D. SFTP

38. Your organization is planning to implement a VPN and wants to ensure it is secure. Which of the following protocols is the BEST choice to use with the VPN?

A. HTTP

B. SFTP

C. IPsec

D. PPTP

39. Which of the following list of protocols use TCP port 22 by default?

    A. FTPS, TLS, SCP

    B. SCP, SFTP, FTPS

    C. HTTPS, SSL, TLS

    D. SSH, SCP, SFTP

    E. SCP, SSH, SSL

40. Bart wants to block access to all external web sites. Which port should he block at the firewall?

    A. TCP 22

    B. TCP 53

    C. UDP 69

    D. TCP 80

41. You need to manage a remote server. Which of the following ports should you open on the firewall between your system and the remote server?

    A. 25 and 3389

    B. 22 and 443

    C. 22 and 3389

    D. 21 and 23

43. One of your web servers was recently attacked and you have been tasked with reviewing firewall logs to see if you can determine how an attacker accessed the system remotely. You identified the following port numbers in log entries: 21, 22, 25, 53, 80, 110, 443, and 3389. Which of the following protocols did the attacker MOST likely use?

    A. Telnet

    B. HTTPS

    C. DNS

    D. RDP

44. Which of the following provides the largest address space?

    A. IPv4

    B. IPv5

    C. IPv6

    D. IPv7

45. While analyzing a firewall log, you notice traffic going out of your network on UDP port 53. What does this indicate?

    A. Connection with a botnet

    B. DNS traffic

    C. SMTP traffic

    D. SFTP traffic

46. You recently learned that a network router has TCP ports 22 and 80 open, but the organization's security policy mandates that these should not be accessible. What should you do?

    A. Disable the FTP and HTTP services on the router.

    B. Disable the DNS and HTTPS services on the router.

    C. Disable the SSH and HTTP services on the router.

    D. Disable the Telnet and Kerberos services on the router.

47. You are assisting a user implement a wireless network in his home. The wireless hardware he has requires the RC4 protocol. What type of security is BEST for this network?

    A. WEP

    B. WPA-TKIP

    C. WPA-AES

    D. WPA2 Enterprise

48. You are planning to deploy a WLAN and you want to ensure it is secure. Which of the following provides the BEST security?

    A. WEP Enterprise

    B. WPA2 TKIP

    C. SSID broadcast

    D. WPA2 CCMP

49. Your organization is planning to implement a wireless network using WPA2 Enterprise. Of the following choices, what is required?

    A. An authentication server with a digital certificate installed on the authentication server

    B. An authentication server with DHCP installed on the authentication server

    C. An authentication server with DNS installed on the authentication server

    D. An authentication server with WEP running on the access point

50. You are assisting a small business owner in setting up a public wireless hot spot for her customers. Which of the following actions are MOST appropriate for this hot spot?

    A. Enabling Open System Authentication

    B. Enabling MAC filtering

    C. Disabling SSID broadcast

    D. Installing Yagi antennas

51. Homer is able to connect to his company's wireless network with his smartphone but not with his laptop computer. Which of the following is the MOST likely reason for this disparity?

A. His company's network has a MAC address filter in place.

B. His company's network has enabled SSID broadcast.

C. His company's network has enabled CCMP.

D. His company's network has enabled WPA2 Enterprise.

52. Your organization maintains a separate wireless network for visitors in a conference room. However, you have recently noticed that people are connecting to this network even when there aren't any visitors in the conference room. You want to prevent these connections, while maintaining easy access for visitors in the conference room. Which of the following is the BEST solution?

A. Disable SSID broadcasting.

B. Enable MAC filtering.

C. Use wireless jamming.

D. Reduce antenna power.

53. Which of the following represents the BEST action to increase security in a wireless network?

A. Replace dipole antennas with Yagi antennas.

B. Replace TKIP with CCMP.

C. Replace WPA with WEP.

D. Disable SSID broadcast.

54. You are planning a wireless network for a business. A core requirement is to ensure that the solution encrypts user credentials when users enter their usernames and passwords. Which of the following BEST meets this requirement?

A. WPA2-PSK

B. WEP over PEAP

C. WPS with LEAP

D. WPA2 over EAP-TTLS

55. A small business owner modified his wireless router with the following settings:

PERMIT 1A:2B:3C:4D:5E:6F

DENY 6F:5E:4D:3C:2B:1A

After saving the settings, an employee reports that he cannot access the wireless network anymore. What is the MOST likely reason that the employee cannot access the network?

A. IP address filtering

B. Hardware address filtering

C. Port filtering

D. URL filtering

56. A team of users in your organization needs a dedicated subnet. For security reasons, other users should not be able to connect to this subnet. Which of the following choices is the BEST solution?

A. Restrict traffic based on port numbers.

B. Restrict traffic based on physical addresses.

C. Implement DNS on the network.

D. Enable SNMP.

57. What type of encryption is used with WPA2 CCMP?

A. AES

B. TKIP

C. RC4

D. SSL

58. Administrators in your organization are planning to implement a wireless network. Management has mandated that they use a RADIUS server and implement a secure wireless authentication method. Which of the following should they use?

    A. LEAP

    B. WPA-PSK

    C. WPA2-PSK

    D. AES

59. Which of the following is the BEST description of why disabling SSID broadcast is not an effective security measure against attackers?

    A. The network name is contained in wireless packets in plaintext.

    B. The passphrase is contained in wireless packets in plaintext.

    C. The SSID is included in MAC filters.

    D. The SSID is not used with WPA2.

60. You need to provide connectivity between two buildings without running any cables. You decide to use two WAPs and a high-gain directional antenna. Which of the following antennas is the BEST choice to meet this need?

    A. Yagi

    B. Omni

    C. Isotropic

    D. Dipole

Practice Test Questions with Answers for Network Security Domain

1. Your organization wants to prevent users from accessing file sharing web sites. Which of the following choices will meet this need?

    A. Content inspection

    B. Malware inspection

    C. URL filter

    D. Web application firewall

1. C is correct. A URL filter blocks access to specific web sites based on their URLs. Proxy servers and unified threat management (UTM) devices include URL filters.

A and B are incorrect. UTM devices include content inspection to identify and filter out different types of files and traffic, and malware inspection to identify and block malware.

D is incorrect. A web application firewall (WAF) protects a web server from incoming attacks.

2. Your organization wants to combine some of the security controls used on the network. What could your organization implement to meet this goal?

    A. SSO

    B. UTM

    C. VPN

    D. VLAN

2. B is correct. A unified threat management (UTM) device combines multiple security controls into a single device.

A is incorrect. Single sign-on allows users to sign on once and access multiple resources without signing on again.

C is incorrect. Users can access a private network over a public network via a virtual private network (VPN).

D is incorrect. You can configure a virtual local area network (VLAN) on a switch to group computers together logically.

3. Which of the following operates on the HIGHEST layer of the OSI model, and is the most effective at blocking application attacks?

    A. IDS

    B. Router

    C. WAF

    D. Stateless firewall

3. C is correct. A web application firewall (WAF) operates on multiple layers up to Layer 7 of the OSI reference model and blocks attacks against a web server.

A is incorrect. An intrusion detection system (IDS) also operates on multiple layers up to Layer 7 of the OSI model; however, it is more effective at detecting attacks than blocking them.

B is incorrect. A router operates on Layer 3 of the OSI model and it can perform packet filtering.

D is incorrect. A stateless firewall only performs packet filtering and isn't effective against Application layer attacks.

4. Which of the following network tools includes sniffing capabilities?

    A. IDS

    B. WAP

    C. VPN

    D. NAC

4. A is correct. Intrusion detection systems (IDSs) and intrusion prevention systems (IPSs) include sniffing capabilities allowing them to inspect packet

streams for malicious activity. None of the other tools have the capability of inspecting packets.

B is incorrect. A wireless access point (WAP) provides access to a wired network for wireless devices.

C is incorrect. A virtual private network (VPN) provides access to an internal network for remote users.

D is incorrect. A network access control (NAC) system inspects clients to ensure they meet minimum security requirements.

5. A HIDS reported a vulnerability on a system using an assigned vulnerability identification number. After researching the number on the vendor's web site, you identify the recommended solution and begin applying it. What type of HIDS is in use?

    A. Network-based

    B. Signature-based

    C. Heuristic-based

    D. Anomaly-based

5. B is correct. If the issue has an assigned number, it must be known, so it is signature-based.

A is incorrect. A host-based intrusion detection system (HIDS) is not network-based.

C and D are incorrect. A heuristic-based (or anomaly-based) detection system catches issues that are not previously known.

6. Management is concerned about malicious activity on your network and wants to implement a security control that will detect unusual traffic on the network. Which of the following is the BEST choice to meet this goal?

    A. Network firewall

    B. Signature-based IDS

C. Anomaly-based IDS

D. Honeypot

6. C is correct. An anomaly-based (also called heuristic or behavior-based) detection system compares current activity with a previously created baseline to detect any anomalies or changes.

A is incorrect. A network firewall blocks and allows traffic, but does not detect unusual traffic.

B is incorrect. Signature-based systems use signatures similar to antivirus software.

D is incorrect. A honeypot is a server designed to look valuable to an attacker and can divert attacks.

7. You need to configure a UTM security appliance to restrict access to peer-to-peer file sharing web sites. What are you MOST likely to configure?

A. Content inspection

B. Malware inspection

C. URL filter

D. Stateless inspection

7. C is correct. You would most likely configure the Uniform Resource Locator (URL) filter on the unified thread management (UTM) security appliance. This would block access to the peer-to-peer sites based on their URL.

A and B are incorrect. Content inspection and malware inspection focus on inspecting the data as it passes through the UTM, but they do not block access to sites.

D is incorrect. Stateless inspection is packet filtering and would be extremely difficult to configure on a firewall for all peer-to-peer web sites.

8. Your organization wants to protect its web server from cross-site scripting attacks. Which of the following choices provides the BEST protection?

    A. WAF

    B. Network-based firewall

    C. Host-based firewall

    D. IDS

8. A is correct. A web application firewall (WAF) is an Application layer firewall designed specifically to protect web servers.

B and C are incorrect. Although both host-based and network-based firewalls provide protection, they aren't necessarily Application layer firewalls, so they do not provide the same level of protection for a web server as a WAF does.

D is incorrect. An intrusion detection system (IDS) can help detect attacks, but it isn't as good as the WAF when protecting the web server.

9. Management recently learned that several employees are using the company network to visit gambling and gaming web sites. They want to implement a security control to prevent this in the future. Which of the following choices would meet this need?

    A. WAF

    B. UTM

    C. DMZ

    D. NIDS

9. B is correct. A unified threat management (UTM) device typically includes a URL filter and can block access to web sites, just as a proxy server can block access to web sites.

B is incorrect. A web application firewall (WAF) protects a web server from incoming attacks.

C is incorrect. A demilitarized zone (DMZ) is a buffered zone between protected and unprotected networks, but it does not include URL filters.

D is incorrect. A network-based intrusion detection system (NIDS) can detect attacks, but doesn't include outgoing URL filters.

10. Which of the following protocols operates on Layer 7 of the OSI model?

    A. IPv6

    B. TCP

    C. ARP

    D. SCP

10. D is correct. Secure Copy (SCP) operates on Layer 7 of the OSI model.

A is incorrect. IPv6 operates on Layer 3.

B is incorrect. TCP operates on Layer 4.

C is incorrect. Address Resolution Protocol (ARP) operates on Layer 3.

11. A network technician incorrectly wired switch connections in your organization's network. It effectively disabled the switch as though it was a victim of a denial-of-service attack. What should be done to prevent this in the future?

    A. Install an IDS.

    B. Only use Layer 2 switches.

    C. Install SNMP on the switches.

    D. Implement STP or RSTP.

11. D is correct. Spanning Tree Protocol (STP) or Rapid STP (RSTP) will prevent switching loop problems. It's rare for a wiring error to take down a switch. However, if two ports on a switch are connected to each other, it creates a switching loop and effectively disables the switch.

A is incorrect. An intrusion detection system (IDS) will not prevent a switching loop.

B is incorrect. Layer 2 switches are susceptible to this problem.

C is incorrect. Administrators use Simple Network Management Protocol (SNMP) to manage and monitor devices, but it doesn't prevent switching loops.

12. Your organization frequently has guests visiting in various conference rooms throughout the building. These guests need access to the Internet via wall jacks, but should not be able to access internal network resources. Employees need access to both the internal network and the Internet. What would BEST meet this need?

    A. PAT and NAT

    B. DMZ and VPN

    C. VLANs and 802.1x

    D. Routers and Layer 3 switches

12. C is correct. An 802.1x server provides port-based authentication and can authenticate clients. Clients that cannot authenticate (the guests in this scenario) can be redirected to a virtual local area network (VLAN) that grants them Internet access, but not access to the internal network. None of the other solutions provides port security or adequate network separation.

A is incorrect. Port Address Translation (PAT) and Network Address Translation (NAT) each translate private IP addresses to public IP addresses.

B is incorrect. A demilitarized zone (DMZ) provides a buffer zone between a public network and a private network for public-facing servers. A virtual private network (VPN) provides access to a private network via a public network.

D is incorrect. Routers work on Layer 3, and Layer 3 switches mimic some of the functionality of routers.

13. Your network currently has a dedicated firewall protecting access to a web server. It is currently configured with the following two rules in the ACL along with an implicit allow rule at the end:

PERMIT TCP ANY ANY 443

PERMIT TCP ANY ANY 80

You have detected DNS requests and zone transfer requests coming through the firewall and you need to block them. Which of the following would meet this goal? (Select TWO. Each answer is a full solution.)

      A. Add the following rule to the firewall: DENY TCP ALL ALL 53.

      B. Add the following rule to the firewall: DENY UDP ALL ALL 53.

      C. Add the following rule to the firewall: DENY TCP ALL ALL 25.

      D. Add the following rule to the firewall: DENY IP ALL ALL 53.

      E. Change the implicit allow rule to implicit deny.

13. D and E are correct. The easiest way is to change the implicit allow rule to implicit deny and that is preferred because it will protect the server from unwanted traffic. You can also deny all IP traffic using port 53 with DENY IP ALL ALL 53.

A and B are incorrect. DNS requests use UDP port 53, and zone transfers use TCP port 53 so both UDP 53 and TCP port 53 need to be blocked. You can achieve that goal with DENY IP ALL ALL 53.

C is incorrect. SMTP uses port 25.

14. What would you configure on a Layer 3 device to allow FTP traffic to pass through?

      A. Router

      B. Implicit deny

      C. Port security

      D. Access control list

14. D is correct. You would configure an access control list (ACL) to allow traffic in or out of a network. A is incorrect. A router is a Layer 3 device and you would configure the ACL on the router.

B is incorrect. The last rule in the ACL would be implicit deny to block all other traffic.

C is incorrect. Port security protects ports by disabling unused ports or using 802.1x, but it cannot block specific types of traffic.

15. What type of device would have the following entries used to define its operation?

permit IP any any eq 80

permit IP any any eq 443

deny IP any any

       A. Layer 2 switch

       B. Proxy server

       C. Web server

       D. Firewall

15. D is correct. These are rules in an access control list (ACL) for a firewall. The first two rules indicate that traffic from any IP address, to any IP address, using ports 80 or 443 is permitted or allowed. The final rule is also known as an implicit deny rule and is placed last in the ACL. It ensures that all traffic that hasn't been previously allowed is denied.

A is incorrect. Layer 2 switches do not use ACLs.

B is incorrect. A proxy server would not use an ACL, although it would use ports 80 and 443 for Hypertext Transfer Protocol (HTTP) and HTTP Secure (HTTPS), respectively.

C is incorrect. A web server wouldn't use an ACL, although it would also use ports 80 and 443.

16. Your organization is hosting a wireless network with an 802.1x server using PEAP. On Thursday, users report they can no longer access the wireless network. Administrators verified the network configuration matches the baseline, there aren't any hardware outages, and the wired network is operational. Which of the following is the MOST likely cause for this problem?

 A. The RADIUS server certificate expired.

 B. DNS is providing incorrect host names.

 C. DHCP is issuing duplicate IP addresses.

 D. MAC filtering is enabled.

16. A is correct. The most likely cause is that the Remote Authentication Dial-In User Service (RADIUS) server certificate expired. An 802.1x server is implemented as a RADIUS server and Protected Extensible Authentication Protocol (PEAP) requires a certificate.

B and C are incorrect. If Domain Name System (DNS) or Dynamic Host Configuration Protocol (DHCP) failed, it would affect both wired and wireless users.

D is incorrect. Media access control (MAC) address filtering might cause this symptom if all MAC addresses were blocked, but the scenario states that there weren't any network configuration changes.

17. What would administrators typically place at the end of an ACL of a firewall?

 A. Allow all all

 B. Timestamp

 C. Password

 D. Implicit deny

17. D is correct. Administrators would place an implicit deny rule at the end of an access control list (ACL) to deny all traffic that hasn't been explicitly allowed. Many firewalls place this rule at the end by default.

A is incorrect. An allow all all rule explicitly allows all traffic and defeats the purpose of a firewall.

B is incorrect. Timestamps aren't needed in an ACL.

C is incorrect. ACLs are in cleartext so should not include passwords.

18. A network administrator needs to open a port on a firewall to support a VPN using PPTP. What ports should the administrator open?

 A. UDP 47

 B. TCP 50

 C. TCP 1723

 D. UDP 1721

18. C is correct. A virtual private network (VPN) using Point-to-Point Tunneling Protocol (PPTP) requires Transmission Control Protocol (TCP) port 1723 open.

A is incorrect. It would also need protocol ID 47 open, but the protocol ID is not a port.

B and D are incorrect. Internet Protocol security (IPsec) uses protocol ID 50 and User Datagram Protocol (UDP) port 1721.

19. You need to divide a single Class B IP address range into several ranges. What would you do?

 A. Subnet the Class B IP address range.

 B. Create a virtual LAN.

 C. Create a DMZ.

 D. Implement STP.

19. A is correct. You can divide any classful IP address range by subnetting it. This breaks up a larger range of IP addresses into smaller network segments or blocks of IP addresses.

B is incorrect. A virtual local area network (VLAN) divides groups of computers logically, but doesn't use IP ranges.

C is incorrect. A demilitarized zone (DMZ) is a buffered zone between a protected network and a public network.

D is incorrect. Spanning Tree Protocol (STP) prevents looping problems caused by incorrect cabling.

20. Your organization hosts a web server and wants to increase its security. You need to separate all web-facing traffic from internal network traffic. Which of the following provides the BEST solution?

    A. VLAN

    B. Firewall

    C. DMZ

    D. WAF

20. C is correct. A demilitarized zone (DMZ) is a buffered zone between a private network and the Internet, and it will separate the web server's web-facing traffic from the internal network.

A is incorrect. You can use a virtual local area network (VLAN) to group computers together based on job function or some other administrative need, but it is created on switches in the internal network.

B is incorrect. A firewall does provide protection for the web server, but doesn't necessarily separate the web-facing traffic from the internal network.

D is incorrect. A web application firewall (WAF) protects a web server from incoming attacks, but it does not necessarily separate Internet and internal network traffic.

21. An automated process isolated a computer in a restricted VLAN because the process noticed the computer's antivirus definitions were not up to date. What is the name of this process?

    A. NFC

    B. NIPS

    C. NIDS

    D. NAC

21. D is correct. Network access control is a group of technologies that can inspect systems and control their access to a network. In this scenario, NAC changed the computer's IP address to quarantine it in a restricted virtual local area network (VLAN).\

A is incorrect. Near field communication (NFC) refers to standards that allow mobile devices to communicate with each other and is not related to VLANs. B and C are incorrect. Network-based intrusion prevention systems (NIPSs) and network-based intrusion detection systems (NIDSs) protect a network from intrusions, but do not quarantine internal systems.

22. Of the following choices, which one is a cloud computing option that allows customers to apply patches to the operating system?

    A. Hybrid cloud

    B. Software as a Service

    C. Infrastructure as a Service

    D. Private

22. C is correct. Infrastructure as a Service (IaaS) is a cloud computing option where the vendor provides access to a computer, but customers must manage the system, including keeping it up to date with current patches.

A is incorrect. A hybrid cloud is a combination of a public cloud and a private cloud.

B is incorrect. Software as a Service (SaaS) provides access to applications, such as email.

D is incorrect. An IaaS solution can be public, private, or a hybrid solution.

23. An organization wants to provide protection against malware attacks. Administrators have installed antivirus software on all computers. Additionally, they implemented a firewall and an IDS on the network. Which of the following BEST identifies this principle?

> A. Implicit deny
>
> B. Layered security
>
> C. Least privilege
>
> D. Flood guard

23. B is correct. Layered security (or defense in depth) implements multiple controls to provide several layers of protection. In this case, the antivirus software provides one layer of protection while the firewall and the intrusion detection system (IDS) provide additional layers.

A is incorrect. Implicit deny blocks access unless it has been explicitly allowed.

C is incorrect. Least privilege ensures that users are granted only the access they need to perform their jobs, and no more.

D is incorrect. A flood guard attempts to block SYN Flood attacks.

24. Your organization has implemented a network design that allows internal computers to share one public IP address. Of the following choices, what did they MOST likely implement?

> A. PAT
>
> B. STP
>
> C. DNAT
>
> D. TLS

24. A is correct. Port Address Translation (PAT) is a form of Network Address Translation (NAT) and it allows many internal devices to share one public IP address.

B is incorrect. Spanning Tree Protocol (STP) prevents switch loop problems and is unrelated to sharing IPs.

C is incorrect. Dynamic Network Address Translation (DNAT) uses multiple public IP addresses instead of just one.

D is incorrect. Transport Layer Security (TLS) secures transmissions for data in transit.

25. A company is implementing a feature that allows multiple servers to operate on a single physical server. What is this?

    A. Virtualization

    B. IaaS

    C. Cloud computing

    D. DLP

25. A is correct. Virtualization allows multiple virtual servers to exist on a single physical server.

B is incorrect. Infrastructure as a Service (IAAS) is a cloud computing option where the vendor provides access to a computer, but customers manage it.

C is incorrect. Cloud computing refers to accessing computing resources via a different location than your local computer.

D is incorrect. Data loss prevention (DLP) techniques examine and inspect data looking for unauthorized data transmissions.

26. Management within your organization wants some users to be able to access internal network resources from remote locations. Which of the following is the BEST choice to meet this need?

A. WAF

B. VPN

C. IDS

D. IPS

26. B is correct. A virtual private network (VPN) provides access to a private network over a public network such as the Internet via remote locations and is the best choice.

A is incorrect. A web application firewall (WAF) provides protection for a web application or a web server.

C and D are incorrect. Intrusion detection systems (IDSs) and intrusion prevention systems (IPSs) protect networks, but do not control remote access.

27. What protocol does IPv6 use for hardware address resolution?

A. ARP

B. NDP

C. RDP

D. SNMP

27. B is correct. IPv6 uses the Neighbor Discovery Protocol (NDP) to resolve IPv6 addresses to media access control (MAC) addresses (also called hardware addresses).

A is incorrect. IPv4 uses the Address Resolution Protocol (ARP) to resolve IPv4 addresses to MAC addresses.

C is incorrect. Remote Desktop Protocol (RDP) is used to connect to remote systems over port TCP 3389.

D is incorrect. Administrators use Simple Network Management Protocol (SNMP) to monitor and manage network devices.

28. What is the default port for SSH?

    A. 22

    B. 23

    C. 25

    D. 80

28. A is correct. Secure Shell (SSH) uses Transmission Control Protocol (TCP) port 22 by default, and it is commonly used with other protocols, such as Secure Copy (SCP) and Secure File Transfer Protocol (SFTP).

B is incorrect. Telnet uses port 23.

C is incorrect. SMTP uses port 25

D is incorrect. HTTP uses port 80.

29. You are configuring a host-based firewall so that it will allow SFTP connections. Which of the following is required?

    A. Allow UDP 21

    B. Allow TCP 21

    C. Allow TCP 22

    D. Allow UDP 22

29. C is correct. You should create a rule to allow traffic using Transmission Control Protocol (TCP) port 22. Secure File Transfer Protocol (SFTP) uses Secure Shell (SSH) on TCP port 22.

B is incorrect. FTP uses TCP port 21.

A and D are incorrect. SSH does not use UDP.

30. You need to send several large files containing proprietary data to a business partner. Which of the following is the BEST choice for this task?

    A. FTP

    B. SNMP

    C. SFTP

    D. SSH

30. C is correct. File Transfer Protocol (FTP) is the best choice to send large files, and Secure File Transfer Protocol (SFTP) is the best choice to send large files that need to be protected with encryption. SFTP encrypts data with Secure Shell (SSH) on port 22.

A is incorrect. FTP data is cleartext and is not suitable for proprietary data.

B is incorrect. Simple Network Management Protocol (SNMP) is used to manage network devices.

D is incorrect. Secure Shell (SSH) provides encryption for other protocols, but is not the best choice to send files without combining it with FTP (as SFTP).

31. Your organization is planning to establish a secure link between one of your mail servers and a business partner's mail server. The connection will use the Internet. What protocol is the BEST choice?

    A. TLS

    B. SMTP

    C. HTTP

    D. SSH

31. A is correct. Transport Layer Security (TLS) is a good choice to create a secure connection between two systems over the Internet. Although the mails servers will likely exchange mail using Simple Mail Transfer Protocol (SMTP), SMTP by itself will not create a secure link. Similarly, Hypertext Transfer Protocol (HTTP) doesn't create a secure link. Although Secure Shell (SSH) creates a secure connection, it isn't used with SMTP.

32. You need to prevent the use of TFTP through your firewall. Which port would you block?

    A. TCP 69

    B. UDP 69

C. TCP 21

D. UDP 21

32. B is correct. You should block UDP port 69 to block Trivial File Transfer Protocol (TFTP).

A is incorrect. TFTP does not use TCP.

C is incorrect. File Transfer Protocol (FTP) uses TCP port 21.

33. You need to enable the use of NetBIOS through a firewall. Which ports should you open?

    A. 137 through 139

    B. 20 and 21

    C. 80 and 443

    D. 22 and 3389

33. A is correct. Network Basic Input/Output System (NetBIOS) uses ports 137 through 139.

B is incorrect. File Transfer Protocol (FTP) uses ports 20 and 21.

C is incorrect. Hypertext Transfer Protocol (HTTP) uses port 80 and HTTP Secure (HTTPS) uses port 443.

D is incorrect. You can connect to remote systems with Secure Shell (SSH) using port 22, and Remote Desktop Protocol (RDP) using port 3389.

34. Lisa wants to manage and monitor the switches and routers in her network. Which of the following protocols would she use?

    A. Telnet

    B. SSH

    C. SNMP

    D. DNS

34. C is correct. Simple Network Management Protocol version 3 (SNMPv3) monitors and manages network devices.

A is incorrect. She can use Telnet to connect to the devices, but not monitor them.

B is incorrect. Secure Shell (SSH) is a more secure alternative than Telnet, but it cannot monitor the devices either.

D is incorrect. Domain Name System (DNS) provides name resolution services.

35. You need to reboot your DNS server. Of the following choices, which type of server are you MOST likely to reboot?

    A. Unix server

    B. Apache server

    C. BIND server

    D. Web server

35. C is correct. Berkeley Internet Name Domain (BIND) is a type of Domain Name System (DNS) software commonly used on the Internet and in some internal networks, so a BIND server is a DNS server.

A is incorrect. BIND runs on Unix servers, but not all Unix servers are BIND servers.

B and D are incorrect. Apache is a type of web server software that runs on Unix and Linux systems.

36. Your organization is increasing security and wants to prevent attackers from mapping out the IP addresses used on your internal network. Which of the following choices is the BEST option?

    A. Implement subnetting.

    B. Implement secure zone transfers.

    C. Block outgoing traffic on UDP port 53.

    D. Add a WAF.

36. B is correct. By implementing secure zone transfers on internal Domain Name System (DNS) servers, it prevents attackers from downloading zone data and mapping out IP addresses and devices.

A is incorrect. Subnetting divides classful IP address ranges into smaller subnets, but it doesn't prevent attacks.

C is incorrect. DNS name resolution queries use UDP port 53, so blocking outgoing traffic on UDP port 53 would prevent internal users from using DNS on the Internet.

D is incorrect. A web application firewall (WAF) protects a web server.

37. Network administrators connect to a legacy server using Telnet. They want to secure these transmissions using encryption at a lower layer of the OSI model. What could they use?

    A. IPv4

    B. IPv6

    C. SSH

    D. SFTP

37. B is correct. IPv6 includes the use of Internet Protocol security (IPsec), so it is the best choice and it operates on Layer 3 of the Open Systems Interconnection (OSI) reference model.

A is incorrect. IPv4 doesn't support IPsec natively.

C is incorrect. Although you can use Secure Shell (SSH) instead of Telnet, they both operate on Layer 7 of the OSI model. IPv6 operates on Layer 3.

D is incorrect. Secure File Transfer Protocol (SFTP) is useful for encrypting large files in transit, but it doesn't encrypt Telnet traffic.

38. Your organization is planning to implement a VPN and wants to ensure it is secure. Which of the following protocols is the BEST choice to use with the VPN?

A. HTTP

B. SFTP

C. IPsec

D. PPTP

38. C is correct. Internet Protocol secure (IPsec) is one of several protocols used to secure virtual private network (VPN) traffic. It is the best choice of the available answers.

A is incorrect. Hypertext Transfer Protocol (HTTP) doesn't provide any security.

B is incorrect. Secure File Transfer Protocol (SFTP) secures FTP transmissions but not VPNs.

D is incorrect. Point-to-Point Tunneling Protocol (PPTP) is an older protocol used with VPNs, but it is not as secure as IPsec.

39. Which of the following list of protocols use TCP port 22 by default?

   A. FTPS, TLS, SCP

   B. SCP, SFTP, FTPS

   C. HTTPS, SSL, TLS

   D. SSH, SCP, SFTP

   E. SCP, SSH, SSL

39. D is correct. Secure Shell (SSH) uses Transmission Control Protocol (TCP) port 22 by default. Secure Copy (SCP) and Secure File Transfer Protocol (SFTP) both use SSH for encryption so they also use port 22 by default.

A and B are incorrect. File Transfer Protocol Secure (FTPS) uses either Secure Sockets Layer (SSL) or Transport Layer Security (TLS), typically on ports 989 or 990.

C is incorrect. Hypertext Transfer Protocol Secure (HTTPS) uses SSL or TLS on port 443.

E is incorrect. TLS and SSL do not have a default port by themselves, but instead use a default port based on the protocols they are encrypting.

40. Bart wants to block access to all external web sites. Which port should he block at the firewall?

    A. TCP 22

    B. TCP 53

    C. UDP 69

    D. TCP 80

40. D is correct. He should block port 80 because web sites use Hypertext Transfer Protocol (HTTP) over TCP port 80.

A is incorrect. Secure Shell (SSH) uses TCP port 22.

B is incorrect. Domain Name System (DNS) uses TCP port 53 for zone transfers.

C is incorrect. Trivial File Transfer Protocol (TFTP) uses UDP port 69.

41. You need to manage a remote server. Which of the following ports should you open on the firewall between your system and the remote server?

    A. 25 and 3389

    B. 22 and 443

    C. 22 and 3389

    D. 21 and 23

41. C is correct. You can manage a remote server using Secure Shell (SSH) on TCP port 22 and Remote Desktop Protocol (RDP) on TCP port 3389. You could also use Telnet on TCP port 23, but SSH is the preferred alternative.

A is incorrect. Simple Mail Transfer Protocol (SMTP) uses TCP port 25.

B is incorrect. Hypertext Transfer Protocol Secure (HTTPS) uses TCP port 443.

D is incorrect. File Transfer Protocol (FTP) uses TCP port 21.

42. While reviewing logs on a firewall, you see several requests for the AAAA record of gcgapremium.com. What is the purpose of this request?

A. To identify the IPv4 address of gcgapremium.com

B. To identify the IPv6 address of gcgapremium.com

C. To identify the mail server for gcgapremium.com

D. To identify any aliases used by gcgapremium.com

42. B is correct. A Domain Name System (DNS) AAAA record identifies the IPv6 address of a given name.

A is incorrect. An A record identifies the IPv4 address of a given name.

C is incorrect. An MX record identifies a mail server.

D is incorrect. A CNAME record identifies aliases.

43. One of your web servers was recently attacked and you have been tasked with reviewing firewall logs to see if you can determine how an attacker accessed the system remotely. You identified the following port numbers in log entries: 21, 22, 25, 53, 80, 110, 443, and 3389. Which of the following protocols did the attacker MOST likely use?

A. Telnet

B. HTTPS

C. DNS

D. RDP

43. D is correct. The attacker most likely used Remote Desktop Protocol (RDP) over port 3389.

A is incorrect. Telnet can connect to systems remotely, but it uses port 23 and that isn't one of the listed ports.

B is incorrect. HTTPS uses port 443 for secure HTTP sessions.

C is incorrect. DNS uses port 53 for name resolution queries and zone transfers.

44. Which of the following provides the largest address space?

    A. IPv4

    B. IPv5

    C. IPv6

    D. IPv7

44. C is correct. Internet Protocol version 6 provides the largest address space using 128 bits to define an IP address.

A is incorrect. IPv4 uses 32 bits.

B is incorrect. IPv5 uses 64 bits but was never adopted.

D is incorrect. IPv7 has not been defined.

45. While analyzing a firewall log, you notice traffic going out of your network on UDP port 53. What does this indicate?

    A. Connection with a botnet

    B. DNS traffic

    C. SMTP traffic

    D. SFTP traffic

45. B is correct. Domain Name System (DNS) traffic uses UDP port 53 by default to resolve host names to IP addresses.

A is incorrect. It is not malicious traffic connecting to a botnet.

C is incorrect. Simple Mail Transfer Protocol (SMTP) uses port 25.

D is incorrect. Secure File Transfer Protocol (SFTP) uses port 22.

46. You recently learned that a network router has TCP ports 22 and 80 open, but the organization's security policy mandates that these should not be accessible. What should you do?

    A. Disable the FTP and HTTP services on the router.

    B. Disable the DNS and HTTPS services on the router.

    C. Disable the SSH and HTTP services on the router.

    D. Disable the Telnet and Kerberos services on the router.

46. C is correct. You should disable the Secure Shell (SSH) and Hypertext Transfer Protocol (HTTP) services because they use TCP ports 22 and 80 by default.

A is incorrect. File Transfer Protocol (FTP) uses ports 20 and 21.

B is incorrect. Domain Name System (DNS) uses port 53. Telnet uses port 23.

D is incorrect. Kerberos uses port 88.

47. You are assisting a user implement a wireless network in his home. The wireless hardware he has requires the RC4 protocol. What type of security is BEST for this network?

    A. WEP

    B. WPA-TKIP

    C. WPA-AES

    D. WPA2 Enterprise

47. B is correct. Temporal Key Integrity Protocol (TKIP) uses RC4 and is compatible with older hardware so Wi-Fi Protected Access (WPA) with TKIP is the best option for this network.

A is incorrect. Wired Equivalent Privacy (WEP) uses RC4, but it is not secure and should not be used.

C is incorrect. WPA with Advanced Encryption Standard (AES) is stronger, but it uses AES instead of RC4.

D is incorrect. Wi-Fi Protected Access II (WPA2) Enterprise requires an 802.1x server and does not use RC4.

48. You are planning to deploy a WLAN and you want to ensure it is secure. Which of the following provides the BEST security?

    A. WEP Enterprise

    B. WPA2 TKIP

C. SSID broadcast

D. WPA2 CCMP

48. D is correct. Wi-Fi Protected Access II (WPA2) with Counter Mode Cipher Block Chaining Message Authentication Code Protocol (CCMP) provides the best security of those listed.

A is incorrect. Wired Equivalent Privacy (WEP) is not secure and is not available in Enterprise mode.

B is incorrect. CCMP is stronger than Temporal Key Integrity Protocol (TKIP).

C is incorrect. Service set identifier (SSID) broadcast indicates the network name is broadcast, but this doesn't provide any security. If SSID broadcast is disabled, it hides the network from casual users, but attackers can still see it.

49. Your organization is planning to implement a wireless network using WPA2 Enterprise. Of the following choices, what is required?

    A. An authentication server with a digital certificate installed on the authentication server

    B. An authentication server with DHCP installed on the authentication server

    C. An authentication server with DNS installed on the authentication server

    D. An authentication server with WEP running on the access point

49. A is correct. WPA2 Enterprise requires an 802.1x authentication server and most implementations require a digital certificate installed on the server.

B and C are incorrect. The network will likely have Dynamic Host Configuration Protocol (DHCP) and Domain Name System (DNS) services, but it isn't necessary to install them on the authentication server.

D is incorrect. Wired Equivalent Privacy (WEP) provides poor security and is not compatible with WPA2 Enterprise.

50. You are assisting a small business owner in setting up a public wireless hot spot for her customers. Which of the following actions are MOST appropriate for this hot spot?

    A. Enabling Open System Authentication

    B. Enabling MAC filtering

    C. Disabling SSID broadcast

    D. Installing Yagi antennas

50. A is correct. Open System Authentication is the best choice of those given for a public wireless hot spot. It is used with Wired Equivalent Privacy (WEP), doesn't require users to enter a preshared key or passphrase, and doesn't require the business owner to give out this information.

B is incorrect. It's also possible to disable security for the hot spot. Media access control (MAC) address filtering would be very difficult to maintain.

C is incorrect. Disabling service set identifier (SSID) broadcasting would make it difficult to find the wireless network.

D is incorrect. Installing a directional Yagi antenna isn't appropriate for a hot spot that needs an omnidirectional antenna.

51. Homer is able to connect to his company's wireless network with his smartphone but not with his laptop computer. Which of the following is the MOST likely reason for this disparity?

    A. His company's network has a MAC address filter in place.

    B. His company's network has enabled SSID broadcast.

    C. His company's network has enabled CCMP.

    D. His company's network has enabled WPA2 Enterprise.

51. A is correct. A media access control (MAC) address filter allows (or blocks) devices based on their MAC addresses, so it is likely that the filter is allowing Homer's smartphone but not allowing his laptop computer.

B is incorrect. Enabling the service set identifier (SSID) makes the network easier to see by casual users, but it does not block access even if SSID broadcast is disabled.

C and D are incorrect. Wi-Fi Protected Access II (WPA2) and Counter Mode Cipher Block Chaining Message Authentication Code Protocol (CCMP) both provide strong security, but they do not differentiate between devices.

52. Your organization maintains a separate wireless network for visitors in a conference room. However, you have recently noticed that people are connecting to this network even when there aren't any visitors in the conference room. You want to prevent these connections, while maintaining easy access for visitors in the conference room. Which of the following is the BEST solution?

    A. Disable SSID broadcasting.

    B. Enable MAC filtering.

    C. Use wireless jamming.

    D. Reduce antenna power.

52. D is correct. Reducing the antenna power will make it more difficult for users outside of the conference room to connect, but will not affect visitors in the conference room.

A is incorrect. Disabling service set identifier (SSID) broadcasting will require visitors to know the SSID and enter it in their device, making it more difficult to access the wireless network.

B is incorrect. Enabling media access control (MAC) address filtering will block visitors until an administrator adds their MAC address.

C is incorrect. Wireless jamming will prevent all mobile devices from connecting to the wireless network.

53. Which of the following represents the BEST action to increase security in a wireless network?

    A. Replace dipole antennas with Yagi antennas.

    B. Replace TKIP with CCMP.

    C. Replace WPA with WEP.

    D. Disable SSID broadcast.

53. B is correct. Counter Mode Cipher Block Chaining Message Authentication Code Protocol (CCMP) provides stronger encryption than Temporal Key Integrity Protocol (TKIP) and is the best choice.

A is incorrect. Replacing omnidirectional dipole antennas with directional Yagi antennas doesn't necessarily increase security and will likely limit availability.

C is incorrect. Wired Equivalent Privacy (WEP) should not be used and is not an improvement over Wi-Fi Protected Access (WPA).

D is incorrect. Disabling service set identifier (SSID) broadcast hides the network from casual users, but is not a security step.

54. You are planning a wireless network for a business. A core requirement is to ensure that the solution encrypts user credentials when users enter their usernames and passwords. Which of the following BEST meets this requirement?

    A. WPA2-PSK

    B. WEP over PEAP

    C. WPS with LEAP

    D. WPA2 over EAP-TTLS

54. D is correct. Wi-Fi Protected Access II (WPA2) over Extensible Authentication Protocol (EAP)-Tunneled Transport Layer Security (EAP-TTLS) is the best solution from the available answers. Because users must

enter their usernames and passwords, an 802.1x solution is required and EAP-TTLS meets this requirement.

A is incorrect. WPA2-preshared key (PSK) does not authenticate users based on their usernames.

B is incorrect. Wired Equivalent Privacy (WEP) is not recommended for use even with Protected EAP (PEAP).

C is incorrect. Wi-Fi Protected Setup (WPS) is a standard designed to simplify the setup of a wireless network, but it does not implement usernames, and Cisco recommends using stronger protocols rather than Lightweight EAP (LEAP).

55. A small business owner modified his wireless router with the following settings:

PERMIT 1A:2B:3C:4D:5E:6F

DENY 6F:5E:4D:3C:2B:1A

After saving the settings, an employee reports that he cannot access the wireless network anymore. What is the MOST likely reason that the employee cannot access the network?

    A. IP address filtering

    B. Hardware address filtering

    C. Port filtering

    D. URL filtering

55. B is correct. Media access control (MAC) address filtering can block or allow access based on a device's MAC address, also known as the hardware address. Both addresses in the scenario are MAC addresses.

A, C, and D are incorrect. These addresses are not Internet Protocol (IP) addresses, port numbers, or Uniform Resource Locators (URLs).

56. A team of users in your organization needs a dedicated subnet. For security reasons, other users should not be able to connect to this subnet. Which of the following choices is the BEST solution?

    A. Restrict traffic based on port numbers.

    B. Restrict traffic based on physical addresses.

    C. Implement DNS on the network.

    D. Enable SNMP.

56. B is correct. Of the given choices, the best answer is to restrict traffic based on physical addresses. This is also known as media access control (MAC) address filtering and is configured on a switch.

A is incorrect. Port numbers are related to protocols, so it wouldn't be feasible to restrict traffic for this group based on protocols.

C is incorrect. Domain Name System (DNS) provides name resolution, but it doesn't restrict traffic.

D is incorrect. Simple Network Management Protocol version 3 (SNMPv3) monitors and manages network devices.

57. What type of encryption is used with WPA2 CCMP?

    A. AES

    B. TKIP

    C. RC4

    D. SSL

57. A is correct. Wi-Fi Protected Access II (WPA2) with Counter Mode Cipher Block Chaining Message Authentication Code Protocol (CCMP) uses Advanced Encryption Standard (AES).

B, C, and D are incorrect. Temporal Key Integrity Protocol (TKIP) and Secure Sockets Layer (SSL) both use Rivest Cipher 4 (RC4), but not AES.

58. Administrators in your organization are planning to implement a wireless network. Management has mandated that they use a RADIUS server and implement a secure wireless authentication method. Which of the following should they use?

    A. LEAP

    B. WPA-PSK

    C. WPA2-PSK

    D. AES

58. A is correct. Enterprise mode implements 802.1x as a Remote Authentication Dial-In User Service (RADIUS) server and Lightweight Extensible Authentication Protocol (LEAP) can secure the authentication channel. LEAP is a Cisco proprietary protocol, but other EAP variations can also be used, such as Protected EAP (PEAP), EAP-Transport Layer Security (EAP-TLS), and EAP Tunneled TLS (EAP-TTLS).

B and C are incorrect. Wi-Fi Protected Access (WPA) and WPA2 using a preshared key (PSK) do not use RADIUS.

D is incorrect. Many security protocols use Advanced Encryption Standard (AES), but AES by itself does not use RADIUS.

59. Which of the following is the BEST description of why disabling SSID broadcast is not an effective security measure against attackers?

    A. The network name is contained in wireless packets in plaintext.

    B. The passphrase is contained in wireless packets in plaintext.

    C. The SSID is included in MAC filters.

    D. The SSID is not used with WPA2.

59. A is correct. The service set identifier (SSID) is the network name and it is included in certain wireless packets in plaintext. Disabling SSID broadcast hides the wireless network from casual users, but not attackers.

B is incorrect. Passphrases are not sent across the network in plaintext and are unrelated to the SSID.

C is incorrect. Media access control (MAC) address filters do not include the SSID.

D is incorrect. Wi-Fi Protected Access II (WPA2) does use the SSID.

60. You need to provide connectivity between two buildings without running any cables. You decide to use two WAPs and a high-gain directional antenna. Which of the following antennas is the BEST choice to meet this need?

A. Yagi

B. Omni

C. Isotropic

D. Dipole

60. A is correct. A Yagi antenna is a high-gain directional antenna with a very narrow radiation pattern and is an ideal choice for this scenario.

C is incorrect. An isotropic antenna is theoretical and indicates the signal goes in all directions equally.

B and D are incorrect. Omnidirectional and dipole antennas attempt to mimic an isotropic antenna, but have stronger gains horizontally then vertically, assuming they are standing vertically.

√ **Get Certified**

√ **Get Ahead**

Network Security Extras

When preparing for the Security+ exam, make sure you know the ports listed in Table 1.1:

Protocol	Port	Protocol	Port
FTP data port (active mode)	TCP 20	NetBIOS (TCP rarely used)	TCP/UDP 137
FTP control port	TCP 21	NetBIOS	UDP 138
SSH	TCP 22	NetBIOS	TCP 139
SCP (uses SSH)	TCP 22	IMAP4	TCP 143
SFTP (uses SSH)	TCP 22	LDAP	TCP 389
Telnet	TCP 23	HTTPS	TCP 443
SMTP	TCP 25	SMTP SSL/TLS	TCP 465
TACACS+	TCP 49	IPsec (for VPN with IKE)	UDP 500
DNS name queries	UDP 53	LDAP/SSL	TCP 636
DNS zone transfers	TCP 53	LDAP/TLS	TCP 636
TFTP	UDP 69	IMAP SSL/TLS	TCP 993
HTTP	TCP 80	POP SSL/TLS	TCP 995
Kerberos	UDP 88	L2TP	UDP 1701
POP3	TCP 110	PPTP	TCP 1723
SNMP	UDP 161	Remote Desktop Protocol (RDP)	TCP/UDP 3389
SNMP trap	UDP 162	Microsoft SQL Server	TCP 1433

Table 1.1: Protocols and ports

Table 1.2 lists the layers in the Open Systems Interconnection (OSI) model. It also lists the relevant devices and protocols that you should know when preparing for the Security+ exam.

Layer Number	Layer Name	Devices	Protocols
1	Physical	Cables, hubs	Ethernet, cabling protocols
2	Data Link	Switches	MAC, ARP, NDP, VLANs
3	Network	Router, Layer 3 switch	IPv4, IPv6, IPsec, ICMP
4	Transport		TCP, UDP
5	Session		
6	Presentation		
7	Application	Proxies, application-proxy firewalls, web application firewalls, web security gateways, UTM security appliances	DNS, FTP, FTPS, HTTP, HTTPS, IMAP4, LDAP, POP3, RDP, SCP, SFTP, SMTP, SNMP, SSH, Telnet, and TFTP

Table 1.2: OSI layers

√ **Get Certified**
   √ **Get Ahead**

Chapter 2 Compliance and Operational Security

Compliance and Operational Security topics are **18 percent** of the CompTIA Security+ exam. The objectives in this domain are:

2.1 Explain the importance of risk related concepts.
- Control types
  - Technical
  - Management
  - Operational
- False positives
- False negatives
- Importance of policies in reducing risk
  - Privacy policy
  - Acceptable use
  - Security policy
  - Mandatory vacations
  - Job rotation
  - Separation of duties
  - Least privilege
- Risk calculation
  - Likelihood
  - ALE
  - Impact
  - SL
  - ARO
  - MTTR
  - MTTF
  - MTBF
- Quantitative vs. qualitative
- Vulnerabilities
- Threat vectors
- Probability / threat likelihood
- Risk-avoidance, transference, acceptance, mitigation, deterrence
- Risks associated with Cloud Computing and Virtualization
- Recovery time objective and recovery point objective

2.2 Summarize the security implications of integrating systems and data with third parties.
- On-boarding/off-boarding business partners
- Social media networks and/or applications
- Interoperability agreements
  - SLA
  - BPA
  - MOU
  - ISA
- Privacy considerations
- Risk awareness
- Unauthorized data sharing
- Data ownership
- Data backups
- Follow security policy and procedures
- Review agreement requirements to verify compliance and performance standards

2.3 Given a scenario, implement appropriate risk mitigation strategies.
- Change management
- Incident management
- User rights and permissions reviews
- Perform routine audits
- Enforce policies and procedures to prevent data loss or theft
- Enforce technology controls
  - Data Loss Prevention (DLP)

2.4 Given a scenario, implement basic forensic procedures.
- Order of volatility
- Capture system image
- Network traffic and logs
- Capture video
- Record time offset
- Take hashes
- Screenshots
- Witnesses
- Track man hours and expense
- Chain of custody
- Big Data analysis

2.5 Summarize common incident response procedures.

- Preparation
- Incident identification
- Escalation and notification
- Mitigation steps
- Lessons learned
- Reporting
- Recovery/reconstitution procedures
- First responder
- Incident isolation
  - Quarantine
  - Device removal
- Data breach
- Damage and loss control

2.6 Explain the importance of security related awareness and training.
- Security policy training and procedures
- Role-based training
- Personally identifiable information
- Information classification
  - High
  - Medium
  - Low
  - Confidential
  - Private
  - Public
- Data labeling, handling and disposal
- Compliance with laws, best practices and standards
- User habits
  - Password behaviors
  - Data handling
  - Clean desk policies
  - Prevent tailgating
  - Personally owned devices
- New threats and new security trends/alerts
  - New viruses
  - Phishing attacks
  - Zero-day exploits
- Use of social networking and P2P
- Follow up and gather training metrics to validate compliance and security posture

2.7 Compare and contrast physical security and environmental controls.

- Environmental controls
  - HVAC
  - Fire suppression
  - EMI shielding
  - Hot and cold aisles
  - Environmental monitoring
  - Temperature and humidity controls
- Physical security
  - Hardware locks
  - Mantraps
  - Video Surveillance
  - Fencing
  - Proximity readers
  - Access list
  - Proper lighting
  - Signs
  - Guards
  - Barricades
  - Biometrics
  - Protected distribution (cabling)
  - Alarms
  - Motion detection
- Control types
  - Deterrent
  - Preventive
  - Detective
  - Compensating
  - Technical
  - Administrative

2.8 Summarize risk management best practices.

- Business continuity concepts
  - Business impact analysis
  - Identification of critical systems and components
  - Removing single points of failure
  - Business continuity planning and testing
  - Risk assessment
  - Continuity of operations
  - Disaster recovery
  - IT contingency planning
  - Succession planning
  - High availability
  - Redundancy
  - Tabletop exercises

- Fault tolerance
  - Hardware
  - RAID
  - Clustering
  - Load balancing
  - Servers
- Disaster recovery concepts
  - Backup plans/policies
  - Backup execution/frequency
  - Cold site
  - Hot site
  - Warm site

2.9 Given a scenario, select the appropriate control to meet the goals of security.
- Confidentiality
  - Encryption
  - Access controls
  - Steganography
- Integrity
  - Hashing
  - Digital signatures
  - Certificates
  - Non-repudiation
- Availability
  - Redundancy
  - Fault tolerance
  - Patching
- Safety
  - Fencing
  - Lighting
  - Locks
  - CCTV
  - Escape plans
  - Drills
  - Escape routes
  - Testing controls

The CompTIA Security+: Get Certified Get Ahead SY0-401 Study Guide (ISBN 1939136024) discusses these topics in much more depth.

√ **Get Certified**

√ **Get Ahead**

Practice Test Questions for
Compliance and Operational Security Domain

1. A security manager needs to identify a policy that will reduce the risk of personnel within an organization colluding to embezzle company funds. Which of the following is the BEST choice?

    A. AUP

    B. Training

    C. Mandatory vacations

    D. Time-of-day restrictions

2. Your organization includes a software development division within the IT department. One developer writes and maintains applications for the Sales and Marketing departments. A second developer writes and maintains applications for the Payroll department. Once a year, they have to switch roles for at least a month. What is the purpose of this practice?

    A. To enforce a separation of duties policy

    B. To enforce a mandatory vacation policy

    C. To enforce a job rotation policy

    D. To enforce an acceptable use policy

3. Which of the following accurately identifies the primary security control classifications?

    A. Role-based, mandatory, and discretionary

    B. Technical, management, and operational

    C. Physical, logical, and technical

    D. Technical and preventive

4. Administrators have noticed an increased workload recently. Which of the following can cause an increased workload from incorrect reporting?

    A. False negatives

    B. False positives

    C. Separation of duties

    D. Signature-based IDSs

5. Which of the following is most closely associated with residual risk?

    A. Risk acceptance

    B. Risk avoidance

    C. Risk deterrence

    D. Risk mitigation

    E. Risk transference

6. You need to calculate the ALE for a server. The value of the server is $3,000, but it has crashed 10 times in the past year. Each time it crashed, it resulted in a 10 percent loss. What is the ALE?

    A. $300

    B. $500

    C. $3,000

    D. $30,000

7. You need to calculate the expected loss of an incident. Which of the following value combinations would you MOST likely use?

    A. ALE and ARO

    B. ALE and SLE

    C. SLE and ARO

    D. ARO and ROI

8. You are helping implement your company's business continuity plan. For one system, the plan requires an RTO of five hours and an RPO of one day. Which of the following would meet this requirement?

    A. Ensure the system can be restored within five hours and ensure it does not lose more than one day of data.

    B. Ensure the system can be restored within one day and ensure it does not lose more than five hours of data.

    C. Ensure the system can be restored between five hours and one day after an outage.

    D. Ensure critical systems can be restored within five hours and noncritical systems can be restored within one day.

9. Your organization is evaluating replacement HVAC systems and is considering increasing current capacities. Which of the following is a potential security benefit of increasing the HVAC capabilities?

    A. Lower MTBF times of hardware components due to lower temperatures

    B. Higher MTBF times of hardware components due to lower temperatures

    C. Lower MTTR times of hardware components due to lower temperatures

    D. Higher MTTR times of hardware components due to lower temperatures

10. An attacker was able to sneak into your building but was unable to open the server room door. He bashed the proximity badge reader with a portable fire extinguisher and the door opened. What is the MOST likely reason that the door opened?

A. The access system was designed to fail-open.

B. The access system was designed to fail-close.

C. The access system was improperly installed.

D. The portable fire extinguisher included a proximity badge.

11. An organization has purchased fire insurance to manage the risk of a potential fire. What method are they using?

A. Risk acceptance

B. Risk avoidance

C. Risk deterrence

D. Risk mitigation

E. Risk transference

12. Lisa needs to calculate the total ALE for a group of servers used in the network. During the past two years, five of the servers failed. The hardware cost to replace each server is $3,500, and the downtime has resulted in $2,500 of additional losses. What is the ALE?

A. $7,000

B. $10,000

C. $15,000

D. $30,000

13. Which of the following BEST describes a false negative?

A. An IDS falsely indicates a buffer overflow attack occurred.

B. Antivirus software reports that a valid application is malware.

C. A locked door opens after a power failure.

D. An IDS does not detect a buffer overflow attack.

14. You are trying to add additional security controls for a database server that includes customer records and need to justify the cost of $1,000 for these controls. The database includes 2,500 records. Estimates indicate a cost of $300 for each record if an attacker successfully gains access to them. Research indicates that there is a 10 percent possibility of a data breach in the next year. What is the ALE?

    A. $300

    B. $37,500

    C. $75,000

    D. $750,000

15. An organizational policy specifies that duties of application developers and administrators must be separated. What is the MOST likely result of implementing this policy?

    A. One group develops program code and the other group deploys the code.

    B. One group develops program code and the other group modifies the code.

    C. One group deploys program code and the other group administers databases.

    D. One group develops databases and the other group modifies databases.

16. Get Certified Get Ahead has outsourced some application development to your organization. Unfortunately, developers at your organization are having problems getting an application module to work and they want to send the module with accompanying data to a third-party vendor for help in resolving the problem. Which of the following should developers consider before doing so?

A. Ensure that data in transit is encrypted.

B. Review NDAs.

C. Identify the classification of the data.

D. Verify the third party has an NDA in place.

17. Two companies have decided to work together on a project and implemented an MOU. Which of the following represents the GREATEST security risk in this situation?

A. An MOU doesn't define responsibilities.

B. An MOU includes monetary penalties if one party doesn't meet its responsibilities.

C. An MOU can impose strict requirements for connections.

D. An MOU doesn't have strict guidelines to protect sensitive data.

18. Your organization is considering storage of sensitive data in a cloud provider. Your organization wants to ensure the data is encrypted while at rest and while in transit. What type of interoperability agreement can your organization use to ensure the data is encrypted while in transit?

A. SLA

B. BPA

C. MOU

D. ISA

19. A network administrator needs to update the operating system on switches used within the network. Assuming the organization is following standard best practices, what should the administrator do first?

A. Submit a request using the baseline configuration process.

B. Submit a request using the incident management process.

C. Submit a request using the change management process.

D. Submit a request using the application patch management process.

20. Management wants to ensure that employees do not print any documents that include customer PII. Which of the following solutions would meet this goal?

    A. HSM

    B. TPM

    C. VLAN

    D. DLP

21. Your organization recently hired an outside security auditor to review internal processes. The auditor identified several employees who had permissions for previously held jobs within the company. What should the organization implement to prevent this in the future?

    A. Design reviews

    B. Code reviews

    C. Baseline review

    D. User rights and permissions reviews

22. Your organization security policy requires that personnel notify security administrators if an incident occurs. However, this is not occurring consistently. Which of the following could the organization implement to ensure security administrators are notified in a timely manner?

    A. Routine auditing

    B. User rights and permissions reviews

    C. Design review

    D. Incident response team

23. After a recent incident, a forensic analyst was given several hard drives to analyze. What should the analyst do first?

A. Take screenshots and capture system images.

B. Take hashes and screenshots.

C. Take hashes and capture system images.

D. Perform antivirus scans and create chain-of-custody documents.

24. A security analyst tagged a computer stating when he took possession of it. What is the BEST explanation for this?

A. To calculate time offset

B. To ensure the system is decommissioned

C. To begin a chain of custody

D. To implement separation of duties

25. An administrator recently learned of an attack on a Virginia-based web server from IP address 72.52.206.134 at 11:35:33 GMT. However, after investigating the logs, he is unable to see any traffic from that IP address at that time. Which of the following is the MOST likely reason why the administrator was unable to identify the attack?

A. He did not account for time offsets.

B. He did not capture an image.

C. The IP address has expired.

D. The logs were erased when the system was rebooted.

26. An incident response team is following typical incident response procedures. Which of the following phases is the BEST choice for analyzing an incident with a goal of identifying steps to prevent a reoccurrence of the incident?

A. Preparation

B. Identification

C. Mitigation

D. Lessons learned

27. Your organization was recently attacked, resulting in a data breach, and attackers captured customer data. Management wants to take steps to better protect customer data. Which of the following will BEST support this goal?

    A. Succession planning and data recovery procedures

    B. Fault tolerance and redundancy

    C. Stronger access controls and encryption

    D. Hashing and digital signatures

28. You are reviewing incident response procedures related to the order of volatility. Which of the following is the LEAST volatile?

    A. Hard disk drive

    B. Memory

    C. RAID-6 cache

    D. CPU cache

29. A security manager is reviewing security policies related to data loss. Which of the following is the security administrator MOST likely to be reviewing?

    A. Clean desk policy

    B. Separation of duties

    C. Job rotation

    D. Change management

30. Security personnel recently released an online training module advising employees not to share personal information on any social media web sites that they visit. What is this advice MOST likely trying to prevent?

    A. Spending time on non-work-related sites

    B. Phishing attack

    C. Cognitive password attacks

    D. Rainbow table attack

31. Your organization blocks access to social media web sites. The primary purpose is to prevent data leakage, such as the accidental disclosure of proprietary information. What is an additional security benefit of this policy?

    A. Improves employee productivity

    B. Enables cognitive password attacks

    C. Prevents P2P file sharing

    D. Protects against banner ad malware

32. Your organization has spent a significant amount of money on training employees on security awareness. Your organization wants to validate the success of this training. Which of the following is the BEST choice?

    A. Implement role-based training.

    B. Use metrics.

    C. Use security policies.

    D. Verify PII.

33. Social engineers have launched several successful phone-based attacks against your organization resulting in several data leaks. Which of the following would be the MOST effective at reducing the success of these attacks?

    A. Implement a BYOD policy.

    B. Update the AUP.

    C. Provide training on data handling.

    D. Implement a program to increase security awareness.

34. A security expert is identifying and implementing several different physical deterrent controls to protect an organization's server room. Which of the following choices would BEST meet this objective?

A. Using hardware locks

B. Utilizing data encryption

C. Performing a vulnerability assessment

D. Training users

35. You need to secure access to a data center. Which of the following choices provides the BEST physical security to meet this need? (Select THREE.)

A. Biometrics

B. Cable locks

C. CCTV

D. Mantrap

36. Your company wants to control access to a restricted area of the building by adding an additional physical security control that includes facial recognition. Which of the following provides the BEST solution?

A. Bollards

B. Guards

C. Palm scanners

D. Video surveillance

37. Thieves recently rammed a truck through the entrance of your company's main building. During the chaos, their partners proceeded to steal a significant amount of IT equipment. Which of the following choices can you use to prevent this from happening again?

A. Bollards

B. Guards

C. CCTV

D. Mantrap

38. A security professional has reported an increase in the number of tailgating violations into a secure data center. What can prevent this?

    A. CCTV

    B. Mantrap

    C. Proximity card

    D. Cipher lock

39. Users are complaining of intermittent connectivity issues. When you investigate, you discover that new network cables for these user systems were run across several fluorescent lights. What environmental control will resolve this issue?

    A. HVAC system

    B. Fire suppression

    C. Humidity controls

    D. EMI shielding

40. Company management suspects an employee is stealing critical project information and selling it to a competitor. They'd like to identify who is doing this, without compromising any live data. What is the BEST option to meet this goal?

    A. Install antivirus software on all user systems.

    B. Implement an IPS.

    C. Implement an IDS.

    D. Add fabricated project data on a honeypot.

41. An organization needs to improve fault tolerance to increase data availability. However, the organization has a limited budget. Which of the following is the BEST choice to meet the organization's needs?

    A. RAID

    B. Backup system

    C. Cluster

    D. UPS

42. Your company's web site experiences a large number of client requests during certain times of the year. Which of the following could your company add to ensure the web site's availability during these times?

    A. Fail-open cluster

    B. Certificates

    C. Web application firewall

    D. Load balancing

43. Your backup policy for a database server dictates that the amount of time needed to perform backups should be minimized. Which of the following backup plans would BEST meet this need?

    A. Full backups on Sunday and full backups every other day of the week

    B. Full backups on Sunday and differential backups every other day of the week

    C. Full backups on Sunday and incremental backups every other day of the week

    D. Differential backups on Sunday and incremental backups every other day of the week

44. An organization is considering an alternate location as part of its business continuity plan. It wants to identify a solution that provides the shortest recovery time. What will it choose?

A. Cold site

B. Warm site

C. Hot site

D. Succession site

45. Your organization is working on its business continuity plan. Management wants to ensure that documents provide detailed information on what technicians should do after an outage. Specifically, they want to list the systems to restore and the order in which to restore them. What document includes this information?

    A. HVAC

    B. BIA

    C. DRP

    D. Succession plan

46. The BCP coordinator at your organization is leading a meeting on-site with key disaster recovery personnel. The purpose of the meeting is to perform a test. What type of test is this?

    A. Functional exercise

    B. Full-blown test

    C. Tabletop exercise

    D. Simulation to perform steps of a plan

47. You are a technician at a small organization. You need to add fault-tolerance capabilities within the business to increase the availability of data. However, you need to keep costs as low as possible. Which of the following is the BEST choice to meet these needs?

    A. Failover cluster

    B. RAID-6

    C. Backups

    D. UPS

48. An organization needs to identify a continuity of operations plan that will allow it to provide temporary IT support during a disaster. The organization does not want to have a dedicated site. Which of the following provides the best solution?

    A. Cold site

    B. Warm site

    C. Hot site

    D. Mobile site

49. Monty Burns is the CEO of the Springfield Nuclear Power Plant. What would the company have in place in case something happens to him?

    A. Business continuity planning

    B. Succession planning

    C. Separation of duties

    D. IT contingency planning

50. A continuity of operations plan for an organization includes the use of a warm site. The BCP coordinator wants to verify that the organization's backup data center is prepared to implement the warm site if necessary. Which of the following is the BEST choice to meet this need?

    A. Perform a review of the disaster recovery plan.

    B. Ask the managers of the backup data center.

    C. Perform a disaster recovery exercise.

    D. Perform a test restore.

51. A security analyst is creating a document that includes the expected monetary loss from a major outage. She is calculating the potential lost sales, fines, and impact on the organization's customers. Which of the following documents is she MOST likely creating?

    A. BCP

    B. BIA

    C. DRP

    D. RPO

52. You want to ensure that messages sent from administrators to managers arrive unchanged. Which security goal are you addressing?

    A. Confidentiality

    B. Integrity

    C. Availability

    D. Authentication

53. Your organization recently implemented two servers that act as failover devices for each other. Which security goal is your organization pursuing?

    A. Safety

    B. Integrity

    C. Confidentiality

    D. Availability

54. Management at your company recently decided to implement additional lighting and fencing around the property. Which security goal is your company MOST likely pursuing?

    A. Confidentiality

    B. Integrity

    C. Availability

    D. Safety

55. Lisa manages network devices in your organization and maintains copies of the configuration files for all the managed routers and switches. On a weekly basis, she creates hashes for these files and compares them with hashes she created on the same files the previous week. Which security goal is she pursuing?

    A. Confidentiality

    B. Integrity

    C. Availability

    D. Safety

56. Lisa hid several plaintext documents within an image file. Which security goal is she pursuing?

    A. Encryption

    B. Integrity

    C. Steganography

    D. Confidentiality

√ Get Certified

√ Get Ahead

Sample Performance-Based Question

Many of the security controls in this chapter can easily be tested in a drag-and-drop or matching type of performance-based question. As long as you know the content, these questions typically aren't any more difficult than a standard multiple-choice question. Here's an example of a performance-based question.

Instructions: You have the following list of controls that you need to use to secure items shown in Figure 2.1:

- Five cable locks
- Four fingerprint readers
- Two proximity badge readers
- One CCTV system
- One mantrap
- One locking cabinet
- One safe

You must use all the items in the list at least once and you must fill all empty boxes in the figure. For example, you must use all five cable locks, not just one cable lock.

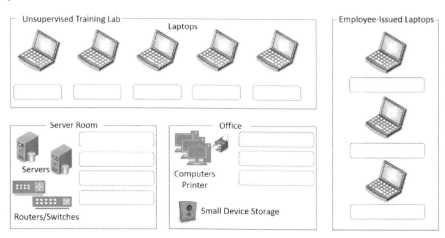

Figure 2.1

√ **Get Certified**

√ **Get Ahead**

Practice Test Questions with Answers for Compliance and Operational Security Domain

1. A security manager needs to identify a policy that will reduce the risk of personnel within an organization colluding to embezzle company funds. Which of the following is the BEST choice?

    A. AUP

    B. Training

    C. Mandatory vacations

    D. Time-of-day restrictions

1. C is correct. Mandatory vacations help to reduce the possibility of fraud and embezzlement.

A is incorrect. An acceptable use policy informs users of company policies and even though users sign them, they don't deter someone considering theft by embezzling funds.

B is incorrect. Training can help reduce incidents by ensuring personnel are aware of appropriate policies.

D is incorrect. Time-of-day restrictions prevent users from logging on during restricted times.

2. Your organization includes a software development division within the IT department. One developer writes and maintains applications for the Sales and Marketing departments. A second developer writes and maintains applications for the Payroll department. Once a year, they have to switch roles for at least a month. What is the purpose of this practice?

    A. To enforce a separation of duties policy

    B. To enforce a mandatory vacation policy

    C. To enforce a job rotation policy

    D. To enforce an acceptable use policy

2. C is correct. This practice enforces a job rotation policy where employees rotate into different jobs, and is designed to reduce potential incidents.

A is incorrect. A separation of duties policy prevents any single person from performing multiple job functions to help prevent fraud, but it doesn't force users to switch roles.

B is incorrect. A mandatory vacation policy requires employees to take time away from their job.

D is incorrect. An acceptable use policy informs users of their responsibilities when using an organization's equipment.

3. Which of the following accurately identifies the primary security control classifications?

      A. Role-based, mandatory, and discretionary

      B. Technical, management, and operational

      C. Physical, logical, and technical

      D. Technical and preventive

3. B is correct. Security controls are classified as technical (implemented by technical means), management (implemented administratively), and operational (for day-to-day operations).

A is incorrect. Access control methods are role-based, rule-based, mandatory, and discretionary.

C is incorrect. Physical and logical are not terms used to describe security control classifications, even though some controls are physical and some are logical.

D is incorrect. Although technical is a security control classification, preventive refers to a security control goal.

4. Administrators have noticed an increased workload recently. Which of the following can cause an increased workload from incorrect reporting?

A. False negatives

B. False positives

C. Separation of duties

D. Signature-based IDSs

4. B is correct. False positives can cause an increased workload because they falsely indicate an alert has occurred.

A is incorrect. A false negative doesn't report an actual attack, so it doesn't increase the workload because administrators are unaware of the attack.

C is incorrect. Separation of duties ensures a single person can't control an entire process, so it is unrelated to increased workload.

D is incorrect. Signature-based intrusion detection systems (IDSs) don't necessarily cause an increased workload unless they have a high incidence of false positives.

5. Which of the following is most closely associated with residual risk?

A. Risk acceptance

B. Risk avoidance

C. Risk deterrence

D. Risk mitigation

E. Risk transference

5. A is correct. Residual risk is the risk that an organization accepts after implementing controls to reduce risk.

B is incorrect. An organization can avoid a risk by not providing a service or not participating in a risky activity.

C is incorrect. Risk deterrence attempts to discourage attacks with preventive controls such as a security guard.

D is incorrect. Risk mitigation reduces risks through internal controls.

D is incorrect. Purchasing insurance is a common method of risk transference.

6. You need to calculate the ALE for a server. The value of the server is $3,000, but it has crashed 10 times in the past year. Each time it crashed, it resulted in a 10 percent loss. What is the ALE?

    A. $300

    B. $500

    C. $3,000

    D. $30,000

6. C is correct. The annual loss expectancy (ALE) is $3,000. It is calculated as single loss expectancy (SLE) × annual rate of occurrence (ARO).

A is incorrect. The SLE is 10 percent of $3,000 ($300) and the ARO is 10. 10 × $300 is $3,000.

B and D are incorrect. The math doesn't give this answers.

7. You need to calculate the expected loss of an incident. Which of the following value combinations would you MOST likely use?

    A. ALE and ARO

    B. ALE and SLE

    C. SLE and ARO

    D. ARO and ROI

7. A is correct. The expected loss is the single loss expectancy (SLE) and you can calculate it with the annual loss expectancy (ALE) and annual rate of occurrence (ARO), as ALE / ARO.

B and C are incorrect. The SLE is what you are trying to determine, so you don't have that value.

D is incorrect. The return on investment (ROI) will not help in identifying the SLE.

8. You are helping implement your company's business continuity plan. For one system, the plan requires an RTO of five hours and an RPO of one day. Which of the following would meet this requirement?

A. Ensure the system can be restored within five hours and ensure it does not lose more than one day of data.

B. Ensure the system can be restored within one day and ensure it does not lose more than five hours of data.

C. Ensure the system can be restored between five hours and one day after an outage.

D. Ensure critical systems can be restored within five hours and noncritical systems can be restored within one day.

8. A is correct. The recovery time objective (RTO) identifies the maximum amount of time it should take to restore a system after an outage.

B, C, and D are incorrect. The recovery point objective (RPO) refers to the amount of data you can afford to lose. RTO only refers to time, not data. RPO refers to data recovery points, not time to restore a system.

9. Your organization is evaluating replacement HVAC systems and is considering increasing current capacities. Which of the following is a potential security benefit of increasing the HVAC capabilities?

A. Lower MTBF times of hardware components due to lower temperatures

B. Higher MTBF times of hardware components due to lower temperatures

C. Lower MTTR times of hardware components due to lower temperatures

D. Higher MTTR times of hardware components due to lower temperatures

9. B is correct. Increasing the heating, ventilation, and air conditioning (HVAC) capacity results in higher mean time between failures (MTBF) times by keeping systems at lower temperatures.

A is incorrect. Lower MTBF times indicate more failures.

C and D are incorrect. Mean time to recover (MTTR) is unrelated to failures or HVAC systems.

10. An attacker was able to sneak into your building but was unable to open the server room door. He bashed the proximity badge reader with a portable fire extinguisher and the door opened. What is the MOST likely reason that the door opened?

    A. The access system was designed to fail-open.

    B. The access system was designed to fail-close.

    C. The access system was improperly installed.

    D. The portable fire extinguisher included a proximity badge.

10. A is correct. In this scenario, the most likely reason that the door opened was because the access system was designed to fail-open for personnel safety.

B is incorrect. If the system was designed to fail-close, then employees would be trapped inside during a fire or other disaster.

C is incorrect. Nothing in the scenario indicates the system was improperly installed.

D is incorrect. A fire extinguisher would not include a proximity badge, and it wouldn't work if the proximity reader was destroyed.

11. An organization has purchased fire insurance to manage the risk of a potential fire. What method are they using?

    A. Risk acceptance

    B. Risk avoidance

    C. Risk deterrence

    D. Risk mitigation

    E. Risk transference

11. E is correct. Purchasing insurance is a common method of risk transference.

A is incorrect. Organizations often accept a risk when the cost of the control exceeds the cost of the risk, and the risk that remains is residual risk.

B is incorrect. An organization can avoid a risk by not providing a service or not participating in a risky activity.

C is incorrect. Risk deterrence attempts to discourage attacks with preventive controls such as a security guard.

D is incorrect. Risk mitigation reduces risks through internal controls.

12. Lisa needs to calculate the total ALE for a group of servers used in the network. During the past two years, five of the servers failed. The hardware cost to replace each server is $3,500, and the downtime has resulted in $2,500 of additional losses. What is the ALE?

    A. $7,000

    B. $10,000

    C. $15,000

    D. $30,000

12. C is correct. The annual loss expectancy (ALE) is $15,000. The single loss expectancy (SLE) is $6,000 ($3,500 + $2,500). The annual rate of occurrence (ARO) is 2.5 (five failures in two years or 5 / 2). You calculate the ARO as SLE × ARO ($6,000 × 2.5).

A, B and D are incorrect. The math ($6,000 × 2.5) doesn't result in the other answers.

13. Which of the following BEST describes a false negative?

A. An IDS falsely indicates a buffer overflow attack occurred.

B. Antivirus software reports that a valid application is malware.

C. A locked door opens after a power failure.

D. An IDS does not detect a buffer overflow attack.

13. D is correct. An intrusion detection system (IDS) should detect a buffer overflow attack and report it, but if it does not, it is a false negative.

A is incorrect. If the IDS falsely indicates an attack occurred, it is a false positive.

B is incorrect. If antivirus software indicates a valid application is malware, it is a false positive.

C is incorrect. A locked door that opens after a power failure is designed to fail-open.

14. You are trying to add additional security controls for a database server that includes customer records and need to justify the cost of $1,000 for these controls. The database includes 2,500 records. Estimates indicate a cost of $300 for each record if an attacker successfully gains access to them. Research indicates that there is a 10 percent possibility of a data breach in the next year. What is the ALE?

    A. $300

    B. $37,500

    C. $75,000

    D. $750,000

14. C is correct. The annual loss expectancy (ALE) is $75,000. The single loss expectancy (SLE) is $750,000 ($300 per record × 2,500 records). The annual rate of occurrence (ARO) is 10 percent or .10. You calculate the ALE as SLE × ARO ($750,000 x .10).

A is incorrect. One single record is $300, but if an attacker can gain access to the database, the attacker can access all 2,500 records.

B is incorrect. If the ARO was .05, the ALE would be $37,500.

D is incorrect. The single loss expectancy (SLE) is $750,000 ($300 per record × 2,500 records).

15. An organizational policy specifies that duties of application developers and administrators must be separated. What is the MOST likely result of implementing this policy?

    A. One group develops program code and the other group deploys the code.

    B. One group develops program code and the other group modifies the code.

    C. One group deploys program code and the other group administers databases.

    D. One group develops databases and the other group modifies databases.

15. A is correct. This describes a separation of duties policy where the application developers create and modify the code, and the administrators deploy the code to live production systems, but neither group can perform both functions.

B is incorrect. Developers would typically develop the original code, and modify it when necessary.

C and D are incorrect. This scenario does not mention databases.

16. Get Certified Get Ahead has outsourced some application development to your organization. Unfortunately, developers at your organization are having problems getting an application module to work and they want to send the module with accompanying data to a third-party vendor for help in resolving the problem. Which of the following should developers consider before doing so?

A. Ensure that data in transit is encrypted.

B. Review NDAs.

C. Identify the classification of the data.

D. Verify the third party has an NDA in place.

16. B is correct. Developers should review the non-disclosure agreements (NDAs) and verify that sharing data with a third party doesn't violate any existing NDAs.

A is incorrect. Encrypting data in transit protects its confidentiality while in transit, but it won't protect it from a third party accessing it after receiving it.

C is incorrect. The classification of the data isn't as relevant as the NDA in this situation.

D is incorrect. An NDA between the third party and your organization isn't relevant, if the NDA between you and the hiring organization states you cannot share the data.

17. Two companies have decided to work together on a project and implemented an MOU. Which of the following represents the GREATEST security risk in this situation?

A. An MOU doesn't define responsibilities.

B. An MOU includes monetary penalties if one party doesn't meet its responsibilities.

C. An MOU can impose strict requirements for connections.

D. An MOU doesn't have strict guidelines to protect sensitive data.

17. D is correct. A memorandum of understanding (MOU) represents an agreement and it doesn't have strict guidelines to protect sensitive data.

A is incorrect. An MOU does define responsibilities between the parties.

B is incorrect. A service level agreement (SLA) might include monetary penalties, but an MOU does not.

C is incorrect. An interconnection security agreement (ISA) includes strict requirements for connections and is often used with an MOU.

18. Your organization is considering storage of sensitive data in a cloud provider. Your organization wants to ensure the data is encrypted while at rest and while in transit. What type of interoperability agreement can your organization use to ensure the data is encrypted while in transit?

    A. SLA

    B. BPA

    C. MOU

    D. ISA

18. D is correct. An interconnection security agreement (ISA) specifies technical and security requirements for secure connections and can ensure data is encrypted while in transit. None of the other agreements address the connection.

A is incorrect. A service level agreement (SLA) stipulates performance expectations of a vendor.

B is incorrect. A business partners agreement (BPA) is a written agreement for business partners.

C is incorrect. A memorandum of understanding (MOU) expresses an understanding between two parties to work together.

19. A network administrator needs to update the operating system on switches used within the network. Assuming the organization is following standard best practices, what should the administrator do first?

    A. Submit a request using the baseline configuration process.

    B. Submit a request using the incident management process.

    C. Submit a request using the change management process.

    D. Submit a request using the application patch management process.

19. C is correct. The network administrator should submit a change using the change management process, which is the same process that is typically used for changes to any devices or systems.

A is incorrect. A baseline configuration identifies the starting configuration.

B is incorrect. Incident management addresses security incidents.

D is incorrect. A regular patch management process typically includes following change management, but application patch management does not apply to devices.

20. Management wants to ensure that employees do not print any documents that include customer PII. Which of the following solutions would meet this goal?

     A. HSM

     B. TPM

     C. VLAN

     D. DLP

20. D is correct. A data loss prevention (DLP) solution can limit documents sent to a printer to be printed using content filters.

A and B are incorrect. A hardware security module (HSM) and a Trusted Platform Module (TPM) both provide full disk encryption, but cannot block documents sent to a printer.

C is incorrect. A virtual local area network (VLAN) segments traffic, but isn't selective about documents sent to a printer.

21. Your organization recently hired an outside security auditor to review internal processes. The auditor identified several employees who had permissions for previously held jobs within the company. What should the organization implement to prevent this in the future?

    A. Design reviews

    B. Code reviews

    C. Baseline review

    D. User rights and permissions reviews

21. D is correct. A user rights and permissions review detects permission bloat situations such as this. Account management controls also help ensure these situations don't occur.

A is incorrect. A design review helps ensure that systems and software are developed properly.

B is incorrect. A code review is a line-by-line review of code by peer programmers.

C is incorrect. A baseline review compares current configurations against baseline settings.

22. Your organization security policy requires that personnel notify security administrators if an incident occurs. However, this is not occurring consistently. Which of the following could the organization implement to ensure security administrators are notified in a timely manner?

    A. Routine auditing

    B. User rights and permissions reviews

    C. Design review

    D. Incident response team

22. A is correct. Routine auditing of the help desk or administrator logs can discover incidents and then match them with reported incidents.

B is incorrect. A review of user rights and permissions helps ensure they are assigned and maintained appropriately, but do not help with ensuring incidents are reported correctly.

C is incorrect. A design review ensures that systems and software are developed properly.

D is incorrect. An incident response team responds to incidents, but they wouldn't necessarily ensure administrators are informed of incidents.

23. After a recent incident, a forensic analyst was given several hard drives to analyze. What should the analyst do first?

    A. Take screenshots and capture system images.

    B. Take hashes and screenshots.

    C. Take hashes and capture system images.

    D. Perform antivirus scans and create chain-of-custody documents.

23. C is correct. Forensic analysts capture images and take hashes before beginning analysis, and they only analyze the image copies, not the original drive.

A and B are incorrect. Screenshots are taken when a computer is running.

D is incorrect. An antivirus scan might modify the drive and chain-of-custody documents are created when evidence is collected.

24. A security analyst tagged a computer stating when he took possession of it. What is the BEST explanation for this?

    A. To calculate time offset

    B. To ensure the system is decommissioned

    C. To begin a chain of custody

    D. To implement separation of duties

24. C is correct. A chain of custody identifies who controlled evidence after it was confiscated. It can start with a tag when a person collects the evidence. Security analysts later create a chain-of-custody log to detail who controlled the evidence at different times.

A is incorrect. Time offset is related to different time zones or times recorded on a video recorder.

B is incorrect. A security analyst would confiscate a computer to analyze it, not decommission it.

D is incorrect. Separation of duties is related to people, not computers.

25. An administrator recently learned of an attack on a Virginia-based web server from IP address 72.52.206.134 at 11:35:33 GMT. However, after investigating the logs, he is unable to see any traffic from that IP address at that time. Which of the following is the MOST likely reason why the administrator was unable to identify the attack?

    A. He did not account for time offsets.

    B. He did not capture an image.

    C. The IP address has expired.

    D. The logs were erased when the system was rebooted.

25. A is correct. The most likely reason is that he did not account for the time offset. The attack occurred at 11:35:33 Greenwich Mean Time (GMT) and the web server is in the Eastern Standard Time (EST) zone in Virginia, which is five hours different from GMT.

B is incorrect. There is no need to capture an image to view logs.

C is incorrect. IP addresses on the Internet do not expire. Logs are written to a hard drive or a central location; they are not erased when a system is rebooted.

D is incorrect.

26. An incident response team is following typical incident response procedures. Which of the following phases is the BEST choice for analyzing an incident with a goal of identifying steps to prevent a reoccurrence of the incident?

    A. Preparation

    B. Identification

C. Mitigation

D. Lessons learned

26. D is correct. You should analyze an incident during the lessons learned stage of incident response with the goal of identifying steps to prevent reoccurrence.

A is incorrect. Preparation is a planning step done before an incident, with the goal of preventing incidents and identifying methods to respond to incidents.

B is incorrect. Identification is the first step after hearing about a potential incident to verify it is an incident.

C is incorrect. Mitigation steps attempt to reduce the effects of the incident.

27. Your organization was recently attacked, resulting in a data breach, and attackers captured customer data. Management wants to take steps to better protect customer data. Which of the following will BEST support this goal?

    A. Succession planning and data recovery procedures

    B. Fault tolerance and redundancy

    C. Stronger access controls and encryption

    D. Hashing and digital signatures

27. C is correct. Strong access controls and encryption are two primary methods of protecting the confidentiality of any data, including customer data.

A is incorrect. Succession planning and data recovery procedures are part of business continuity.

B is incorrect. Fault tolerance and redundancy increase the availability of data.

D is incorrect. Hashing and digital signatures provide integrity.

28. You are reviewing incident response procedures related to the order of volatility. Which of the following is the LEAST volatile?

A. Hard disk drive

B. Memory

C. RAID-6 cache

D. CPU cache

28. A is correct. Data on a hard disk drive is the least volatile of those listed.

B, C, and D are incorrect. All other sources are some type of memory, which will be lost if a system is turned off. This includes data in a redundant array of inexpensive disks 6 (RAID-6) cache, normal memory, and the central processing unit's (CPU's) memory.

29. A security manager is reviewing security policies related to data loss. Which of the following is the security administrator MOST likely to be reviewing?

A. Clean desk policy

B. Separation of duties

C. Job rotation

D. Change management

29. A is correct. A clean desk policy requires users to organize their areas to reduce the risk of possible data theft and password compromise.

B is incorrect. A separation of duties policy separates individual tasks of an overall function between different people.

C is incorrect. Job rotation policies require employees to change roles on a regular basis.

D is incorrect. Change management helps reduce intended outages from changes.

30. Security personnel recently released an online training module advising employees not to share personal information on any social media web sites that they visit. What is this advice MOST likely trying to prevent?

A. Spending time on non-work-related sites

B. Phishing attack

C. Cognitive password attacks

D. Rainbow table attack

30. C is correct. A cognitive password attack utilizes information that a person would know, such as the name of their first pet or their favorite color. If this information is available on Facebook or another social media site, attackers can use it to change the user's password.

A is incorrect. This advice has nothing to do with employees visiting the sites, only with what they post.

B is incorrect. Although attackers may use this information in a phishing attack, they can also launch phishing attacks without this information.

D is incorrect. A rainbow table attack is a password attack, but it uses a database of precalculated hashes.

31. Your organization blocks access to social media web sites. The primary purpose is to prevent data leakage, such as the accidental disclosure of proprietary information. What is an additional security benefit of this policy?

A. Improves employee productivity

B. Enables cognitive password attacks

C. Prevents P2P file sharing

D. Protects against banner ad malware

31. D is correct. The primary benefit is protection against banner ad malware, also known as malvertisements.

A is incorrect. Although the policy might result in improved employee productivity, this is not a security benefit.

B is incorrect. You want to prevent cognitive password attacks, not enable them.

C is incorrect. Although organizations typically try to prevent peer-to-peer (P2P) file sharing, this is done by blocking access to P2P sites, not social media sites.

32. Your organization has spent a significant amount of money on training employees on security awareness. Your organization wants to validate the success of this training. Which of the following is the BEST choice?

    A. Implement role-based training.

    B. Use metrics.

    C. Use security policies.

    D. Verify PII.

32. B is correct. Metrics are measurements and you can use them to validate the success of a security awareness program.

A is incorrect. Role-based training is targeted training, but it does not validate the success of training.

C is incorrect. Training would typically teach employees about a security policy, but the policy doesn't provide measurements.

D is incorrect. Personally Identifiable Information (PII) might be part of the training, but PII cannot validate training.

33. Social engineers have launched several successful phone-based attacks against your organization resulting in several data leaks. Which of the following would be the MOST effective at reducing the success of these attacks?

    A. Implement a BYOD policy.

    B. Update the AUP.

    C. Provide training on data handling.

    D. Implement a program to increase security awareness.

33. D is correct. The best choice of the available answers is to implement a program to increase security awareness, and it could focus on social engineering attacks.

A and B are incorrect. A bring your own device (BYOD) policy or an acceptable use policy (AUP) doesn't apply in this scenario.

C is incorrect. Training is useful, but training users on data handling won't necessarily educate them on social engineering attacks.

34. A security expert is identifying and implementing several different physical deterrent controls to protect an organization's server room. Which of the following choices would BEST meet this objective?

    A. Using hardware locks

    B. Utilizing data encryption

    C. Performing a vulnerability assessment

    D. Training users

34. A is correct. A hardware lock is a physical security control. It's also a deterrent control because it would deter someone from entering.

B is incorrect. Data encryption is a technical control designed to protect data and is not a physical security control.

C is incorrect. A vulnerability assessment is a management control designed to discover vulnerabilities, but it is not a physical control.

D is incorrect. Training users is an effective preventive control, but it is not a physical control.

35. You need to secure access to a data center. Which of the following choices provides the BEST physical security to meet this need? (Select THREE.)

    A. Biometrics

    B. Cable locks

C. CCTV

D. Mantrap

35. A, C, and D are correct. A biometric reader used for access control, a mantrap, and a closed-circuit television (CCTV) system all provide strong physical security for accessing a data center.

B is incorrect. Cable locks are effective theft deterrents for mobile devices such as laptops, but they don't protect data centers.

36. Your company wants to control access to a restricted area of the building by adding an additional physical security control that includes facial recognition. Which of the following provides the BEST solution?

A. Bollards

B. Guards

C. Palm scanners

D. Video surveillance

36. B is correct. Security guards can protect access to restricted areas with facial recognition and by checking identities of personnel before letting them in.

A is incorrect. Bollards are effective barricades to block vehicles, but they do not block personnel.

C is incorrect. Palm scanners are effective biometric access devices, but they do not use facial recognition.

D is incorrect. Video surveillance can monitor who goes in and out of an area, but it cannot control the access.

37. Thieves recently rammed a truck through the entrance of your company's main building. During the chaos, their partners proceeded to steal a significant amount of IT equipment. Which of the following choices can you use to prevent this from happening again?

    A. Bollards

    B. Guards

    C. CCTV

    D. Mantrap

37. A is correct. Bollards are effective barricades that can block vehicles.

B is incorrect. Guards can restrict access for personnel, but they cannot stop trucks from ramming through a building.

C is incorrect. Closed-circuit television (CCTV) or a similar video surveillance system can monitor the entrance, but it won't stop the attack.

D is incorrect. Mantraps prevent tailgating, but they most likely won't stop a truck.

38. A security professional has reported an increase in the number of tailgating violations into a secure data center. What can prevent this?

    A. CCTV

    B. Mantrap

    C. Proximity card

    D. Cipher lock

38. B is correct. A mantrap is highly effective at preventing unauthorized entry and can also be used to prevent tailgating.

A is incorrect. CCTV provides video surveillance and it can record unauthorized entry, but it can't prevent it.

C is incorrect. A proximity card is useful as an access control mechanism, but it won't prevent tailgating, so it isn't as useful as a mantrap.

D is incorrect. A cipher lock is a door access control, but it can't prevent tailgating.

39. Users are complaining of intermittent connectivity issues. When you investigate, you discover that new network cables for these user systems were

run across several fluorescent lights. What environmental control will resolve this issue?

  A. HVAC system

  B. Fire suppression

  C. Humidity controls

  D. EMI shielding

39. D is correct. Electromagnetic interference (EMI) shielding provides protection against EMI sources such as fluorescent lights.

A is incorrect. Heating, ventilation, and air conditioning systems provide protection from overheating.

B is incorrect. Fire suppression systems provide protection from fire.

C is incorrect. Humidity controls provide protection against electrostatic discharge (ESD) and condensation.

40. Company management suspects an employee is stealing critical project information and selling it to a competitor. They'd like to identify who is doing this, without compromising any live data. What is the BEST option to meet this goal?

  A. Install antivirus software on all user systems.

  B. Implement an IPS.

  C. Implement an IDS.

  D. Add fabricated project data on a honeypot.

40. D is correct. Fabricated data on a honeypot could lure the malicious insider and entice him to access it.

A is incorrect. Antivirus software blocks malware.

B and C are incorrect. An intrusion prevention system (IPS) and an intrusion detection system (IDS) each detect attacks, but won't detect someone accessing data on a server.

41. An organization needs to improve fault tolerance to increase data availability. However, the organization has a limited budget. Which of the following is the BEST choice to meet the organization's needs?

    A. RAID

    B. Backup system

    C. Cluster

    D. UPS

41. A is correct. A redundant array of inexpensive disks (RAID) system would provide fault tolerance for disk drives and increase data availability if drives fail.

B is incorrect. A backup system improves data availability because you can restore data after data is lost or corrupt. However, a backup system does not provide fault tolerance.

C is incorrect. A cluster provides fault tolerance at the server level and ensures a service continues to operate even if a server fails. However, a cluster is more expensive than a RAID.

D is incorrect. An uninterruptible power supply (UPS) provides short-term power after a power failure but does not directly increase data availability.

42. Your company's web site experiences a large number of client requests during certain times of the year. Which of the following could your company add to ensure the web site's availability during these times?

    A. Fail-open cluster

    B. Certificates

    C. Web application firewall

    D. Load balancing

42. D is correct. Load balancing shifts the load among multiple systems and can increase the site's availability by adding additional nodes when necessary.

A is incorrect. A failover cluster also provides high availability, but there is no such thing as a fail-open cluster.

B is incorrect. Certificates help ensure confidentiality and integrity, but do not assist with availability.

C is incorrect. A web application firewall helps protect a web server against attacks, but it does not increase availability from normal client requests.

43. Your backup policy for a database server dictates that the amount of time needed to perform backups should be minimized. Which of the following backup plans would BEST meet this need?

    A. Full backups on Sunday and full backups every other day of the week

    B. Full backups on Sunday and differential backups every other day of the week

    C. Full backups on Sunday and incremental backups every other day of the week

    D. Differential backups on Sunday and incremental backups every other day of the week

43. C is correct. A full/incremental backup strategy is best with one full backup on one day and incremental backups on the other days.

A is incorrect. A full backup every day would require the most time every day.

B is incorrect. Differential backups become steadily larger as the week progresses and take more time to back up than incremental backups.

D is incorrect. Backups must start with a full backup, so a differential/incremental backup strategy is not possible.

44. An organization is considering an alternate location as part of its business continuity plan. It wants to identify a solution that provides the shortest recovery time. What will it choose?

    A. Cold site

    B. Warm site

    C. Hot site

    D. Succession site

44. C is correct. A hot site has the shortest recovery time, but it is also the most expensive.

A and B are incorrect. Cold sites have the longest recovery time, and warm sites are shorter than cold sites but not as quick as hot sites.

D is incorrect. Succession site isn't a valid type of alternate location.

45. Your organization is working on its business continuity plan. Management wants to ensure that documents provide detailed information on what technicians should do after an outage. Specifically, they want to list the systems to restore and the order in which to restore them. What document includes this information?

    A. HVAC

    B. BIA

    C. DRP

    D. Succession plan

45. C is correct. The disaster recovery plan (DRP) typically includes a hierarchical list of critical systems that identifies what to restore and in what order.

A is incorrect. Heating, ventilation, and air conditioning (HVAC) is not a document.

B is incorrect. The business impact analysis (BIA) identifies critical systems and components but does not include recovery methods or procedures.

D is incorrect. Succession planning refers to people, not systems, and it clarifies who can make decisions during a disaster.

46. The BCP coordinator at your organization is leading a meeting on-site with key disaster recovery personnel. The purpose of the meeting is to perform a test. What type of test is this?

    A. Functional exercise

    B. Full-blown test

    C. Tabletop exercise

    D. Simulation to perform steps of a plan

46. C is correct. A tabletop exercise is discussion-based and is typically performed in a classroom or conference room setting. Because this is a meeting led by the business continuity plan (BCP) coordinator, it is a tabletop exercise.

A, B, and D are incorrect. Functional exercises are hands-on exercises and include simulations and full-blown tests.

47. You are a technician at a small organization. You need to add fault-tolerance capabilities within the business to increase the availability of data. However, you need to keep costs as low as possible. Which of the following is the BEST choice to meet these needs?

    A. Failover cluster

    B. RAID-6

    C. Backups

    D. UPS

47. B is correct. A redundant array of inexpensive disks 6 (RAID-6) subsystem provides fault tolerance for disks, and increases data availability.

A is incorrect. A failover cluster provides fault tolerance for servers and can increase data availability but is significantly more expensive than a RAID subsystem.

C is incorrect. Backups help ensure data availability, but they do not help with fault tolerance.

D is incorrect. An uninterruptible power supply (UPS) provides fault tolerance for power, but not necessarily for data.

48. An organization needs to identify a continuity of operations plan that will allow it to provide temporary IT support during a disaster. The organization does not want to have a dedicated site. Which of the following provides the best solution?

    A. Cold site

    B. Warm site

    C. Hot site

    D. Mobile site

48. D is correct. A mobile site is a self-contained transportable unit that can be moved around without having a dedicated site.

A, B, and C are incorrect. Cold sites, warm sites, and hot sites are dedicated locations.

49. Monty Burns is the CEO of the Springfield Nuclear Power Plant. What would the company have in place in case something happens to him?

    A. Business continuity planning

    B. Succession planning

    C. Separation of duties

    D. IT contingency planning

49. B is correct. Succession planning identifies people within an organization who can fill leadership positions if they become vacant. It is also helpful

during a disaster by ensuring people understand their roles and responsibilities.

A is incorrect. A succession planning chart is often in a business continuity plan (BCP), but business continuity planning is much broader than just succession planning.

C is incorrect. A separation of duties policy separates individual tasks of an overall function between different people.

D is incorrect. IT contingency planning focuses on recovery of IT systems.

50. A continuity of operations plan for an organization includes the use of a warm site. The BCP coordinator wants to verify that the organization's backup data center is prepared to implement the warm site if necessary. Which of the following is the BEST choice to meet this need?

    A. Perform a review of the disaster recovery plan.

    B. Ask the managers of the backup data center.

    C. Perform a disaster recovery exercise.

    D. Perform a test restore.

50. C is correct. The best way to test elements of a business continuity plan (BCP) or disaster recovery plan (DRP) is to test the plan by performing a disaster recovery exercise.

A and B are incorrect. Asking managers if they are ready and reviewing the plan are both helpful, but not as effective as an exercise.

D is incorrect. Performing a test restore verifies the backup capabilities, but not necessarily the steps required when implementing a warm site.

51. A security analyst is creating a document that includes the expected monetary loss from a major outage. She is calculating the potential lost sales, fines, and impact on the organization's customers. Which of the following documents is she MOST likely creating?

A. BCP

B. BIA

C. DRP

D. RPO

51. B is correct. A business impact analysis (BIA) includes information on potential monetary losses and is the most likely document of those listed that would include this information.

A is incorrect. A business continuity plan (BCP) includes a BIA, but the BIA is more likely to include this information than the BCP is.

C is incorrect. A disaster recovery plan (DRP) includes methods used to recover from an outage.

D is incorrect. The recovery point objective (RPO) refers to the amount of data you can afford to lose but does not include monetary losses.

52. You want to ensure that messages sent from administrators to managers arrive unchanged. Which security goal are you addressing?

    A. Confidentiality

    B. Integrity

    C. Availability

    D. Authentication

52. B is correct. Integrity provides assurances that data has not been modified, and integrity is commonly enforced with hashing.

A is incorrect. Confidentiality prevents unauthorized disclosure of data but doesn't address modifications of data.

C is incorrect. Availability ensures systems are up and operational when needed and uses fault tolerance and redundancy methods.

D is incorrect. Authentication provides proof that users are who they claim to be.

53. Your organization recently implemented two servers that act as failover devices for each other. Which security goal is your organization pursuing?

    A. Safety

    B. Integrity

    C. Confidentiality

    D. Availability

53. D is correct. Your organization is pursuing availability. A failover cluster uses redundant servers to ensure a service will continue to operate even if one of the servers fail.

A is incorrect. Safety methods provide safety for personnel and other assets.

B is incorrect. Integrity methods ensure that data has not been modified.

C is incorrect. Confidentiality methods such as encryption prevent the unauthorized disclosure of data.

54. Management at your company recently decided to implement additional lighting and fencing around the property. Which security goal is your company MOST likely pursuing?

    A. Confidentiality

    B. Integrity

    C. Availability

    D. Safety

54. D is correct. Lighting and fencing are two methods that can enhance the security goal of safety.

A is incorrect. Confidentiality is enhanced with encryption and access controls.

B is incorrect. Integrity is enhanced with hashing, certificates, and digital signatures.

C is incorrect. Availability is enhanced with redundancy and fault-tolerance procedures.

55. Lisa manages network devices in your organization and maintains copies of the configuration files for all the managed routers and switches. On a weekly basis, she creates hashes for these files and compares them with hashes she created on the same files the previous week. Which security goal is she pursuing?

     A. Confidentiality

     B. Integrity

     C. Availability

     D. Safety

55. B is correct. She is pursing integrity by verifying the configuration files have not changed. By verifying that the hashes are the same, she also verifies that the configuration files are the same.

A is incorrect. Confidentiality is enforced with encryption, access controls, and steganography.

C is incorrect. Availability ensures systems are up and operational when needed.

D is incorrect. Safety goals help ensure the safety of personnel and/or other assets.

56. Lisa hid several plaintext documents within an image file. Which security goal is she pursuing?

     A. Encryption

     B. Integrity

     C. Steganography

     D. Confidentiality

56. D is correct. Hiding files in another file is one way to achieve the security goal of confidentiality.

A is incorrect. Encryption is the best way to achieve confidentiality, but simply hiding files within a file doesn't encrypt the data.

B is incorrect. Hashing methods and digital signatures provide integrity.
C is incorrect. In this scenario, Lisa is using steganography as the method by hiding files within a file, but the goal is confidentiality.

Sample Performance-Based Question Answer

Many of the security controls in this chapter can easily be tested in a drag-and-drop or matching type of performance-based question. As long as you know the content, these questions typically aren't any more difficult than a standard multiple-choice question. Here's an example of a performance-based question.

Instructions: You have the following list of controls that you need to use to secure items shown in Figure 2.1:

- Five cable locks
- Four fingerprint readers
- Two proximity badge readers
- One CCTV system
- One mantrap
- One locking cabinet
- One safe

You must use all the items in the list at least once and you must fill all empty boxes in the figure. For example, you must use all five cable locks, not just one cable lock.

Figure 2.2 shows the solution to the matching security controls question.

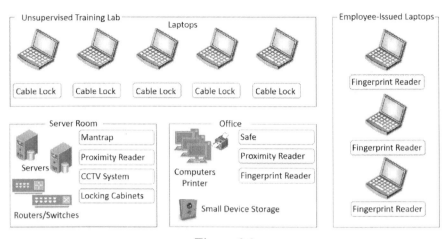

Figure 2.2

- **Unsupervised training lab.** The biggest risk to these laptops is theft and the best theft deterrent for the laptops is cable locks. Because you have five laptops and five cable locks, this uses all of your cable locks for this question.

- **Employee-issued laptops.** Of the remaining controls, only fingerprint readers provide protection for the laptops. Additional controls such as encryption and cable locks might also be useful. However, the scenario doesn't include encryption, and it was appropriate to use all the cable locks to protect the laptops in the unsupervised training lab.

- **Server room.** The server room holds much more important data than the lab or the office so it requires the strongest access controls available. In the scenario, you have the following access controls, which you should use with the server room.

  o **Mantrap.** This prevents anyone from tailgating into the server room.

  o **Proximity badge reader.** This provides an added measure of security and you can configure it with the mantrap. (This leaves one proximity badge reader you'll need to use somewhere else.)

- o **CCTV system.** This provides video surveillance and identifies anyone that enters or exits the server room.
- o **Locking cabinets.** These secure the equipment bays (also called equipment cabinets) by locking and preventing access to equipment within them. Without much context, it's difficult to determine if "locking cabinets" refers to equipment cabinets or office cabinets. However, the office has a safe, so an additional locking cabinet isn't necessary.

- **Office.** You can use the leftover controls to secure the office.
  - o **Safe.** This is a freebie because the figure shows a picture of a safe.
  - o **Proximity badge reader.** You started with two proximity badge readers and used one for the server room. This leaves one for the office. You cannot use this to protect employee-issued laptops and it isn't appropriate for an unsupervised training lab that you want people to be able to freely access.
  - o **Fingerprint reader.** You have one fingerprint reader left after using three with the employee-issued laptops. You can use it on one of the computers here.

√ **Get Certified**

√ **Get Ahead**

Chapter 3 Threats and Vulnerabilities

Threats and Vulnerabilities topics are **20 percent** of the CompTIA Security+ exam. The objectives in this domain are:

3.1 Explain types of malware.
- Adware
- Virus
- Spyware
- Trojan
- Rootkits
- Backdoors
- Logic bomb
- Botnets
- Ransomware
- Polymorphic malware
- Armored virus

3.2 Summarize various types of attacks.
- Man-in-the-middle
- DDoS
- DoS
- Replay
- Smurf attack
- Spoofing
- Spam
- Phishing
- Spim
- Vishing
- Spear phishing
- Xmas attack
- Pharming
- Privilege escalation
- Malicious insider threat
- DNS poisoning and ARP poisoning

- Transitive access
- Client-side attacks
- Password attacks
  - Brute force
  - Dictionary attacks
  - Hybrid
  - Birthday attacks
  - Rainbow tables
- Typo squatting/URL hijacking
- Watering hole attack

3.3 Summarize social engineering attacks and the associated effectiveness with each attack.

- Shoulder surfing
- Dumpster diving
- Tailgating
- Impersonation
- Hoaxes
- Whaling
- Vishing
- Principles (reasons for effectiveness)
  - Authority
  - Intimidation
  - Consensus/Social proof
  - Scarcity
  - Urgency
  - Familiarity/liking
  - Trust

3.4 Explain types of wireless attacks.

- Rogue access points
- Jamming/Interference
- Evil twin
- War driving
- Bluejacking
- Bluesnarfing
- War chalking
- IV attack
- Packet sniffing
- Near field communication
- Replay attacks
- WEP/WPA attacks

- WPS attacks

3.5 Explain types of application attacks.
- Cross-site scripting
- SQL injection
- LDAP injection
- XML injection
- Directory traversal/command injection
- Buffer overflow
- Integer overflow
- Zero-day
- Cookies and attachments
- LSO (Locally Shared Objects)
- Flash Cookies
- Malicious add-ons
- Session hijacking
- Header manipulation
- Arbitrary code execution / remote code execution

3.6 Analyze a scenario and select the appropriate type of mitigation and deterrent techniques.
- Monitoring system logs
  - Event logs
  - Audit logs
  - Security logs
  - Access logs
- Hardening
  - Disabling unnecessary services
  - Protecting management interfaces and applications
  - Password protection
  - Disabling unnecessary accounts
- Network security
  - MAC limiting and filtering
  - 802.1x
  - Disabling unused interfaces and unused application service port
  - Rogue machine detection
- Security posture (Chapters 4, 5)
  - Initial baseline configuration
  - Continuous security monitoring
  - Remediation
- Reporting

- o Alarms
- o Alerts
- o Trends
- Detection controls vs. prevention controls
  - o IDS vs. IPS
  - o Camera vs. guard

3.7 Given a scenario, use appropriate tools and techniques to discover security threats and vulnerabilities.

- Interpret results of security assessment tools
- Tools
  - o Protocol analyzer
  - o Vulnerability scanner
  - o Honeypots
  - o Honeynets
  - o Port scanner
  - o Passive vs. active tools
  - o Banner grabbing
- Risk calculations
  - o Threat vs. likelihood
- Assessment types
  - o Risk
  - o Threat
  - o Vulnerability
- Assessment technique
  - o Baseline reporting
  - o Code review
  - o Determine attack surface
  - o Review architecture
  - o Review designs

3.8 Explain the proper use of penetration testing versus vulnerability scanning.

- Penetration testing
  - o Verify a threat exists
  - o Bypass security controls
  - o Actively test security controls
  - o Exploiting vulnerabilities
- Vulnerability scanning
  - o Passively testing security controls
  - o Identify vulnerability
  - o Identify lack of security controls
  - o Identify common misconfigurations

- o Intrusive vs. non-intrusive
- o Credentialed vs. non-credentialed
- o False positive
- Black box
- White box
- Gray box

The CompTIA Security+: Get Certified Get Ahead SY0-401 Study Guide (ISBN 1939136024) discusses these topics in much more depth.

√ **Get Certified**

√ **Get Ahead**

Practice Test Questions for Threats and Vulnerabilities Domain

1. Which of the following types of malware is the MOST difficult to reverse engineer?

    A. Logic bomb

    B. Trojan

    C. Armored virus

    D. Ransomware

2. A recent antivirus scan on a server detected a Trojan. A technician removed the Trojan, but a security administrator expressed concern that unauthorized personnel might be able to access data on the server. The security administrator decided to check the server further. Of the following choices, what is the administrator MOST likely looking for on this server?

    A. Backdoor

    B. Logic bomb

    C. Rootkit

    D. Botnet

3. After Maggie turned on her computer, she saw a message indicating that unless she made a payment, her hard drive would be formatted. What does this indicate?

    A. Armored virus

    B. Ransomware

    C. Backdoor

    D. Trojan

4. A security administrator recently noticed abnormal activity on a workstation. It is connecting to computers outside the organization's internal network, using uncommon ports. Using a security toolkit, the administrator discovered the computer is also running several hidden processes. Which of the following choices BEST indicates what the administrator has found?

> A. Rootkit
>
> B. Backdoor
>
> C. Spam
>
> D. Trojan

5. Of the following malware types, which one is MOST likely to monitor a user's computer?

> A. Trojan
>
> B. Spyware
>
> C. Adware
>
> D. Ransomware

6. Bart installed code designed to enable his account automatically, three days after anyone disables it. What does this describe?

> A. Logic bomb
>
> B. Rootkit
>
> C. Armored virus
>
> D. Ransomware

7. Marge reports that she keeps receiving unwanted emails about personal loans. What does this describe?

> A. Phishing
>
> B. Spear phishing
>
> C. Spam
>
> D. Vishing

8. A recent spear phishing attack that appeared to come from your organization's CEO resulted in several employees revealing their passwords to attackers. Management wants to implement a security control to provide assurances to employees that email that appears to come from the CEO actually came from the CEO. Which of the following should be implemented?

    A. Digital signatures

    B. Spam filter

    C. Training

    D. Metrics

9. A penetration tester is tasked with gaining information on one of your internal servers and he enters the following command: telnet server1 80. What is the purpose of this command?

    A. Identify if server1 is running a service using port 80 and is reachable.

    B. Launch an attack on server1 sending 80 separate packets in a short period of time.

    C. Use Telnet to remotely administer server1.

    D. Use Telnet to start an RDP session.

10. Which of the following tools is the LEAST invasive and can verify if security controls are in place?

    A. Pentest

    B. Protocol analyzer

    C. Vulnerability scan

    D. Host enumeration

11. An organization has a legacy server within the DMZ. It is running older software that is not compatible with current patches, so it remains unpatched. Management accepts the risk on this system, but wants to know if attackers can access the internal network if they successfully compromise this server. Which of the following is the MOST appropriate test?

    A. Vulnerability scan

    B. Port scan

    C. Code review

    D. Pentest

12. Your organization has hired a group of external testers to perform a black box penetration test. One of the testers asks you to provide information about your internal network. What should you provide?

    A. A list of IP ranges and the types of security devices operational on the network

    B. Network diagrams but without internal IP addresses

    C. Some network diagrams and some IP addresses, but not all

    D. Nothing

13. Lisa needs to identify if a risk exists on a web application and if attackers can potentially bypass security controls. However, she should not actively test the application. Which of the following is the BEST choice?

    A. Perform a penetration test.

    B. Perform a port scan.

    C. Perform a vulnerability scan.

    D. Perform traffic analysis with a sniffer.

14. A recent vulnerability scan reported that a web application server is missing some patches. However, after inspecting the server, you realize that the patches are for a protocol that administrators removed from the server. Which of the following is the BEST explanation for this disparity?

    A. False negative

    B. False positive

    C. Lack of patch management tools

    D. The patch isn't applied

15. Some protocols include timestamps and sequence numbers. These components help protect against what type of attacks?

    A. Smurf

    B. Replay

    C. Flood guards

    D. Salting

16. An application stores user passwords in a hashed format. Which of the following can decrease the likelihood that attackers can discover these passwords?

    A. Rainbow tables

    B. MD5

    C. Salt

    D. Smurf

17. A user complains that his system is no longer able to access the blogs.getcertifiedgetahead.com site. Instead, his browser goes to a different site. After investigation, you notice the following entries in the user's hosts file:

127.0.0.1 localhost

72.52.230.233 blogs.getcertifiedgetahead.com

What is the BEST explanation for this entry?

    A. A pharming attack

    B. A whaling attack

    C. Session hijacking

    D. A phishing attack

18. Security analysts recently discovered that users in your organization are inadvertently installing malware on their systems after visiting the comptai.org web site. Users have a legitimate requirement to visit the comptia.org web site. What is the MOST likely explanation for this activity?

    A. Smurf

    B. Typo squatting

    C. Fuzzing

    D. Replay

19. You are troubleshooting an intermittent connectivity issue with a web server. After examining the logs, you identify repeated connection attempts from various IP addresses. You realize these connection attempts are overloading the server, preventing it from responding to other connections. Which of the following is MOST likely occurring?

    A. DDoS attack

    B. DoS attack

    C. Smurf attack

    D. Salting attack

20. A network administrator needs to ensure the company's network is protected against smurf attacks. What should the network administrator do?

    A. Install flood guards.

    B. Use salting techniques.

    C. Verify border routers block directed broadcasts.

    D. Ensure protocols use timestamps and sequence numbers.

21. Security experts at your organization have determined that your network has been repeatedly attacked from multiple entities in a foreign country. Research indicates these are coordinated and sophisticated attacks. What BEST describes this activity?

    A. Fuzzing

    B. Sniffing

    C. Spear phishing

    D. Advanced persistent threat

22. Security administrators are reviewing security controls and their usefulness. Which of the following attacks will account lockout controls prevent? (Choose TWO.)

    A. DNS poisoning

    B. Replay

    C. Brute force

    D. Buffer overflow

    E. Dictionary

23. A security administrator at a shopping mall discovered two wireless cameras pointing at an automatic teller machine. These cameras were not installed by mall personnel and are not authorized. What is the MOST likely goal of these cameras?

A. Tailgating

B. Dumpster diving

C. Vishing

D. Shoulder surfing

24. Bart is in a break area outside the office. He told Lisa that he forgot his badge inside and asked Lisa to let him follow her when she goes back inside. What does this describe?

A. Spear phishing

B. Whaling

C. Mantrap

D. Tailgating

25. While cleaning out his desk, Bart threw several papers containing PII into the recycle bin. Which type of attack can exploit this action?

A. Vishing

B. Dumpster diving

C. Shoulder surfing

D. Tailgating

26. Attackers are targeting C-level executives in your organization. Which type of attack is this?

A. Phishing

B. Vishing

C. Spam

D. Whaling

27. Homer received an email advertising the newest version of a popular smartphone, which is not available elsewhere. It includes a malicious link. Which of the following principles is the email author using?

    A. Authority

    B. Intimidation

    C. Scarcity

    D. Trust

28. A recent change in an organization's security policy states that monitors need to be positioned so that they cannot be viewed from outside any windows. What is the purpose of this policy?

    A. Reduce success of phishing

    B. Reduce success of shoulder surfing

    C. Reduce success of dumpster diving

    D. Reduce success of impersonation

29. A web developer is using methods to validate user input in a web site application. This ensures the application isn't vulnerable to all of the following attacks except one. Which of the following attacks are NOT prevented by validating user input?

    A. XSS

    B. SQL injection

    C. Buffer overflow

    D. Command injection

    E. Whaling

30. A war driver is capturing traffic from a wireless network. When an authorized client connects, the attacker is able to implement a brute force

attack to discover the encryption key. What type of attack did this war driver use?

    A. WPS attack

    B. IV attack

    C. Packet injection

    D. WPA cracking

31. Your organization hosts three wireless networks for different purposes. A recent site survey audit discovered the information shown in the following table:

SSID	Security	Channel	Power
GetCertifiedVisitors	WPA2	1	71 dBm
GetCertifiedEmployee	WPA2	2	94 dBm
GetCertifiedEmployees	WPA2	3	73 dBm
GetCertifiedKiosk	WPA2	5	79 dBm

What does this indicate?

    A. Evil twin

    B. Rogue access point

    C. Interference

    D. Near field communication

32. An attacker is able to access email contact lists on your smartphone. What type of attack is this?

    A. Bluesnarfing

    B. War chalking

    C. War driving

    D. Bluejacking

33. Which of the following is an attack against a mobile device?

    A. War chalking

    B. SSID hiding

    C. Evil twin

    D. Bluejacking

34. Which of the following wireless security mechanisms is subject to a spoofing attack?

    A. WEP

    B. IV

    C. WPA2 Enterprise

    D. MAC address filtering

35. You are reviewing logs from a wireless survey within your organization's network due to a suspected attack and you notice the following entries:

MAC	SSID	Encryption	Power
12:AB:34:CD:56:EF	GetCertifiedGetAhead	WPA2	47
12:AB:34:CD:56:EF	GetCertifiedGetAhead	WPA2	62
56:CD:34:EF:12:AB	GetCertifiedGetAhead	WPA2	20
12:AB:34:CD:56:EF	GetCertifiedGetAhead	WPA2	57
12:AB:34:CD:56:EF	GetCertifiedGetAhead	WPA2	49

Of the following choices, what is the MOST likely explanation of these entries?

    A. An evil twin is in place.

    B. Power of the AP needs to be adjusted.

    C. A rogue AP is in place.

    D. The AP is being pharmed.

36. Mobile users in your network report that they frequently lose connectivity with the wireless network on some days, but on other days they don't have any problems. Which of the following types of attacks could cause this?

    A. IV

    B. Wireless jamming

    C. Replay

    D. WPA cracking

37. Your organization recently suffered a loss from malware that wasn't previously known by any trusted sources. Which type of attack is this?

    A. Phishing attack

    B. Zero-day

    C. Buffer overflow

    D. Integer overflow

38. An application on one of your database servers has crashed several times recently. Examining detailed debugging logs, you discover that just prior to crashing, the database application is receiving a long series of x90 characters. What is MOST likely occurring?

    A. SQL injection

    B. Buffer overflow

    C. XML injection

    D. Zero-day

39. While creating a web application, a developer adds code to limit data provided by users. The code prevents users from entering special characters. Which of the following attacks will this code MOST likely prevent?

    A. Sniffing

    B. Spoofing

    C. XSS

    D. Pharming

40. Which of the following is an attack against servers hosting a directory service?

    A. XSS

    B. LDAP

    C. XSRF

    D. Fuzzing

41. Your organization hosts a web site within a DMZ and the web site accesses a database server in the internal network. ACLs on firewalls prevent any connections to the database server except from the web server. Database fields holding customer data are encrypted and all data in transit between the web site server and the database server are encrypted. Which of the following represents the GREATEST risk to the data on the server?

    A. Theft of the database server

    B. XML injection

    C. SQL injection

    D. Sniffing

42. Checking the logs of a web server, you see the following entry:
198.252.69.129 --[1/Sep/2013:05:20]"GET
/index.php?username=ZZZZZZZZZZZZZZZZZZZZBBBBBBBBCCCC
CCCHTTP/1.1" "http://gcgapremium.com/security/" "Chrome31"
Which of the following is the BEST choice to explain this entry?

    A. A SQL injection attack

    B. A pharming attack

    C. A phishing attack

    D. A buffer overflow attack

43. Looking at logs for an online web application, you see that someone has entered the following phrase into several queries:

' or '1'='1' --

Which of the following is the MOST likely explanation for this?

    A. A buffer overflow attack

    B. An XSS attack

    C. A SQL injection attack

    D. An LDAP injection attack

44. You need to reduce the attack surface of a web server. Which of the following is a preventive control that will assist with this goal?

    A. Disabling unnecessary services

    B. Identifying the initial baseline configuration

    C. Using hardware locks

    D. Monitoring logs for trends

45. Your organization has several switches used within the network. You need to implement a security control to secure the switch from physical access. What should you do?

    A. Disable unused ports.

    B. Implement an implicit deny rule.

    C. Disable STP.

    D. Enable SSH.

46. An organization recently updated its security policy. A new requirement dictates a need to increase protection from rogue devices plugging into physical ports. Which of the following choices provides the BEST protection?

    A. Disable unused ports

    B. Implement 802.1x

    C. Enable MAC limiting

    D. Enable MAC filtering

47. Your organization hosts a web-based server that remote administrators access via Telnet. Management wants to increase their rights to prosecute unauthorized personnel who access this server. Which of the following is the BEST choice?

    A. Enable SSH instead of Telnet.

    B. Enable banner ads.

    C. Enable FTP logging.

    D. Add a warning banner.

48. Of the following choices, what can you use to divert malicious attacks on your network away from valuable data to worthless fabricated data?

    A. IPS

    B. Proxy server

    C. Web application firewall

    D. Honeypot

49. You need to monitor the security posture of several servers in your organization and keep a security administrator aware of their status. Which of the following tasks will BEST help you meet this goal?

    A. Establishing baseline reporting

    B. Determining attack surface

    C. Implementing patch management

    D. Enabling sandboxing

50. You want to identify all of the services running on a server. Which of the following tools is the BEST choice to meet this goal?

    A. Penetration test

    B. Protocol analyzer

    C. Sniffer

    D. Port scanner

51. Your organization develops web application software, which it sells to other companies for commercial use. Your organization wants to ensure that the software isn't susceptible to common vulnerabilities, such as buffer overflow attacks and race conditions. What should the organization implement to ensure software meets this standard?

    A. Input validation

    B. Change management

    C. Code review

    D. Regression testing

52. A network administrator needs to identify the type of traffic and packet flags used in traffic sent from a specific IP address. Which of the following is the BEST tool to meet this need?

    A. UTM security appliance

    B. Router logs

    C. Protocol analyzer

    D. Vulnerability scan

53. While analyzing a packet capture log, you notice the following entry:
16:12:50, src 10.80.1.5:3389, dst 192.168.1.100:8080, syn/ack
Of the following choices, what is the BEST explanation of this entry?

    A. An HTTP connection attempt

    B. An RDP connection attempt

    C. An FTP connection attempt

    D. A buffer overflow attack

54. A security company wants to gather intelligence about current methods attackers are using against its clients. What can it use?

A. Vulnerability scan

B. Honeynet

C. MAC address filtering

D. Evil twin

55. Bart is performing a vulnerability assessment. Which of the following BEST represents the goal of this task?

A. Identify services running on a system.

B. Determine if vulnerabilities can be exploited.

C. Determine if input validation is in place.

D. Identify the system's security posture.

56. A network administrator is attempting to identify all traffic on an internal network. Which of the following tools is the BEST choice?

A. Black box test

B. Protocol analyzer

C. Penetration test

D. Baseline review

57. Your organization develops web application software, which it sells to other companies for commercial use. To ensure the software is secure, your organization uses a peer assessment to help identify potential security issues related to the software. Which of the following is the BEST term for this process?

A. Code review

B. Change management

C. Routine audit

D. Rights and permissions review

58. Your organization plans to deploy new systems within the network within the next six months. What should your organization implement to ensure these systems are developed properly?

    A. Code review

    B. Design review

    C. Baseline review

    D. Attack surface review

59. You need to periodically check the configuration of a server and identify any changes. What are you performing?

    A. Code review

    B. Design review

    C. Attack surface review

    D. Baseline review

60. You are troubleshooting issues between two servers on your network and need to analyze the network traffic. Of the following choices, what is the BEST tool to capture and analyze this traffic?

    A. Switch

    B. Protocol analyzer

    C. Firewall

    D. NIDS

61. You recently completed a vulnerability scan on your network. It reported that several servers are missing key operating system patches. However, after checking the servers, you've verified the servers have these patches installed. Which of the following BEST describes this?

A. False negative

B. Misconfiguration on servers

C. False positive

D. Servers not hardened

√ Get Certified

√ Get Ahead

Practice Test Questions with Answers for Threats and Vulnerabilities Domain

1. Which of the following types of malware is the MOST difficult to reverse engineer?

    A. Logic bomb

    B. Trojan

    C. Armored virus

    D. Ransomware

1. C is correct. An armored virus uses one or more techniques to make it difficult for antivirus researchers to reverse engineer it.

A is incorrect. A logic bomb executes in response to an event, but it is often implemented with simple code.

B is incorrect. A Trojan appears to be something beneficial, but it includes a malicious component.

D is incorrect. Ransomware takes control of a user's system or data and then demands payment as ransom.

2. A recent antivirus scan on a server detected a Trojan. A technician removed the Trojan, but a security administrator expressed concern that unauthorized personnel might be able to access data on the server. The security administrator decided to check the server further. Of the following choices, what is the administrator MOST likely looking for on this server?

    A. Backdoor

    B. Logic bomb

    C. Rootkit

    D. Botnet

2. A is correct. The security administrator is most likely looking for a backdoor because Trojans commonly create backdoors, and a backdoor allows unauthorized personnel to access data on the system.

B and C are incorrect. Logic bombs and rootkits can create backdoor accounts, but Trojans don't create logic bombs and would rarely install a rootkit.

D is incorrect. The computer might be joined to a botnet, but it wouldn't be a botnet.

3. After Maggie turned on her computer, she saw a message indicating that unless she made a payment, her hard drive would be formatted. What does this indicate?

    A. Armored virus

    B. Ransomware

    C. Backdoor

    D. Trojan

3. B is correct. Ransomware attempts to take control of a user's system or data and then demands ransom to return control.

A is incorrect. An armored virus uses one or more techniques to make it more difficult to reverse engineer.

C is incorrect. It's possible that Maggie's computer was infected with a Trojan, which created a backdoor.

D is incorrect. However, not all Trojans or backdoor accounts demand payment as ransom.

4. A security administrator recently noticed abnormal activity on a workstation. It is connecting to computers outside the organization's internal network, using uncommon ports. Using a security toolkit, the administrator discovered the computer is also running several hidden processes. Which of the following choices BEST indicates what the administrator has found?

A. Rootkit

B. Backdoor

C. Spam

D. Trojan

4. A is correct. A rootkit typically runs processes that are hidden and it also attempts to connect to computers via the Internet.

B is incorrect. Although an attacker might have used a backdoor to gain access to the user's computer and install the rootkit, backdoors don't run hidden processes.

C is incorrect. Spam is unwanted email and is unrelated to this question.

D is incorrect. A Trojan is malware that looks like it's beneficial, but is malicious.

5. Of the following malware types, which one is MOST likely to monitor a user's computer?

A. Trojan

B. Spyware

C. Adware

D. Ransomware

5. B is correct. Spyware monitors a user's computer and activity.

A is incorrect. Trojans often install backdoor accounts, but they don't necessarily monitor systems and activity.

C is incorrect. Adware typically causes pop-up windows for advertising, and although it might monitor the user to target ads, not all adware monitors users.

D is incorrect. Ransomware is primarily concerned with getting the user to make a ransom payment.

6. Bart installed code designed to enable his account automatically, three days after anyone disables it. What does this describe?

    A. Logic bomb

    B. Rootkit

    C. Armored virus

    D. Ransomware

6. A is correct. A logic bomb is code that executes in response to an event. In this scenario, the logic bomb executes when it discovers the account is disabled (indicating Bart is no longer employed at the company). In this scenario, the logic bomb is creating a backdoor.

B is incorrect. A rootkit includes hidden processes, but it does not activate in response to an event.

C is incorrect. An armored virus uses techniques to resist reverse engineering.

D is incorrect. Ransomware demands payment as ransom.

7. Marge reports that she keeps receiving unwanted emails about personal loans. What does this describe?

    A. Phishing

    B. Spear phishing

    C. Spam

    D. Vishing

7. C is correct. Spam is unwanted emails from any source.

A and B are incorrect. Phishing and spear phishing are types of attacks using email.

D is incorrect. Vishing is similar to phishing but it uses telephone technology.

8. A recent spear phishing attack that appeared to come from your organization's CEO resulted in several employees revealing their passwords to attackers. Management wants to implement a security control to provide

assurances to employees that email that appears to come from the CEO actually came from the CEO. Which of the following should be implemented?

> A. Digital signatures
>
> B. Spam filter
>
> C. Training
>
> D. Metrics

8. A is correct. A digital signature provides assurances of who sent an email and meets the goal of this scenario.

B is incorrect. Although a spam filter might filter a spear phishing attack, it does not provide assurances about who sent an email.

C is incorrect. A training program would help educate employees about attacks and would help prevent the success of these attacks, but it doesn't provide assurances about who sent an email.

D is incorrect. Metrics can measure the success of a training program.

9. A penetration tester is tasked with gaining information on one of your internal servers and he enters the following command: telnet server1 80. What is the purpose of this command?

> A. Identify if server1 is running a service using port 80 and is reachable.
>
> B. Launch an attack on server1 sending 80 separate packets in a short period of time.
>
> C. Use Telnet to remotely administer server1.
>
> D. Use Telnet to start an RDP session.

9. A is correct. This command sends a query to server1 over port 80 and if the server is running a service on port 80, it will connect. This is a common beginning command for a banner grabbing attempt.

B is incorrect. It does not send 80 separate packets.

C is incorrect. If 80 was omitted, Telnet would attempt to connect using its default port of 23 and attempt to create a Telnet session.

D is incorrect. Remote Desktop Protocol (RDP) uses port 3389 and is not relevant in this scenario.

10. Which of the following tools is the LEAST invasive and can verify if security controls are in place?

> A. Pentest
>
> B. Protocol analyzer
>
> C. Vulnerability scan
>
> D. Host enumeration

10. C is correct. A vulnerability scan can verify if security controls are in place, and it does not try to exploit these controls using any invasive methods.

A is incorrect. A pentest (or penetration test) can verify if security controls are in place, but it is invasive and can potentially compromise a system.

B is incorrect. A protocol analyzer is not invasive, but it cannot determine if security controls are in place.

D is incorrect. Host enumeration identifies hosts on a network, but does not check for security controls.

11. An organization has a legacy server within the DMZ. It is running older software that is not compatible with current patches, so it remains unpatched. Management accepts the risk on this system, but wants to know if attackers can access the internal network if they successfully compromise this server. Which of the following is the MOST appropriate test?

> A. Vulnerability scan
>
> B. Port scan
>
> C. Code review
>
> D. Pentest

11. D is correct. A pentest (or penetration test) attempts to compromise the server and then attempts to access the internal network.

A is incorrect. A vulnerability scan is passive. It does not attempt to compromise a system, so it cannot verify if an attacker can access the internal network.

B is incorrect. A port scan only identifies open ports.

C is incorrect. A code review is useful for newly developed software, but there isn't any indication that the original code is available for the legacy server.

12. Your organization has hired a group of external testers to perform a black box penetration test. One of the testers asks you to provide information about your internal network. What should you provide?

> A. A list of IP ranges and the types of security devices operational on the network
>
> B. Network diagrams but without internal IP addresses
>
> C. Some network diagrams and some IP addresses, but not all
>
> D. Nothing

12. D is correct. Black box testers should not have access to any information before starting the test, so technicians and administrators should not provide any information if asked.

A, B, and C are incorrect. It's appropriate to give white box testers all the information on the network, and give gray box testers some information on the internal network.

13. Lisa needs to identify if a risk exists on a web application and if attackers can potentially bypass security controls. However, she should not actively test the application. Which of the following is the BEST choice?

    A. Perform a penetration test.

    B. Perform a port scan.

    C. Perform a vulnerability scan.

    D. Perform traffic analysis with a sniffer.

13. C is correct. A vulnerability scan identifies vulnerabilities that attackers can potentially exploit, and vulnerability scanners perform passive testing.

A is incorrect. A penetration test actively tests the application and can potentially compromise the system.

B is incorrect. A port scan only identifies open ports.

D is incorrect. A sniffer can capture traffic for analysis, but it doesn't check for security controls.

14. A recent vulnerability scan reported that a web application server is missing some patches. However, after inspecting the server, you realize that the patches are for a protocol that administrators removed from the server. Which of the following is the BEST explanation for this disparity?

    A. False negative

    B. False positive

    C. Lack of patch management tools

    D. The patch isn't applied

14. B is correct. A false positive on a vulnerability scan indicates that a vulnerability is positively detected, but the vulnerability doesn't actually exist.

A is incorrect. A false negative indicates that the vulnerability scan did not detect a vulnerability that does exist on a system.

C is incorrect. False positives can occur even if an organization has a strong patch management process in place.

D is incorrect. Although it's true that the patch isn't applied, it's also true that the patch cannot be applied because it is for a protocol that administrators removed.

15. Some protocols include timestamps and sequence numbers. These components help protect against what type of attacks?

>A. Smurf

>B. Replay

>C. Flood guards

>D. Salting

15. B is correct. Timestamps and sequence numbers act as countermeasures against replay attacks.

A is incorrect. Blocking directed broadcasts prevents smurf attacks.

C is incorrect. Flood guards protect against SYN (synchronize) attacks.

D is incorrect. Salting protects against brute force attacks on passwords.

16. An application stores user passwords in a hashed format. Which of the following can decrease the likelihood that attackers can discover these passwords?

>A. Rainbow tables

>B. MD5

>C. Salt

>D. Smurf

16. C is correct. A password salt is additional random characters added to a password before hashing the password, and it decreases the success of password attacks.

A is incorrect. Rainbow tables are used by attackers and contain precomputed hashes.

B is incorrect. Message digest 5 (MD5) is a hashing algorithm that creates hashes, but the scenario already states that passwords are hashed.

D is incorrect. Smurf is a type of attack using a directed broadcast and is not related to passwords.

17. A user complains that his system is no longer able to access the blogs.getcertifiedgetahead.com site. Instead, his browser goes to a different site. After investigation, you notice the following entries in the user's hosts file:

127.0.0.1 localhost

72.52.230.233 blogs.getcertifiedgetahead.com

What is the BEST explanation for this entry?

    A. A pharming attack

    B. A whaling attack

    C. Session hijacking

    D. A phishing attack

17. A is correct. A pharming attack attempts to redirect users from one web site to another web site. Although this is often done using DNS poisoning, it can also be done by rewriting the hosts file in a user's system. The 127.0.0.1 localhost entry is the default entry in the hosts file, and the second entry redirects the user to a different site.

B is incorrect. Whaling is a phishing attack that targets high-level executives.

C is incorrect. In session hijacking, an attacker records a user's credentials and uses them to impersonate the user.

D is incorrect. Phishing is the practice of sending email to users with the purpose of tricking them into revealing personal information (such as bank account information).

18. Security analysts recently discovered that users in your organization are inadvertently installing malware on their systems after visiting the comptai.org web site. Users have a legitimate requirement to visit the comptia.org web site. What is the MOST likely explanation for this activity?

    A. Smurf

    B. Typo squatting

C. Fuzzing

D. Replay

18. B is correct. Typo squatting (or URL hijacking) uses a similar domain name to redirect traffic. In this scenario, the last two letters in CompTIA are swapped in the malicious domain name, and that site is attempting to download malware onto the user systems.

A is incorrect. A smurf attack is unrelated to web sites.

C is incorrect. Fuzzing tests an application's ability to handle random data.

D is incorrect. A replay attack attempts to replay data with the intent of impersonating one of the parties.

19. You are troubleshooting an intermittent connectivity issue with a web server. After examining the logs, you identify repeated connection attempts from various IP addresses. You realize these connection attempts are overloading the server, preventing it from responding to other connections. Which of the following is MOST likely occurring?

    A. DDoS attack

    B. DoS attack

    C. Smurf attack

    D. Salting attack

19. A is correct. A distributed denial-of-service (DDoS) attack includes attacks from multiple systems with the goal of depleting the target's resources and this scenario indicates multiple connection attempts from different IP addresses.

B is incorrect. A DoS attack comes from a single system, and a SYN flood is an example of a DoS attack.

C is incorrect. A smurf attack doesn't attempt to connect to systems but instead sends pings.

D is incorrect. Salting is a method used to prevent brute force attacks to discover passwords.

20. A network administrator needs to ensure the company's network is protected against smurf attacks. What should the network administrator do?

   A. Install flood guards.

   B. Use salting techniques.

   C. Verify border routers block directed broadcasts.

   D. Ensure protocols use timestamps and sequence numbers.

20. C is correct. Smurf attacks are blocked by preventing routers from passing directed broadcasts, especially border routers with direct access to the Internet.

A is incorrect. Flood guards protect against SYN (synchronize) flood attacks.

B is incorrect. Salting techniques add additional characters to passwords to thwart brute force attacks.

D is incorrect. Timestamps and sequence numbers are useful to protect against replay attacks, but not smurf attacks.

21. Security experts at your organization have determined that your network has been repeatedly attacked from multiple entities in a foreign country. Research indicates these are coordinated and sophisticated attacks. What BEST describes this activity?

   A. Fuzzing

   B. Sniffing

   C. Spear phishing

   D. Advanced persistent threat

21. D is correct. An advanced persistent threat is a group of highly organized individuals, typically from a foreign country, with the ability to coordinate sophisticated attacks.

A is incorrect. Fuzzing is the practice of sending unexpected input to an application for testing and can be used in a security assessment.

B is incorrect. Sniffing is the practice of capturing traffic with a protocol analyzer.

C is incorrect. Spear phishing is a targeted phishing attack.

22. Security administrators are reviewing security controls and their usefulness. Which of the following attacks will account lockout controls prevent? (Choose TWO.)

> A. DNS poisoning
>
> B. Replay
>
> C. Brute force
>
> D. Buffer overflow
>
> E. Dictionary

22. C and E are correct. Brute force and dictionary attacks attempt to guess passwords, but an account lockout control locks an account after the wrong password is guessed too many times. The other attacks are not password attacks, so they aren't mitigated using account lockout controls.

A is incorrect. Domain name system (DNS) poisoning attempts to redirect web browsers to malicious URLs.

B is incorrect. Replay attacks attempt to capture packets to impersonate one of the parties in an online session.

D is incorrect. Buffer overflow attacks attempt to overwhelm online applications with unexpected code or data.

23. A security administrator at a shopping mall discovered two wireless cameras pointing at an automatic teller machine. These cameras were not installed by mall personnel and are not authorized. What is the MOST likely goal of these cameras?

    A. Tailgating

    B. Dumpster diving

    C. Vishing

    D. Shoulder surfing

23. D is correct. Shoulder surfing is the practice of peering over a person's shoulder to discover information. In this scenario, the attacker is using the wireless cameras to discover PINs as users enter them.

A is incorrect. Tailgating is the practice of following closely behind someone else without using credentials.

B is incorrect. Dumpster diving is the practice of searching trash dumpsters for information.

C is incorrect. Vishing is a form of phishing using the phone.

24. Bart is in a break area outside the office. He told Lisa that he forgot his badge inside and asked Lisa to let him follow her when she goes back inside. What does this describe?

    A. Spear phishing

    B. Whaling

    C. Mantrap

    D. Tailgating

24. D is correct. Tailgating is the practice of following closely behind someone else without using credentials. In this scenario, Bart might be an employee who forgot his badge, or he might be a social engineer trying to get in by tailgating.

A and B are incorrect. Spear phishing and whaling are two types of phishing with email.

C is incorrect. Mantraps prevent tailgating.

25. While cleaning out his desk, Bart threw several papers containing PII into the recycle bin. Which type of attack can exploit this action?

    A. Vishing

    B. Dumpster diving

    C. Shoulder surfing

    D. Tailgating

25. B is correct. Dumpster divers look through trash or recycling containers for valuable paperwork, such as documents that include Personally Identifiable Information (PII). Instead, paperwork should be shredded or incinerated.

A is incorrect. Vishing is a form of phishing that uses the phone.

C is incorrect. Shoulder surfers attempt to view monitors or screens, not papers.

D is incorrect. Tailgating is the practice of following closely behind someone else, without using proper credentials.

26. Attackers are targeting C-level executives in your organization. Which type of attack is this?

    A. Phishing

    B. Vishing

    C. Spam

    D. Whaling

26. D is correct. Whaling is a type of phishing that targets high-level executives, such as CEOs, CIOs, and CFOs.

A is incorrect. Because whaling is more specific than phishing, phishing isn't the best answer.

B is incorrect. Vishing is similar to phishing, but it uses the phone instead.

C is incorrect. Spam is unwanted email, but spam isn't necessarily malicious.

27. Homer received an email advertising the newest version of a popular smartphone, which is not available elsewhere. It includes a malicious link. Which of the following principles is the email author using?

    A. Authority

    B. Intimidation

    C. Scarcity

    D. Trust

27. C is correct. The attacker is using scarcity to entice the user to click the link. A user might realize that clicking on links from unknown sources is risky, but the temptation of getting the new smartphone might cause the user to ignore the risk.

A, B, and D are incorrect. None of the principles uses advertising for new products.

28. A recent change in an organization's security policy states that monitors need to be positioned so that they cannot be viewed from outside any windows. What is the purpose of this policy?

    A. Reduce success of phishing

    B. Reduce success of shoulder surfing

    C. Reduce success of dumpster diving

    D. Reduce success of impersonation

28. B is correct. Shoulder surfing is the practice of viewing data by looking over someone's shoulder and it includes looking at computer monitors. Positioning monitors so that they cannot be viewed through a window reduces this threat.

A is incorrect. Phishing is an email attack.

C is incorrect. Dumpster diving is the practice of looking through dumpsters.

D is incorrect. Social engineers often try to impersonate others to trick them.

29. A web developer is using methods to validate user input in a web site application. This ensures the application isn't vulnerable to all of the following attacks except one. Which of the following attacks are NOT prevented by validating user input?

    A. XSS

    B. SQL injection

    C. Buffer overflow

    D. Command injection

    E. Whaling

29. E is correct. Whaling is a phishing attack using email that targets executives and cannot be prevented with input validation.

A, B, C, and D are incorrect. Input validation can prevent cross-site scripting (XSS), SQL injection, buffer overflow, and command injection attacks.

30. A war driver is capturing traffic from a wireless network. When an authorized client connects, the attacker is able to implement a brute force attack to discover the encryption key. What type of attack did this war driver use?

    A. WPS attack

    B. IV attack

    C. Packet injection

    D. WPA cracking

30. D is correct. A Wi-Fi Protected Access (WPA) cracking attack captures traffic and then performs an offline brute force attack to discover the encryption key.

A is incorrect. Wi-Fi Protected Setup (WPS) attacks also use a brute force attack, but do not need to wait for an authorized client to connect.

B and C are incorrect. Initialization vector (IV) attacks often use packet injection techniques to generate more traffic in Wired Equivalent Privacy (WEP) attacks.

31. Your organization hosts three wireless networks for different purposes. A recent site survey audit discovered the information shown in the following table:

SSID	Security	Channel	Power
GetCertifiedVisitors	WPA2	1	71 dBm
GetCertifiedEmployee	WPA2	2	94 dBm
GetCertifiedEmployees	WPA2	3	73 dBm
GetCertifiedKiosk	WPA2	5	79 dBm

What does this indicate?

    A. Evil twin

    B. Rogue access point

    C. Interference

    D. Near field communication

31. B is correct. This indicates a rogue access point because the organization is hosting three wireless networks, but the survey found four. A rogue access point typically has a similar name (such as GetCertifiedGetEmployee in this example).

A is incorrect. An evil twin will have the exact name as an authorized WAP.

C is incorrect. An interference or jamming attack would make it difficult to connect to the access points causing users to disconnect often.

D is incorrect. Near field communication (NFC) refers to two devices communicating when they are close to each other and is unrelated to this scenario.

32. An attacker is able to access email contact lists on your smartphone. What type of attack is this?

    A. Bluesnarfing

    B. War chalking

    C. War driving

    D. Bluejacking

32. A is correct. Attackers are able to access data (including email contact lists) on a smartphone in a bluesnarfing attack.

B is incorrect. War chalking is the practice of marking the location of wireless networks.

C is incorrect. War driving is the practice of looking for wireless networks, often by driving around.

D is incorrect. Bluejacking is the practice of sending unsolicited messages to other Bluetooth devices.

33. Which of the following is an attack against a mobile device?

    A. War chalking

    B. SSID hiding

    C. Evil twin

    D. Bluejacking

33. D is correct. Bluejacking is the practice of sending unsolicited messages to other Bluetooth devices.

A is incorrect. War chalking is the practice of marking the location of wireless networks, sometimes using chalk.

B is incorrect. You can disable service set identifier (SSID) broadcasting to hide the SSID from casual users, but this isn't an attack.

C is incorrect. An evil twin is a rogue access point with the same SSID as a legitimate access point. It can be used to launch attacks against any wireless devices, but it isn't an attack against only mobile devices.

34. Which of the following wireless security mechanisms is subject to a spoofing attack?

    A. WEP

    B. IV

    C. WPA2 Enterprise

    D. MAC address filtering

34. D is correct. Media access control (MAC) address filtering is vulnerable to spoofing attacks because attackers can easily change MAC addresses on network interface cards (NICs).

A and B are incorrect. Wired Equivalent Privacy (WEP) can be cracked using an initialization vector (IV) attack, but not by spoofing.

C is incorrect. WPA2 Enterprise requires users to enter credentials, so it isn't susceptible to a spoofing attack.

35. You are reviewing logs from a wireless survey within your organization's network due to a suspected attack and you notice the following entries:

MAC	SSID	Encryption	Power
12:AB:34:CD:56:EF	GetCertifiedGetAhead	WPA2	47
12:AB:34:CD:56:EF	GetCertifiedGetAhead	WPA2	62
56:CD:34:EF:12:AB	GetCertifiedGetAhead	WPA2	20
12:AB:34:CD:56:EF	GetCertifiedGetAhead	WPA2	57
12:AB:34:CD:56:EF	GetCertifiedGetAhead	WPA2	49

Of the following choices, what is the MOST likely explanation of these entries?

    A. An evil twin is in place.

    B. Power of the AP needs to be adjusted.

    C. A rogue AP is in place.

    D. The AP is being pharmed.

35. A is correct. The logs indicate an evil twin is in place. An evil twin is a rogue wireless access point with the same service set identifier (SSID) as a live wireless access point. The SSID is GetCertifiedGetAhead and most of the entries are from an access point (AP) with a media access control (MAC) address of 12:AB:34:CD:56:EF. However one entry shows a MAC of 56:CD:34:EF:12:AB, indicating an evil twin with the same name as the legitimate AP.

B is incorrect. Power can be adjusted if necessary to reduce the visibility of the AP, but there isn't any indication this is needed. The power of the evil twin is lower, indicating it is in a different location farther away. C is incorrect. A rogue AP is an unauthorized AP and although the evil twin is unauthorized, it is more correct to identify this as an evil twin because that is more specific. Generically, a rogue AP has a different SSID.

D is incorrect. A pharming attack redirects a web site's traffic to another web site, but this isn't indicated in this question at all.

36. Mobile users in your network report that they frequently lose connectivity with the wireless network on some days, but on other days they don't have any problems. Which of the following types of attacks could cause this?

    A. IV

    B. Wireless jamming

    C. Replay

    D. WPA cracking

36. B is correct. A wireless jamming attack is a type of denial-of-service (DoS) attack that can cause wireless devices to lose their association with access points and disconnect them from the network. None of the other attacks are DoS attacks.

A is incorrect. An initialization vector (IV) is a specific type of attack on Wired Equivalent Privacy (WEP) to crack the key.

C is incorrect. A replay attack captures traffic with the goal of replaying it later to impersonate one of the parties in the original transmission.

D is incorrect. Wi-Fi Protected Access (WPA) cracking attacks attempt to discover the passphrase.

37. Your organization recently suffered a loss from malware that wasn't previously known by any trusted sources. Which type of attack is this?

    A. Phishing attack

    B. Zero-day

    C. Buffer overflow

    D. Integer overflow

37. B is correct. A zero-day exploit is one that isn't known by trusted sources such as antivirus vendors or operating system vendors.

A, C, and D are incorrect. Trusted sources know about many phishing attacks, buffer overflow attacks, and integer overflow attacks.

38. An application on one of your database servers has crashed several times recently. Examining detailed debugging logs, you discover that just prior to crashing, the database application is receiving a long series of x90 characters. What is MOST likely occurring?

    A. SQL injection

    B. Buffer overflow

    C. XML injection

    D. Zero-day

38. B is correct. Buffer overflow attacks include a series of no operation (NOP) commands, such as hexadecimal 90 (x90). When successful, they can crash applications and expose memory, allowing attackers to run malicious code on the system.

A and C are incorrect. SQL injection attacks and Extensible Markup Language (XML) injection attacks do not use NOP commands.

D is incorrect. Zero-day attacks are unknown or undocumented, but attacks using NOP commands are known.

39. While creating a web application, a developer adds code to limit data provided by users. The code prevents users from entering special characters. Which of the following attacks will this code MOST likely prevent?

    A. Sniffing

    B. Spoofing

    C. XSS

    D. Pharming

39. C is correct. A cross-site scripting (XSS) attack can be blocked by using input validation techniques to filter special characters such as the < and > characters used in HTML code. None of the other attackers requires the use of special characters.

A is incorrect. Sniffing captures data with a protocol analyzer.

B is incorrect. Spoofing hides the identity of the original entity.

D is incorrect. Pharming redirects a user from one web site to another web site.

40. Which of the following is an attack against servers hosting a directory service?

    A. XSS

    B. LDAP

    C. XSRF

    D. Fuzzing

40. B is correct. A Lightweight Directory Application Protocol (LDAP) injection attack attempts to access data on servers hosting a directory service, such as a Microsoft domain controller hosting Active Directory.

A and C are incorrect. Cross-site scripting (XSS) and cross-site request forgery (XSRF) attacks attack web servers, not directory service servers.

D is incorrect. Fuzzing sends random data to see if the application can handle it, but it doesn't necessarily target servers hosting a directory service.

41. Your organization hosts a web site within a DMZ and the web site accesses a database server in the internal network. ACLs on firewalls prevent any connections to the database server except from the web server. Database fields holding customer data are encrypted and all data in transit between the web site server and the database server are encrypted. Which of the following represents the GREATEST risk to the data on the server?

    A. Theft of the database server

    B. XML injection

    C. SQL injection

    D. Sniffing

41. C is correct. A SQL injection attack allows an attacker to send commands to the database server to access data. Encryption protects it on the server and in transit, but the web server can decrypt it.

A is incorrect. Because the data in the database server is encrypted, theft of the server isn't a significant risk.

B is incorrect. There aren't any indications that the database server is replying with Extensible Markup Language (XML) data, so an XML injection attack isn't a risk.

D is incorrect. Because data is encrypted while in transit, sniffing isn't a significant risk.

42. Checking the logs of a web server, you see the following entry:

198.252.69.129 --[1/Sep/2013:05:20]"GET
/index.php?username=ZZZZZZZZZZZZZZZZZZZZZBBBBBBBBCCCC
CCCHTTP/1.1" "http://gcgapremium.com/security/" "Chrome31"

Which of the following is the BEST choice to explain this entry?

    A. A SQL injection attack

    B. A pharming attack

    C. A phishing attack

    D. A buffer overflow attack

42. D is correct. A buffer overflow attack sends more data or unexpected data to a system in the hopes of overloading it and causing a problem. In this case, it is sending a series of letters as the username (?username=ZZZZ....), which is likely longer than any expected username. Input validation can prevent this from succeeding.

A is incorrect. A SQL injection attack uses specific SQL code, not random letters or characters.

B is incorrect. A pharming attack attempts to redirect users from one web site to another web site.

C is incorrect. A phishing attack sends unwanted email to users.

43. Looking at logs for an online web application, you see that someone has entered the following phrase into several queries:
' or '1'='1' --

Which of the following is the MOST likely explanation for this?

    A. A buffer overflow attack

    B. An XSS attack

    C. A SQL injection attack

    D. An LDAP injection attack

43. C is correct. Attackers use the phrase in SQL injection attacks to query or modify databases.

A is incorrect. A buffer overflow attack sends more data or unexpected data to an application with the goal of accessing system memory.

B is incorrect. A cross-site scripting (XSS) attack attempts to insert HTML or JavaScript code into a web site or email.

D is incorrect. A Lightweight Directory Application Protocol (LDAP) injection attack attempts to inject LDAP commands to query a directory service database.

44. You need to reduce the attack surface of a web server. Which of the following is a preventive control that will assist with this goal?

    A. Disabling unnecessary services

    B. Identifying the initial baseline configuration

    C. Using hardware locks

    D. Monitoring logs for trends

44. A is correct. Disabling unnecessary services is one of several steps you can take to harden a server and it is a preventive control.

B is incorrect. Identifying the initial baseline configuration is useful to determine the security posture of the system, but by itself it doesn't prevent attacks.

C is incorrect. Hardware locks are useful to protect a server room where a web server operates, but it doesn't reduce the attack surface.

D is incorrect. Monitoring logs and trend analysis are detective controls, not preventive controls.

45. Your organization has several switches used within the network. You need to implement a security control to secure the switch from physical access. What should you do?

A. Disable unused ports.

B. Implement an implicit deny rule.

C. Disable STP.

D. Enable SSH.

45. A is correct. You can provide added security by disabling unused physical ports on the switch. If someone gains physical access to the switch by plugging in a computer to one of its unused ports, that person will not be able to connect to the network.

B is incorrect. An implicit deny rule is placed at the end of an access control list on a router to deny traffic that hasn't been explicitly allowed, but it doesn't not affect physical ports differently.

C is incorrect. Spanning Tree Protocol (STP) prevents switching loop problems and should be enabled.

D is incorrect. Secure Shell (SSH) encrypts traffic but doesn't protect a switch.

46. An organization recently updated its security policy. A new requirement dictates a need to increase protection from rogue devices plugging into physical ports. Which of the following choices provides the BEST protection?

A. Disable unused ports

B. Implement 802.1x

C. Enable MAC limiting

D. Enable MAC filtering

46. B is correct. IEEE 802.1x is a port-based authentication protocol and it requires systems to authenticate before they are granted access to the network. If an attacker plugged a rogue device into a physical port, the 802.1x server would block it from accessing the network.

A is incorrect. Disabling unused ports is a good practice, but it doesn't prevent an attacker from unplugging a system from a used port and plugging the rogue device into the port.

C and D are incorrect. While MAC limiting and filtering will provide some protection against rogue devices, an 802.1x server provides much stronger protection.

47. Your organization hosts a web-based server that remote administrators access via Telnet. Management wants to increase their rights to prosecute unauthorized personnel who access this server. Which of the following is the BEST choice?

    A. Enable SSH instead of Telnet.

    B. Enable banner ads.

    C. Enable FTP logging.

    D. Add a warning banner.

47. D is correct. A warning banner displayed when personnel log on could inform them that unauthorized access is restricted and is the best choice of those given.

A is incorrect. Although Secure Shell (SSH) is a more secure alternative than Telnet, it doesn't impact the ability of prosecuting personnel.

B is incorrect. Banner ads are used on web sites, not within a Telnet session.

C is incorrect. File Transfer Protocol (FTP) logging wouldn't log Telnet sessions.

48. Of the following choices, what can you use to divert malicious attacks on your network away from valuable data to worthless fabricated data?

    A. IPS

    B. Proxy server

    C. Web application firewall

    D. Honeypot

48. D is correct. A honeypot can divert malicious attacks to a harmless area of your network, such as away from production servers holding valid data.

A is incorrect. An intrusion prevention system (IPS) can block attacks, but it doesn't divert it.

B is incorrect. A proxy server can filter and cache content from web pages, but doesn't divert attacks.

C is incorrect. A web application firewall (WAF) is an additional firewall designed to protect a web application.

49. You need to monitor the security posture of several servers in your organization and keep a security administrator aware of their status. Which of the following tasks will BEST help you meet this goal?

    A. Establishing baseline reporting

    B. Determining attack surface

    C. Implementing patch management

    D. Enabling sandboxing

49. A is correct. Establishing baseline reporting processes allows you to monitor the systems and identify any changes from the baseline that might affect their security posture.

B is incorrect. You would determine the attack surface prior to establishing a baseline.

C is incorrect. Patch management is important, but it doesn't monitor the overall security posture of systems.

D is incorrect. Sandboxing allows you to isolate systems for testing, but isn't used for online production systems.

50. You want to identify all of the services running on a server. Which of the following tools is the BEST choice to meet this goal?

    A. Penetration test

    B. Protocol analyzer

    C. Sniffer

    D. Port scanner

50. D is correct. A port scanner identifies open ports on a system and is commonly used to determine what services are running on the system.

A is incorrect. A penetration test attempts to exploit a vulnerability.

B and C are incorrect. A protocol analyzer (also called a sniffer) could analyze traffic and discover protocols in use, but this would be much more difficult than using a port scanner.

51. Your organization develops web application software, which it sells to other companies for commercial use. Your organization wants to ensure that the software isn't susceptible to common vulnerabilities, such as buffer overflow attacks and race conditions. What should the organization implement to ensure software meets this standard?

    A. Input validation

    B. Change management

    C. Code review

    D. Regression testing

51. C is correct. A code review goes line-by-line through the software code looking for vulnerabilities, such as buffer overflows and race conditions.

A is incorrect. Input validation helps prevent buffer overflows but not race conditions.

B is incorrect. Change management controls help prevent unintended outages from unauthorized changes.

D is incorrect. Regression testing is a type of testing used to ensure that new patches do not cause errors.

52. A network administrator needs to identify the type of traffic and packet flags used in traffic sent from a specific IP address. Which of the following is the BEST tool to meet this need?

    A. UTM security appliance

    B. Router logs

    C. Protocol analyzer

    D. Vulnerability scan

52. C is correct. A protocol analyzer (or sniffer) can capture traffic sent over a network and identify the type of traffic, the source of the traffic, and protocol flags used within individual packets.

A is incorrect. A unified threat management (UTM) security appliance combines multiple security solutions into a single solution but doesn't typically capture traffic.

B is incorrect. Router logs identify the type of traffic going through it, but do not include packet flag data.

D is incorrect. A vulnerability scan identifies vulnerabilities on a network.

53. While analyzing a packet capture log, you notice the following entry:
16:12:50, src 10.80.1.5:3389, dst 192.168.1.100:8080, syn/ack
Of the following choices, what is the BEST explanation of this entry?

    A. An HTTP connection attempt

    B. An RDP connection attempt

    C. An FTP connection attempt

    D. A buffer overflow attack

53. B is correct. This log entry indicates that a source (src) system with an IP of 10.80.1.5 sent a connection attempt using port 3389, which is the Remote Desktop Protocol (RDP) port, at time 4:12:50 p.m. The destination (dst) was sent to IP 192.168.1.100 using a common proxy server listening port of 8080.

A is incorrect. Hypertext Transfer Protocol (HTTP) uses port 80, not port 3389.

C is incorrect. File Transfer Protocol (FTP) uses ports 20 and 21, not port 3389.

D is incorrect. A buffer overflow attack sends unexpected data, but this entry indicates that it is a SYN/ACK (synchronize/acknowledge) packet establishing a connection.

54. A security company wants to gather intelligence about current methods attackers are using against its clients. What can it use?

    A. Vulnerability scan

    B. Honeynet

    C. MAC address filtering

    D. Evil twin

54. B is correct. A honeynet is a fake network designed to look valuable to attackers and can help security personnel learn about current attack methods. In this scenario, the security company can install honeynets in its customers' networks to lure the attackers.

A is incorrect. A vulnerability scan detects vulnerabilities, but attackers may not try to exploit them.

C is incorrect. Media access control (MAC) address filtering is a form of network access control, but can't be used to detect or learn about attacks.

D is incorrect. An evil twin is a rogue access point with the same SSID as an authorized access point.

55. Bart is performing a vulnerability assessment. Which of the following BEST represents the goal of this task?

    A. Identify services running on a system.

    B. Determine if vulnerabilities can be exploited.

C. Determine if input validation is in place.

D. Identify the system's security posture.

55. D is correct. A vulnerability assessment identifies a system or network's security posture.

A is incorrect. A port scanner identifies services running on a system.

B is incorrect. A penetration test determines if vulnerabilities can be exploited.

C is incorrect. Although a vulnerability assessment might verify if input validation methods are in place, it includes much more.

56. A network administrator is attempting to identify all traffic on an internal network. Which of the following tools is the BEST choice?

A. Black box test

B. Protocol analyzer

C. Penetration test

D. Baseline review

56. B is correct. You can use a protocol analyzer (or sniffer) to capture traffic on a network, and then analyze the capture to identify and quantify all the traffic on the network.

A and C are incorrect. Penetration tests (including black box tests) attempt to identify and exploit vulnerabilities.

D is incorrect. A baseline review can identify changes from standard configurations, but they don't necessarily identify all traffic on a network.

57. Your organization develops web application software, which it sells to other companies for commercial use. To ensure the software is secure, your organization uses a peer assessment to help identify potential security issues related to the software. Which of the following is the BEST term for this process?

    A. Code review

    B. Change management

    C. Routine audit

    D. Rights and permissions review

57. A is correct. Peers, such as other developers, perform code reviews going line-by-line through the software code looking for vulnerabilities, such as buffer overflows and race conditions.

B is incorrect. Change management helps prevent unintended outages from configuration changes.

C is incorrect. Routine audits review processes and procedures, but not software code.

D is incorrect. A user rights and permissions review ensures users have appropriate privileges.

58. Your organization plans to deploy new systems within the network within the next six months. What should your organization implement to ensure these systems are developed properly?

    A. Code review

    B. Design review

    C. Baseline review

    D. Attack surface review

58. B is correct. A design review ensures that systems and software are developed properly.

A is incorrect. A code review is appropriate if the organization is developing its own software for these new systems, but the scenario doesn't indicate this.

C is incorrect. A baseline review identifies changes from the initial baseline configuration, but couldn't be done for systems that aren't deployed yet.

D is incorrect. Identifying the attack surface, including the required protocols and services, would likely be part of the design review, but the design review does much more.

59. You need to periodically check the configuration of a server and identify any changes. What are you performing?

 A. Code review

 B. Design review

 C. Attack surface review

 D. Baseline review

59. D is correct. A baseline review identifies changes from the original deployed configuration. The original configuration is also known as the baseline.

A is incorrect. A code review checks internally developed software for vulnerabilities.

B is incorrect. A design review verifies the design of software or applications to ensure they are developed properly.

C is incorrect. Determining the attack surface is an assessment technique, but it does not identify changes.

60. You are troubleshooting issues between two servers on your network and need to analyze the network traffic. Of the following choices, what is the BEST tool to capture and analyze this traffic?

 A. Switch

 B. Protocol analyzer

 C. Firewall

 D. NIDS

60. B is correct. A protocol analyzer (also called a sniffer) is the best choice to capture and analyze network traffic.

A is incorrect. Although the traffic probably goes through a switch, the switch doesn't capture the traffic in such a way that you can analyze it.

C is incorrect. It's unlikely that the traffic is going through a firewall between two internal servers and even if it did, the best you could get is data from the firewall log, but this wouldn't provide the same level of detail as a capture from the sniffer.

D is incorrect. A network intrusion detection system (NIDS) detects traffic, but it isn't the best tool to capture and analyze it.

61. You recently completed a vulnerability scan on your network. It reported that several servers are missing key operating system patches. However, after checking the servers, you've verified the servers have these patches installed. Which of the following BEST describes this?

    A. False negative

    B. Misconfiguration on servers

    C. False positive

    D. Servers not hardened

61. C is correct. In this scenario, the vulnerability scanner reported a false positive indicating that the servers had a vulnerability, but in reality, the servers did not have the vulnerability.

A is incorrect. A false negative occurs if a vulnerability scanner does not report a known vulnerability.

B and D are incorrect. There isn't any indication that the servers are misconfigured and they are not hardened.

√ Get Certified
√ Get Ahead

Chapter 4 Application, Data and Host Security

Application, Data, and Host Security topics are **15 percent** of the CompTIA Security+ exam. The objectives in this domain are:

4.1 Explain the importance of application security controls and techniques.

- Fuzzing
- Secure coding concepts
    - Error and exception handling
    - Input validation
- Cross-site scripting prevention
- Cross-site Request Forgery (XSRF) prevention
- Application configuration baseline (proper settings)
- Application hardening
- Application patch management
- NoSQL databases vs. SQL databases
- Server-side vs. Client-side validation

4.2 Summarize mobile security concepts and technologies.

- Device security
    - Full device encryption
    - Remote wiping
    - Lockout
    - Screen-locks
    - GPS
    - Application control
    - Storage segmentation
    - Asset tracking
    - Inventory control
    - Mobile device management
    - Device access control
    - Removable storage
    - Disabling unused features
- Application security
    - Key management

- o Credential management
- o Authentication
- o Geo-tagging
- o Encryption
- o Application whitelisting
- o Transitive trust/authentication
- BYOD concerns
  - o Data ownership
  - o Support ownership
  - o Patch management
  - o Antivirus management
  - o Forensics
  - o Privacy
  - o On-boarding/off-boarding
  - o Adherence to corporate policies
  - o User acceptance
  - o Architecture/infrastructure considerations
  - o Legal concerns
  - o Acceptable use policy
  - o On-board camera/video

4.3 Given a scenario, select the appropriate solution to establish host security.

- Operating system security and settings
- OS hardening
- Anti-malware
  - o Antivirus
  - o Anti-spam
  - o Anti-spyware
  - o Pop-up blockers
- Patch management
- White listing vs. black listing applications
- Trusted OS
- Host-based firewalls
- Host-based intrusion detection
- Hardware security
  - o Cable locks
  - o Safe
  - o Locking cabinets
- Host software baselining
- Virtualization
  - o Snapshots

- o Patch compatibility
- o Host availability/elasticity
- o Security control testing
- o Sandboxing

4.4 Implement the appropriate controls to ensure data security.

- Cloud storage
- SAN
- Handling Big Data
- Data encryption
  - o Full disk
  - o Database
  - o Individual files
  - o Removable media
  - o Mobile devices
- Hardware based encryption devices
  - o TPM
  - o HSM
  - o USB encryption
  - o Hard drive
- Data in-transit, Data at-rest, Data in-use
- Permissions/ACL
- Data policies
  - o Wiping
  - o Disposing
  - o Retention
  - o Storage

4.5 Compare and contrast alternative methods to mitigate security risks in static environments.

- Environments
  - o SCADA
  - o Embedded (Printer, Smart TV, HVAC control)
  - o Android
  - o iOS
  - o Mainframe
  - o Game consoles
  - o In-vehicle computing systems
- Methods
  - o Network segmentation
  - o Security layers
  - o Application firewalls
  - o Manual updates

- o Firmware version control
- o Wrappers
- o Control redundancy and diversity

The CompTIA Security+: Get Certified Get Ahead SY0-401 Study Guide (ISBN 1939136024) discusses these topics in much more depth.

√ Get Certified
√ Get Ahead

Practice Test Questions for
Application, Data and Host Security Domain

1. Administrators ensure server operating systems are updated at least once a month with relevant patches, but they do not track other software updates. Of the following choices, what is the BEST choice to mitigate risks on these servers?

      A. Application change management

      B. Application patch management

      C. Whole disk encryption

      D. Application hardening

2. Homer noticed that several generators within the nuclear power plant have been turning on without user interaction. Security investigators discovered that an unauthorized file was installed and causing these generators to start at timed intervals. Further, they determined this file was installed during a visit by external engineers. What should Homer recommend to mitigate this threat in the future?

      A. Create an internal CA.

      B. Implement WPA2 Enterprise.

      C. Implement patch management processes.

      D. Configure the SCADA within a VLAN.

3. Web developers are implementing error and exception handling in a web site application. Which of the following represents a best practice for this?

A. Displaying a detailed error message but logging generic information on the error

B. Displaying a generic error message but logging detailed information on the error

C. Displaying a generic error message and logging generic information on the error

D. Displaying a detailed error message and logging detailed information on the error

4. Homer recently received an email thanking him for a purchase that he did not make. He asked an administrator about it and the administrator noticed a pop-up window, which included the following code:

```
<body onload="document.getElementByID('myform').submit()">
    <form id="myForm" action="gcgapremium.com/purchase.php"
method="post"
<input name="Buy Now" value="Buy Now" />
    </form>
</body>
```

What is the MOST likely explanation?

A. XSRF

B. Buffer overflow

C. SQL injection

D. Fuzzing

5. Your organization is preparing to deploy a web-based application, which will accept user input. Which of the following will test the reliability of this application to maintain availability and data integrity?

A. Secure coding

B. Input validation

C. Error handling

D. Fuzzing

6. A code review of a web application discovered that the application is not performing boundary checking. What should the web developer add to this application to resolve this issue?

    A. XSRF

    B. XSS

    C. Input validation

    D. Fuzzing

7. Lisa has scanned all the user computers in the organization as part of a security audit. She is creating an inventory of these systems, including a list of applications running on each computer and the application versions. What is she MOST likely trying to identify?

    A. System architecture

    B. Application baseline

    C. Code vulnerabilities

    D. Attack surface

8. A web developer wants to reduce the chances of an attacker successfully launching XSRF attacks against a web site application. Which of the following provides the BEST protection?

    A. Client-side input validation

    B. Web proxy

    C. Antivirus software

    D. Server-side input validation

9. Your company has recently provided mobile devices to several employees. A security manager has expressed concerns related to data saved on these devices. Which of the following would BEST address these concerns?

    A. Disabling the use of removable media

    B. Installing an application that tracks the location of the device

    C. Implementing a BYOD policy

    D. Enabling geo-tagging

10. Your company provides electrical and plumbing services to homeowners. Employees use tablets during service calls to record activity, create invoices, and accept credit card payments. Which of the following would BEST prevent disclosure of customer data if any of these devices are lost or stolen?

    A. Mobile device management

    B. Disabling unused features

    C. Remote wiping

    D. GPS tracking

11. Which of the following represents a primary security concern when authorizing mobile devices on a network?

    A. Cost of the device

    B. Compatibility

    C. Virtualization

    D. Data security

12. Of the following choices, what are valid security controls for mobile devices?

    A. Screen locks, device encryption, and remote wipe

    B. Host-based firewalls, pop-up blockers, and SCADA access

    C. Antivirus software, voice encryption, and NAC

    D. Remote lock, NAC, and locking cabinets

13. You want to deter an attacker from using brute force to gain access to a mobile device. What would you configure?

    A. Remote wiping

    B. Account lockout settings

    C. Geo-tagging

    D. RFID

14. Management within your company is considering allowing users to connect to the corporate network with their personally owned devices. Which of the following represents a security concern with this policy?

    A. Inability to ensure devices are up to date with current system patches

    B. Difficulty in locating lost devices

    C. Cost of the devices

    D. Devices might not be compatible with applications within the network

15. An updated security policy identifies authorized applications for company-issued mobile devices. Which of the following would prevent users from installing other applications on these devices?

    A. Geo-tagging

    B. Authentication

    C. ACLs

    D. Whitelisting

16. Your organization has issued mobile devices to several key personnel. These devices store sensitive information. What can administrators implement to prevent data loss from these devices if they are stolen?

A. Inventory control

B. GPS tracking

C. Full device encryption

D. Geo-tagging

17. Homer wants to ensure that other people cannot view data on his mobile device if he leaves it unattended. What should he implement?

A. Encryption

B. Cable lock

C. Screen lock

D. Remote wiping

18. Management wants to implement a system that will provide automatic notification when personnel remove devices from the building. Which of the following security controls will meet this requirement?

A. Video monitoring

B. RFID

C. Geo-tagging

D. Account lockout

19. Maggie is compiling a list of approved software for desktop operating systems within a company. What is the MOST likely purpose of this list?

A. Host software baseline

B. Baseline reporting

C. Application configuration baseline

D. Code review

20. Your organization wants to ensure that employees do not install or play operating system games, such as solitaire and FreeCell, on their computers. Which of the following is the BEST choice to prevent this?

    A. Security policy

    B. Application whitelisting

    C. Anti-malware software

    D. Antivirus software

21. An IT department recently had its hardware budget reduced, but the organization still expects them to maintain availability of services. Of the following choices, what would BEST help them maintain availability with a reduced budget?

    A. Failover clusters

    B. Virtualization

    C. Bollards

    D. Hashing

22. You are preparing to deploy a new application on a virtual server. The virtual server hosts another server application that employees routinely access. Which of the following is the BEST method to use when deploying the new application?

    A. Take a snapshot of the VM before deploying the new application.

    B. Take a snapshot of the VM after deploying the new application.

    C. Apply blacklisting techniques on the server for the new applications.

    D. Back up the server after installing the new application.

23. A recent risk assessment identified several problems with servers in your organization. They occasionally reboot on their own and the operating

systems do not have current security fixes. Administrators have had to rebuild some servers from scratch due to mysterious problems. Which of the following solutions will mitigate these problems?

A. Virtualization

B. Sandboxing

C. IDS

D. Patch management

24. You manage a group of computers in an isolated network without Internet access. You need to update the antivirus definitions manually on these computers. Which of the following choices is the MOST important concern?

A. Running a full scan of the systems before installing the new definitions

B. Running a full scan of the systems after installing the new definitions

C. Ensuring the definition file hash is equal to the hash on the antivirus vendor's web site

D. Ensuring the update includes all signature definitions

25. A user wants to reduce the threat of an attacker capturing her personal information while she surfs the Internet. Which of the following is the BEST choice?

A. Antivirus software

B. Anti-spyware software

C. Pop-up blocker

D. Whitelisting

26. Bart is complaining that new browser windows keep opening on his computer. Which of the following is the BEST choice to stop these in the future?

    A. Malware

    B. Adware

    C. Pop-up blocker

    D. Antivirus software

27. Network administrators identified what appears to be malicious traffic coming from an internal computer, but only when no one is logged on to the computer. You suspect the system is infected with malware. It periodically runs an application that attempts to connect to web sites over port 80 with Telnet. After comparing the computer with a list of services from the standard image, you verify this application is very likely the problem. What process allowed you to make this determination?

    A. Banner grabbing

    B. Hardening

    C. Whitelisting

    D. Baselining

28. You want to test new security controls before deploying them. Which of the following technologies provides the MOST flexibility to meet this goal?

    A. Baselines

    B. Hardening techniques

    C. Virtualization technologies

    D. Patch management programs

29. An organization recently suffered a significant outage after a technician installed an application update on a vital server during peak hours. The server

remained down until administrators were able to install a previous version of the application on the server. What could the organization implement to prevent a reoccurrence of this problem?

    A. Do not apply application patches to server applications.

    B. Apply the patches during nonpeak hours.

    C. Apply hardening techniques.

    D. Create a patch management policy.

30. Your organization wants to reduce the amount of money it is losing due to thefts. Which of the following is the BEST example of an equipment theft deterrent?

    A. Remote wiping

    B. Cable locks

    C. Strong passwords

    D. Disk encryption

31. You suspect that an executable file on a web server is malicious and includes a zero-day exploit. Which of the following steps can you take to verify your suspicious?

    A. Perform a code review.

    B. Perform an architecture review.

    C. Perform a design review.

    D. Perform an operating system baseline comparison.

32. A software vendor recently developed a patch for one of its applications. Before releasing the patch to customers, the vendor needs to test it in different environments. Which of the following solutions provides the BEST method to test the patch in different environments?

A. Baseline image

B. BYOD

C. Virtualized sandbox

D. Change management

33. Your organization has been receiving a significant amount of spam with links to malicious web sites. You want to stop the spam. Of the following choices, what provides the BEST solution?

A. Add the domain to a block list

B. Use a URL filter

C. Use a MAC filter

D. Add antivirus software

34. A recent vulnerability assessment identified several issues related to an organization's security posture. Which of the following issues is MOST likely to affect the organization on a day-to-day basis?

A. Natural disasters

B. Lack of antivirus software

C. Lack of protection for data at rest

D. Lack of protection for data in transit

35. A user recently worked with classified data on an unclassified system. You need to sanitize all the reclaimed space on this system's hard drives while keeping the system operational. Which of the following methods will BEST meet this goal?

A. Use a cluster tip wiping tool.

B. Use a file shredding tool.

C. Degauss the disk.

D. Physically destroy the disk.

36. Which of the following is the MOST likely negative result if administrators do not implement access controls correctly on an encrypted USB hard drive?

    A. Data can be corrupted.

    B. Security controls can be bypassed.

    C. Drives can be geo-tagged.

    D. Data is not encrypted.

37. Your organization hosts a web site with a back-end database. The database stores customer data, including credit card numbers. Which of the following is the BEST way to protect the credit card data?

    A. Full database encryption

    B. Whole disk encryption

    C. Database column encryption

    D. File-level encryption

38. Bart copied an encrypted file from his desktop computer to his USB drive and discovered that the copied file isn't encrypted. He asks you what he can do to ensure files he's encrypted remain encrypted when he copies them to a USB drive. What would you recommend as the BEST solution to this problem?

    A. Use file-level encryption.

    B. Convert the USB to FAT32.

    C. Use whole disk encryption on the desktop computer.

    D. Use whole disk encryption on the USB drive.

39. You are comparing different encryption methods. Which method includes a storage root key?

A. HSM

B. NTFS

C. VSAN

D. TPM

40. Your organization issues users a variety of different mobile devices. However, management wants to reduce potential data losses if the devices are lost or stolen. Which of the following is the BEST technical control to achieve this goal?

    A. Cable locks

    B. Risk assessment

    C. Disk encryption

    D. Hardening the systems

41. Your organization recently purchased several new laptop computers for employees. You're asked to encrypt the laptop's hard drives without purchasing any additional hardware. What would you use?

    A. TPM

    B. HSM

    C. VM escape

    D. DLP

42. Network administrators in your organization need to administer firewalls, security appliances, and other network devices. These devices are protected with strong passwords, and the passwords are stored in a file listing these passwords. Which of the following is the BEST choice to protect this password list?

A. File encryption

B. Database field encryption

C. Full database encryption

D. Whole disk encryption

43. Your organization is considering the purchase of new computers. A security professional stresses that these devices should include TPMs. What benefit does a TPM provide? (Choose all that apply.)

    A. It uses hardware encryption, which is quicker than software encryption.

    B. It uses software encryption, which is quicker than hardware encryption.

    C. It includes an HSM file system.

    D. It stores RSA keys.

44. What functions does an HSM include?

    A. Reduces the risk of employees emailing confidential information outside the organization

    B. Provides webmail to clients

    C. Provides full drive encryption

    D. Generates and stores keys used with servers

45. Your company is planning on implementing a policy for users so that they can connect their mobile devices to the network. However, management wants to restrict network access for these devices. They should have Internet access and be able to access some internal servers, but management wants to ensure that they do not have access to the primary network where company-owned devices operate. Which of the following will BEST meet this goal?

A. WPA2 Enterprise

B. VPN

C. GPS

D. VLAN

46. Lisa oversees and monitors processes at a water treatment plant using SCADA systems. Administrators recently discovered malware on her system that was connecting to the SCADA systems. Although they removed the malware, management is still concerned. Lisa needs to continue using her system and it's not possible to update the SCADA systems. What can mitigate this risk?

A. Install HIPS on the SCADA systems.

B. Install a firewall on the border of the SCADA network.

C. Install a NIPS on the border of the SCADA network.

D. Install a honeypot on the SCADA network.

47. A security analyst is evaluating a critical industrial control system. The analyst wants to ensure the system has security controls to support availability. Which of the following will BEST meet this need?

A. Using at least two firewalls to create a DMZ

B. Installing a SCADA system

C. Implementing control redundancy and diversity

D. Using an embedded system

Practice Test Questions with Answers for Application, Data and Host Security Domain

1. Administrators ensure server operating systems are updated at least once a month with relevant patches, but they do not track other software updates. Of the following choices, what is the BEST choice to mitigate risks on these servers?

     A. Application change management

     B. Application patch management

     C. Whole disk encryption

     D. Application hardening

1. B is correct. Application patch management practices ensure that applications are kept up to date with relevant patches, similar to how the operating systems are kept up to date with patches. Application change management helps control changes to the applications. Whole disk encryption helps protect confidentiality, but is unrelated to this question. Application hardening secures the applications when they are deployed, but doesn't keep them up to date with current patches.

2. Homer noticed that several generators within the nuclear power plant have been turning on without user interaction. Security investigators discovered that an unauthorized file was installed and causing these generators to start at timed intervals. Further, they determined this file was installed during a visit by external engineers. What should Homer recommend to mitigate this threat in the future?

     A. Create an internal CA.

     B. Implement WPA2 Enterprise.

     C. Implement patch management processes.

     D. Configure the SCADA within a VLAN.

2. D is correct. The generators are likely controlled within a supervisory control and data acquisition (SCADA) system and isolating them within a virtual local area network (VLAN) will protect them from unauthorized access.

A is incorrect. An internal certificate authority (CA) issues and manages certificates within a Public Key Infrastructure (PKI), but there isn't any indication certificates are in use.

B is incorrect. Wi-Fi Protected Access II (WPA2) secures wireless networks, but doesn't protect SCADA networks.

C is incorrect. Patch management processes help ensure systems are kept up to date with patches, but this doesn't apply in this scenario.

3. Web developers are implementing error and exception handling in a web site application. Which of the following represents a best practice for this?

> A. Displaying a detailed error message but logging generic information on the error
>
> B. Displaying a generic error message but logging detailed information on the error
>
> C. Displaying a generic error message and logging generic information on the error
>
> D. Displaying a detailed error message and logging detailed information on the error

3. B is correct. You should display a generic error message but log detailed information on the error.

A and D are incorrect. Detailed error messages to the user are often confusing to them and give attackers information they can use against the system.

C is incorrect. Logging generic information makes it more difficult to troubleshoot the problem later.

4. Homer recently received an email thanking him for a purchase that he did not make. He asked an administrator about it and the administrator noticed a pop-up window, which included the following code:

```
<body onload="document.getElementByID('myform').submit()">
   <form id="myForm" action="gcgapremium.com/purchase.php"
method="post"
<input name="Buy Now" value="Buy Now" />
   </form>
</body>
```

What is the MOST likely explanation?

    A. XSRF

    B. Buffer overflow

    C. SQL injection

    D. Fuzzing

4. A is correct. A cross-site request forgery attack (XSRF) causes users to perform actions without their knowledge. This scenario indicates the user visited a web site, most likely through a malicious link, and the link initiated a purchase. None of the other attacks cause unsuspecting users to make purchases.

B is incorrect. A buffer overflow attacks a web site and attempts to access system memory.

C is incorrect. A SQL injection attack attempts to access data on a database server.

D is incorrect. Fuzzing sends random data to an application to test its ability to handle the random data.

5. Your organization is preparing to deploy a web-based application, which will accept user input. Which of the following will test the reliability of this application to maintain availability and data integrity?

    A. Secure coding

    B. Input validation

    C. Error handling

    D. Fuzzing

5. D is correct. Fuzzing can test the application's ability to maintain availability and data integrity for some scenarios. Fuzzing sends random data to an application to verify the random data doesn't crash the application or expose the system to a data breach.

A, B, and C are incorrect. Secure coding practices such as input validation and error- and exception-handling techniques protect applications, but do not test them.

6. A code review of a web application discovered that the application is not performing boundary checking. What should the web developer add to this application to resolve this issue?

    A. XSRF

    B. XSS

    C. Input validation

    D. Fuzzing

6. C is correct. The lack of input validation is a common coding error and it includes boundary or limit checking to validate data before using it.

A and B are incorrect. Proper input validation prevents many problems such as cross-site request forgery (XSRF), cross-site scripting (XSS), buffer overflow, and command injection attacks.

D is incorrect. Fuzzing injects extra data and tests the effectiveness of input validation.

7. Lisa has scanned all the user computers in the organization as part of a security audit. She is creating an inventory of these systems, including a list of

applications running on each computer and the application versions. What is she MOST likely trying to identify?

    A. System architecture

    B. Application baseline

    C. Code vulnerabilities

    D. Attack surface

7. B is correct. Administrators create a list of applications installed on systems as part of an application baseline (also called a host software baseline).

A is incorrect. An architecture review typically looks at the network architecture, not individual systems.

C is incorrect. A code review looks for vulnerabilities within code, but applications are compiled so the code is not easily available for review.

D is incorrect. The attack surface looks at much more than just applications and includes protocols and services.

8. A web developer wants to reduce the chances of an attacker successfully launching XSRF attacks against a web site application. Which of the following provides the BEST protection?

    A. Client-side input validation

    B. Web proxy

    C. Antivirus software

    D. Server-side input validation

8. D is correct. Validating and filtering input using server-side input validation can restrict the use of special characters needed in cross-site request forgery (XSRF) attacks.

A is incorrect. Both server-side and client-side input validation is useful, but client-side input validation can be bypassed, so it should not be used alone.

B is incorrect. A web proxy can filter URLs, but it cannot validate data. Additionally, web proxies can be used to bypass client-side input validation techniques.

C is incorrect. Antivirus software cannot detect XSRF attacks.

9. Your company has recently provided mobile devices to several employees. A security manager has expressed concerns related to data saved on these devices. Which of the following would BEST address these concerns?

    A. Disabling the use of removable media

    B. Installing an application that tracks the location of the device

    C. Implementing a BYOD policy

    D. Enabling geo-tagging

9. A is correct. Disabling the use of mobile media on the devices will reduce the potential of data loss from these devices. It would make it more difficult to copy data to and from the devices.

B is incorrect. Tracking the location won't affect data.

C is incorrect. The devices are provided by the company, so a bring your own device (BYOD) policy isn't relevant.

D is incorrect. Geo-tagging only refers to geographic location information attached to pictures posted on social media sites.

10. Your company provides electrical and plumbing services to homeowners. Employees use tablets during service calls to record activity, create invoices, and accept credit card payments. Which of the following would BEST prevent disclosure of customer data if any of these devices are lost or stolen?

    A. Mobile device management

    B. Disabling unused features

    C. Remote wiping

    D. GPS tracking

10. C is correct. Remote wiping sends a signal to a device and erases all data, which would prevent disclosure of customer data.

A is incorrect. Mobile device management helps ensure devices are kept up to date with current patches.

B is incorrect. Disabling unused features is a basic hardening step for mobile devices, but doesn't help if the device is lost.

D is incorrect. Global positioning system (GPS) tracking helps locate the device, but doesn't necessarily prevent data disclosure if the device cannot be retrieved.

11. Which of the following represents a primary security concern when authorizing mobile devices on a network?

    A. Cost of the device

    B. Compatibility

    C. Virtualization

    D. Data security

11. D is correct. Protecting data is a primary security concern when authorizing mobile devices on a network, often because mobile devices are more difficult to manage.

A is incorrect. The cost of the devices is trivial when compared with the cost of other network devices and the value of data.

B is incorrect. Compatibility issues aren't a major concern and typically only affect the ability to use an application.

C is incorrect. Virtualization techniques can be used with mobile devices allowing users to access virtual desktops, but these enhance security.

12. Of the following choices, what are valid security controls for mobile devices?

A. Screen locks, device encryption, and remote wipe

B. Host-based firewalls, pop-up blockers, and SCADA access

C. Antivirus software, voice encryption, and NAC

D. Remote lock, NAC, and locking cabinets

12. A is correct. Screen locks, device encryption, and remote wipe are all valid security controls for mobile devices.

B is incorrect. It's rare for mobile devices to have firewalls, but granting them access to supervisory control and data acquisition (SCADA) systems doesn't protect mobile devices or SCADA systems.

C and D are incorrect. Network access control (NAC) provides protection for networks, not mobile devices.

13. You want to deter an attacker from using brute force to gain access to a mobile device. What would you configure?

A. Remote wiping

B. Account lockout settings

C. Geo-tagging

D. RFID

13. B is correct. Account lockout settings are useful on any type of device, including mobile devices and desktop systems. An account lockout setting locks a device after a specified number of incorrect password or PIN guesses; some devices can be configured to erase all the data on the device after too many incorrect guesses.

A is incorrect. Remote wiping erases all the data.

C is incorrect. Geo-tagging provides geographic location for pictures posted to social media sites.

D is incorrect. Radio-frequency identification (RFID) can be used for automated inventory control to detect movement of devices.

14. Management within your company is considering allowing users to connect to the corporate network with their personally owned devices. Which of the following represents a security concern with this policy?

    A. Inability to ensure devices are up to date with current system patches

    B. Difficulty in locating lost devices

    C. Cost of the devices

    D. Devices might not be compatible with applications within the network

14. A is correct. A core security concern with bring your own device (BYOD) policies is ensuring that they are up to date with current patches and have up-to-date antivirus signature files.

B is incorrect. Tools are available to locate lost devices even if they are employee-owned.

C is incorrect. The cost of the devices is not a security concern and not a concern to the company because employees pay for their own devices.

D is incorrect. Although ensuring that the devices are compatible with network applications is a concern, it only affects availability of the application for a single user.

15. An updated security policy identifies authorized applications for company-issued mobile devices. Which of the following would prevent users from installing other applications on these devices?

    A. Geo-tagging

    B. Authentication

    C. ACLs

    D. Whitelisting

15. D is correct. Whitelisting identifies authorized software and prevents users from installing or running any other software.

A is incorrect. Geo-tagging adds location information to media such as photographs, but the scenario only refers to applications.

B is incorrect. Authentication allows users to prove their identity, such as with a username and password, but isn't relevant in this question.

C is incorrect. Access control lists (ACLs) are used with routers, firewalls, and files, but do not restrict installation of applications.

16. Your organization has issued mobile devices to several key personnel. These devices store sensitive information. What can administrators implement to prevent data loss from these devices if they are stolen?

    A. Inventory control

    B. GPS tracking

    C. Full device encryption

    D. Geo-tagging

16. C is correct. Full device encryption helps prevent data loss in the event of theft of a mobile device storing sensitive information. Other security controls (not listed as answers in this question) that help prevent loss of data in this situation are a screen lock, account lockout, and remote wipe capabilities.

A is incorrect. Inventory control methods help ensure devices aren't lost or stolen.

B is incorrect. Global positioning system (GPS) tracking helps locate the device.

D is incorrect. Geo-tagging includes geographical information with pictures posted to social media sites.

17. Homer wants to ensure that other people cannot view data on his mobile device if he leaves it unattended. What should he implement?

    A. Encryption

    B. Cable lock

C. Screen lock

D. Remote wiping

17. C is correct. A screen lock locks a device until the proper passcode is entered and prevents access to mobile devices when they are left unattended.

A is incorrect. Encryption protects data, especially if the device is lost or stolen.

B is incorrect. A cable lock is used with laptops to prevent them from being stolen.

D is incorrect. Remote wiping can erase data on a lost or stolen device.

18. Management wants to implement a system that will provide automatic notification when personnel remove devices from the building. Which of the following security controls will meet this requirement?

A. Video monitoring

B. RFID

C. Geo-tagging

D. Account lockout

18. B is correct. Radio-frequency identification (RFID) provides automated inventory control and can detect movement of devices.

A is incorrect. Video monitoring might detect removal of devices, but it does not include automatic notification.

C is incorrect. Geo-tagging provides geographic location for pictures posted to social media sites.

D is incorrect. Account lockout controls lock accounts when the incorrect password is entered too many times.

19. Maggie is compiling a list of approved software for desktop operating systems within a company. What is the MOST likely purpose of this list?

    A. Host software baseline

    B. Baseline reporting

    C. Application configuration baseline

    D. Code review

19. A is correct. A host software baseline (also called an application baseline) identifies a list of approved software for systems and compares it with installed applications.

B is incorrect. Baseline reporting is a process that monitors systems for changes and reports discrepancies.

C is incorrect. An application configuration baseline identifies proper settings for applications.

D is incorrect. A code review looks at the actual code of the software, and doesn't just create a list.

20. Your organization wants to ensure that employees do not install or play operating system games, such as solitaire and FreeCell, on their computers. Which of the following is the BEST choice to prevent this?

    A. Security policy

    B. Application whitelisting

    C. Anti-malware software

    D. Antivirus software

20. B is correct. Application whitelisting identifies authorized applications and prevents users from installing or running any other applications. Alternately, you can use a blacklist to identify specific applications that cannot be installed or run on a system.

A is incorrect. A security policy (such as an acceptable use policy) can state a rule to discourage this behavior, but it doesn't enforce the rule by preventing users from installing or running the software.

C and D are incorrect. Anti-malware software and antivirus software can detect and block malware, but not applications.

21. An IT department recently had its hardware budget reduced, but the organization still expects them to maintain availability of services. Of the following choices, what would BEST help them maintain availability with a reduced budget?

    A. Failover clusters

    B. Virtualization

    C. Bollards

    D. Hashing

21. B is correct. Virtualization provides increased availability because it is much easier to rebuild a virtual server than a physical server after a failure. Virtualization supports a reduced budget because virtual servers require less hardware, less space in a data center, less power, and less heating and air conditioning.

A is incorrect. Failover clusters are more expensive.

C is incorrect. Bollards are physical barriers that block vehicles.

D is incorrect. Hashing provides integrity, not availability.

22. You are preparing to deploy a new application on a virtual server. The virtual server hosts another server application that employees routinely access. Which of the following is the BEST method to use when deploying the new application?

    A. Take a snapshot of the VM before deploying the new application.

    B. Take a snapshot of the VM after deploying the new application.

    C. Apply blacklisting techniques on the server for the new applications.

    D. Back up the server after installing the new application.

22. A is correct. Taking a snapshot of the virtual machine (VM) before deploying it ensures that the VM can be reverted to the original configuration if the new application causes problems.

B is incorrect. Taking a snapshot after the installation doesn't allow you to revert the image.

C is incorrect. Blacklisting prevents an application from running, so it isn't appropriate for a new application deployed on a server.

D is incorrect. Backing up the server might be appropriate before installing the new application but not after.

23. A recent risk assessment identified several problems with servers in your organization. They occasionally reboot on their own and the operating systems do not have current security fixes. Administrators have had to rebuild some servers from scratch due to mysterious problems. Which of the following solutions will mitigate these problems?

    A. Virtualization

    B. Sandboxing

    C. IDS

    D. Patch management

23. D is correct. Patch management procedures ensure that systems are kept up to date with current security fixes and patches and help eliminate problems with known attack methods. The scenario indicates that these systems have been attacked, exploiting the vulnerabilities caused by not patching them.

A is incorrect. Virtualization will have the same problems if the systems are not kept up to date.

B is incorrect. Sandboxing isolates systems for testing, but there isn't any indication these servers should be isolated.

C is incorrect. An intrusion detection system (IDS) might identify some attacks, but the systems will still be exploited if they aren't patched.

24. You manage a group of computers in an isolated network without Internet access. You need to update the antivirus definitions manually on these computers. Which of the following choices is the MOST important concern?

    A. Running a full scan of the systems before installing the new definitions

    B. Running a full scan of the systems after installing the new definitions

    C. Ensuring the definition file hash is equal to the hash on the antivirus vendor's web site

    D. Ensuring the update includes all signature definitions

24. C is correct. When downloading files as important as antivirus definitions, it's important to ensure they do not lose data integrity, and you can do so by verifying the hashes.

A and B are incorrect. It's not necessary to run a full scan either before or after installing new definitions, but the new definitions will help.

D is incorrect. An update will only include new definitions, not all signature definitions.

25. A user wants to reduce the threat of an attacker capturing her personal information while she surfs the Internet. Which of the following is the BEST choice?

    A. Antivirus software

    B. Anti-spyware software

    C. Pop-up blocker

    D. Whitelisting

25. B is correct. Anti-spyware is the best choice to protect an individual's personal information while online.

A is incorrect. Many antivirus software applications include anti-spyware components, but not all of them do.

C is incorrect. A pop-up blocker prevents pop-up windows, caused by adware.

D is incorrect. Whitelisting identifies specific applications authorized on a system, but does not necessarily prevent the theft of personal information.

26. Bart is complaining that new browser windows keep opening on his computer. Which of the following is the BEST choice to stop these in the future?

    A. Malware

    B. Adware

    C. Pop-up blocker

    D. Antivirus software

26. C is correct. A pop-up blocker is the best choice to stop these windows, which are commonly called pop-up windows.

A and B are incorrect. They might be the result of malware or adware, but more malware or adware will not stop them.

D is incorrect. Some antivirus software may block the pop-ups, but a pop-up blocker is the best choice.

27. Network administrators identified what appears to be malicious traffic coming from an internal computer, but only when no one is logged on to the computer. You suspect the system is infected with malware. It periodically runs an application that attempts to connect to web sites over port 80 with Telnet. After comparing the computer with a list of services from the standard image, you verify this application is very likely the problem. What process allowed you to make this determination?

A. Banner grabbing

B. Hardening

C. Whitelisting

D. Baselining

27. D is correct. The standard image is the baseline and by comparing the list of services in the baseline with the services running on the suspect computer, you can identify unauthorized services. In this scenario, Telnet must not be in the baseline, but it is running on the suspect computer.

A is incorrect. It's possible an attacker has hijacked the computer to perform banner-grabbing attacks against external web sites, but banner grabbing doesn't verify the problem on the computer.

B is incorrect. Hardening makes a computer more secure than the default configuration, but it is done before creating a baseline.

C is incorrect. Whitelisting identifies authorized applications and prevents unauthorized applications from running.

28. You want to test new security controls before deploying them. Which of the following technologies provides the MOST flexibility to meet this goal?

A. Baselines

B. Hardening techniques

C. Virtualization technologies

D. Patch management programs

28. C is correct. Virtualization provides a high degree of flexibility when testing security controls because testers can easily rebuild virtual systems or revert them using a snapshot.

A is incorrect. Baselines provide a known starting point, but aren't flexible because they stay the same.

B is incorrect. Hardening techniques make systems more secure than their default configuration.

D is incorrect. Patch management programs ensure patches are deployed, but do not test security controls.

29. An organization recently suffered a significant outage after a technician installed an application update on a vital server during peak hours. The server remained down until administrators were able to install a previous version of the application on the server. What could the organization implement to prevent a reoccurrence of this problem?

    A. Do not apply application patches to server applications.

    B. Apply the patches during nonpeak hours.

    C. Apply hardening techniques.

    D. Create a patch management policy.

29. D is correct. An application patch management policy includes plans for identifying, testing, scheduling, and deploying updates. Patches are often applied to test systems before they are applied to live production systems and this would prevent this outage.

A is incorrect. Server applications should be kept up to date with patches.

B is incorrect. Although applying patches during nonpeak hours is a good recommendation, it would have still caused an outage in this scenario.

C is incorrect. Hardening techniques makes a system more secure, but won't protect systems from a faulty patch.

30. Your organization wants to reduce the amount of money it is losing due to thefts. Which of the following is the BEST example of an equipment theft deterrent?

    A. Remote wiping

    B. Cable locks

    C. Strong passwords

    D. Disk encryption

30. B is correct. Cable locks are effective equipment theft deterrents for laptops and other systems.

A is incorrect. Remote wiping can erase data on stolen systems, but it doesn't deter thefts.

C is incorrect. Strong passwords help prevent someone from accessing a stolen device, but it doesn't deter thefts.

D is incorrect. Disk encryption can protect the data after a device is stolen, but it doesn't deter theft.

31. You suspect that an executable file on a web server is malicious and includes a zero-day exploit. Which of the following steps can you take to verify your suspicious?

    A. Perform a code review.

    B. Perform an architecture review.

    C. Perform a design review.

    D. Perform an operating system baseline comparison.

31. D is correct. An operating system baseline comparison is the best choice of the available answers. It can verify if the file is in the baseline, or was added after the server was deployed.

A is incorrect. A code review is possible if you have access to the original code, but this isn't easily possible with an executable file.

B and C are incorrect. Code reviews look at the code before it is released and architecture reviews look at architecture designs, but neither of these identifies malicious files after a web server has been deployed.

32. A software vendor recently developed a patch for one of its applications. Before releasing the patch to customers, the vendor needs to test it in different environments. Which of the following solutions provides the BEST method to test the patch in different environments?

A. Baseline image

B. BYOD

C. Virtualized sandbox

D. Change management

32. C is correct. A virtualized sandbox provides a simple method of testing patches and would be used with snapshots so that the virtual machine (VM) can easily be reverted to the original state.

A is incorrect. A baseline image is a starting point of a single environment.

B is incorrect. Bring your own device (BYOD) refers to allowing employee-owned mobile devices in a network, and is not related to this question.

D is incorrect. Change management practices ensure changes are not applied until they are approved and documented.

33. Your organization has been receiving a significant amount of spam with links to malicious web sites. You want to stop the spam. Of the following choices, what provides the BEST solution?

A. Add the domain to a block list

B. Use a URL filter

C. Use a MAC filter

D. Add antivirus software

33. A is correct. You can block emails from a specific domain sending spam by adding the domain to a block list. While the question doesn't indicate that the spam is coming from a single domain, this is still the best answer of the given choices.

B is incorrect. A URL filter blocks outgoing traffic and can be used to block the links to the malicious web sites in this scenario, but it doesn't stop the email.

C is incorrect. Switches use MAC filters to restrict access within a network.

D is incorrect. Antivirus software does not block spam.

34. A recent vulnerability assessment identified several issues related to an organization's security posture. Which of the following issues is MOST likely to affect the organization on a day-to-day basis?

    A. Natural disasters

    B. Lack of antivirus software

    C. Lack of protection for data at rest

    D. Lack of protection for data in transit

34. B is correct. Malware is a constant threat and without antivirus software, systems are sure to become infected in a short period of time.

A is incorrect. Natural disasters are a risk, but not on a day-to-day basis.

C and D are incorrect. Encryption protects data at rest and data in transit, but a lack of encryption isn't likely to affect the organization on a day-to-day basis.

35. A user recently worked with classified data on an unclassified system. You need to sanitize all the reclaimed space on this system's hard drives while keeping the system operational. Which of the following methods will BEST meet this goal?

    A. Use a cluster tip wiping tool.

    B. Use a file shredding tool.

    C. Degauss the disk.

    D. Physically destroy the disk.

35. A is correct. A cluster tip wiping tool sanitizes reclaimed space on hard drives. The cluster tip is the extra space in the last cluster of a file, which can hold remnants of data.

B is incorrect. A file shredding tool successfully erases a file, but does not affect clusters in reclaimed space.

C and D are incorrect. Degaussing the disk magnetically erases it, and physically destroying the disk is the most secure method protecting its confidentiality, but both of these methods take the system out of operation.

36. Which of the following is the MOST likely negative result if administrators do not implement access controls correctly on an encrypted USB hard drive?

    A. Data can be corrupted.

    B. Security controls can be bypassed.

    C. Drives can be geo-tagged.

    D. Data is not encrypted.

36. B is correct. If access controls are not implemented correctly, an attacker might be able to bypass them and access the data.

A is incorrect. The incorrect implementation of the access controls won't corrupt the data.

C is incorrect. Files such as pictures posted on social media can be geo-tagged, but this is unrelated to a hard drive.

D is incorrect. The scenario says the drive is encrypted, so the data is encrypted.

37. Your organization hosts a web site with a back-end database. The database stores customer data, including credit card numbers. Which of the following is the BEST way to protect the credit card data?

    A. Full database encryption

    B. Whole disk encryption

    C. Database column encryption

    D. File-level encryption

37. C is correct. Database column (or field) encryption is the best choice because it can be used to encrypt the fields holding credit card data, but not fields that don't need to be encrypted.

A and B are incorrect. Full database encryption and whole disk encryption aren't appropriate because everything doesn't need to be encrypted to protect the credit card data.

D is incorrect. File-level encryption isn't appropriate on a database and will often make it inaccessible to the database application.

38. Bart copied an encrypted file from his desktop computer to his USB drive and discovered that the copied file isn't encrypted. He asks you what he can do to ensure files he's encrypted remain encrypted when he copies them to a USB drive. What would you recommend as the BEST solution to this problem?

    A. Use file-level encryption.

    B. Convert the USB to FAT32.

    C. Use whole disk encryption on the desktop computer.

    D. Use whole disk encryption on the USB drive.

38. D is correct. The best solution is to use whole disk encryption on the USB drive.

A and B are incorrect. The scenario indicates Bart is using file-level encryption (such as NTFS encryption) on the desktop computer, but the USB drive doesn't support it, possibly because it's formatted as a FAT32 drive. The result is that the system decrypts the file before copying it to the USB drive. Another solution is to convert the USB to NTFS.

D is incorrect. Whole disk encryption on the desktop computer wouldn't protect files copied to the USB drive.

39. You are comparing different encryption methods. Which method includes a storage root key?

    A. HSM

    B. NTFS

    C. VSAN

    D. TPM

39. D is correct. A Trusted Platform Module (TPM) includes a storage root key. The TPM generates this key when a user activates the TPM.

A is incorrect. A hardware security module (HSM) uses RSA keys, but not a storage root key.

B is incorrect. NT File System (NTFS) supports encryption with Encrypting File System (EFS).

C is incorrect. A virtual storage area network (VSAN) is a virtualization technique, and it doesn't provide encryption.

40. Your organization issues users a variety of different mobile devices. However, management wants to reduce potential data losses if the devices are lost or stolen. Which of the following is the BEST technical control to achieve this goal?

    A. Cable locks

    B. Risk assessment

    C. Disk encryption

    D. Hardening the systems

40. C is correct. Disk encryption is a strong technical control that can mitigate potential data losses if mobile devices are lost or stolen.

A is incorrect. Cable locks are preventive controls that can prevent the theft of mobile devices such as laptops, but they don't protect the data after the device is stolen.

B is incorrect. A risk assessment is a management control.

D is incorrect. Hardening systems helps make them more secure than their default configuration, but doesn't necessarily protect data after the device is lost.

41. Your organization recently purchased several new laptop computers for employees. You're asked to encrypt the laptop's hard drives without purchasing any additional hardware. What would you use?

    A. TPM

    B. HSM

    C. VM escape

    D. DLP

41. A is correct. A Trusted Platform Module (TPM) is included in many new laptops and it provides a mechanism for vendors to perform hard drive encryption. Because the TPM components are included, this solution does not require purchasing additional hardware.

B is incorrect. An HSM is a removable hardware device and is not included with laptops, so it requires an additional purchase.

C is incorrect. A VM escape attack runs on a virtual system, and if successful, it allows the attacker to control the physical host server and all other virtual servers on the physical server.

D is incorrect. A network-based data loss prevention (DLP) system can examine and analyze network traffic and detect if confidential company data is included.

42. Network administrators in your organization need to administer firewalls, security appliances, and other network devices. These devices are protected with strong passwords, and the passwords are stored in a file listing these passwords. Which of the following is the BEST choice to protect this password list?

A. File encryption

B. Database field encryption

C. Full database encryption

D. Whole disk encryption

42. A is correct. The best choice is file encryption to protect the passwords in this list.

B is incorrect. If the passwords were stored in a database, it would be appropriate to encrypt the fields in the database holding the passwords.

C is incorrect. It's rarely desirable to encrypt an entire database.

D is incorrect. Whole disk encryption is appropriate for mobile devices.

43. Your organization is considering the purchase of new computers. A security professional stresses that these devices should include TPMs. What benefit does a TPM provide? (Choose all that apply.)

A. It uses hardware encryption, which is quicker than software encryption.

B. It uses software encryption, which is quicker than hardware encryption.

C. It includes an HSM file system.

D. It stores RSA keys.

43. A and D are correct. A Trusted Platform Module (TPM) is a hardware chip that stores RSA encryption keys and uses hardware encryption, which is quicker than software encryption.

B is incorrect. A TPM does not use software encryption.

C is incorrect. An HSM is a removable hardware device that uses hardware encryption, but it does not have a file system and TPM does not provide HSM as a benefit.

44. What functions does an HSM include?

    A. Reduces the risk of employees emailing confidential information outside the organization

    B. Provides webmail to clients

    C. Provides full drive encryption

    D. Generates and stores keys used with servers

44. D is correct. A hardware security module (HSM) is a removable device that can generate and store RSA keys used with servers for data encryption.

A is incorrect. A data loss prevention (DLP) device is a device that can reduce the risk of employees emailing confidential information outside the organization.

B is incorrect. Software as a Service (SaaS) provides software or applications, such as webmail, via the cloud.

C is incorrect. A Trusted Platform Module (TPM) provides full drive encryption and is included in many laptops.

45. Your company is planning on implementing a policy for users so that they can connect their mobile devices to the network. However, management wants to restrict network access for these devices. They should have Internet access and be able to access some internal servers, but management wants to ensure that they do not have access to the primary network where company-owned devices operate. Which of the following will BEST meet this goal?

    A. WPA2 Enterprise

    B. VPN

    C. GPS

    D. VLAN

45. D is correct. A virtual local area network (VLAN) provides network segmentation and can prevent employee owned devices from accessing the primary network.

A is incorrect. WPA2 Enterprise provides strong security for the devices by ensuring they authenticate through an 802.1x server, but this doesn't segment them on a separate network.

B is incorrect. A virtual private network (VPN) allows remote employees to connect to a private network, but is unrelated to this question.

C is incorrect. A global positioning system (GPS) is useful for locating lost devices but not segmenting network traffic.

46. Lisa oversees and monitors processes at a water treatment plant using SCADA systems. Administrators recently discovered malware on her system that was connecting to the SCADA systems. Although they removed the malware, management is still concerned. Lisa needs to continue using her system and it's not possible to update the SCADA systems. What can mitigate this risk?

> A. Install HIPS on the SCADA systems.
>
> B. Install a firewall on the border of the SCADA network.
>
> C. Install a NIPS on the border of the SCADA network.
>
> D. Install a honeypot on the SCADA network.

46. C is correct. A network intrusion prevention system (NIPS) installed on the supervisory control and data acquisition (SCADA) network can intercept malicious traffic coming into the network and is the best choice of those given.

A is incorrect. The scenario states you cannot update the SCADA systems, so you cannot install a host-based IPS (HIPS) on any of them.

B is incorrect. A firewall provides a level of protection. However, it wouldn't be able to differentiate between valid traffic sent by Lisa and malicious traffic sent by malware from Lisa's system.

D is incorrect. A honeypot might be useful to observe malicious traffic, but wouldn't prevent it.

47. A security analyst is evaluating a critical industrial control system. The analyst wants to ensure the system has security controls to support availability. Which of the following will BEST meet this need?

    A. Using at least two firewalls to create a DMZ

    B. Installing a SCADA system

    C. Implementing control redundancy and diversity

    D. Using an embedded system

47. C is correct. A critical industrial control system implies a supervisory control and data acquisition (SCADA) system and ensuring that the system incorporates diversity into a redundant design will best meet this need of the available choices.

A is incorrect. A demilitarized zone (DMZ) provides some protection against Internet attacks, but critical industrial control systems rarely have direct Internet access.

B is incorrect. The goal in the question is to protect the SCADA system, but the SCADA system isn't a security control.

D is incorrect. The scenario is describing an embedded system.

√ Get Certified

                √ Get Ahead

Chapter 5 Access Control and Identity Management

Access Control and Identity Management topics are **15 percent** of the CompTIA Security+ exam. The objectives in this domain are:

5.1 Compare and contrast the function and purpose of authentication services.

- RADIUS
- TACACS+
- Kerberos
- LDAP
- XTACACS
- SAML
- Secure LDAP

5.2 Given a scenario, select the appropriate authentication, authorization or access control.

- Identification vs. authentication vs. authorization
- Authorization
  - Least privilege
  - Separation of duties
  - ACLs
  - Mandatory access
  - Discretionary access
  - Rule-based access control
  - Role-based access control
  - Time of day restrictions
- Authentication
  - Tokens
  - Common access card
  - Smart card
  - Multifactor authentication
  - TOTP
  - HOTP
  - CHAP
  - PAP

- o Single sign-on
- o Access control
- o Implicit deny
- o Trusted OS
- Authentication factors
  - o Something you are
  - o Something you have
  - o Something you know
  - o Somewhere you are
  - o Something you do
- Identification
  - o Biometrics
  - o Personal identification verification card
  - o Username
- Federation
- Transitive trust/authentication

5.3 Install and configure security controls when performing account management, based on best practices.

- Mitigate issues associated with users with multiple account/roles and/or shared accounts
- Account policy enforcement
  - o Credential management
  - o Group policy
  - o Password complexity
  - o Expiration
  - o Recovery
  - o Disablement
  - o Lockout
  - o Password history
  - o Password reuse
  - o Password length
  - o Generic account prohibition
- Group based privileges
- User assigned privileges
- User access reviews
- Continuous monitoring

The CompTIA Security+: Get Certified Get Ahead SY0-401 Study Guide (ISBN 1939136024) discusses these topics in much more depth.

√ **Get Certified**

√ **Get Ahead**

Practice Test Questions for Access Control and Identity Management Domain

1. Which of the following authentication services uses tickets for user credentials?

    A. RADIUS

    B. Diameter

    C. Kerberos

    D. LDAP

2. Your network uses an authentication service based on the X.500 specification. When encrypted, it uses TLS. Which authentication service is your network using?

    A. SAML

    B. Diameter

    C. RADIUS

    D. LDAP

3. A user calls into the help desk and asks the help-desk professional to reset his password. Which of the following choices is the BEST choice for what the help-desk professional should do before resetting the password?

    A. Verify the user's original password.

    B. Disable the user's account.

    C. Verify the user's identity.

    D. Enable the user's account.

4. Your organization recently made an agreement with third parties for the exchange of authentication and authorization information. The solution uses an XML-based open standard. Which of the following is the MOST likely solution being implemented?

    A. RADIUS

    B. Diameter

    C. TACACS+

    D. SAML

5. The Retirement Castle uses groups for ease of administration and management. They recently hired Jasper as their new accountant. Jasper needs access to all the files and folders used by the Accounting department. What should the administrator do to give Jasper appropriate access?

    A. Create an account for Jasper and add the account to the Accounting group.

    B. Give Jasper the password for the Guest account.

    C. Create an account for Jasper and use rule-based access control for accounting.

    D. Create an account for Jasper and add the account to the Administrators group.

6. Which of the following choices provide authentication services for remote users and devices? (Select TWO.)

    A. Kerberos

    B. RADIUS

    C. Secure LDAP

    D. Diameter

7. Your company recently began allowing workers to telecommute from home one or more days a week. However, your company doesn't currently have a remote access solution. They want to implement an AAA solution that supports different vendors. Which of the following is the BEST choice?

    A. TACACS+

    B. RADIUS

    C. Circumference

    D. SAML

8. A network includes a ticket-granting ticket server used for authentication. What authentication service does this network use?

    A. TACACS+

    B. SAML

    C. LDAP

    D. Kerberos

9. You are modifying a configuration file used to authenticate Unix accounts against an external server. The file includes phrases such as DC=Server1 and DC=Com. Which authentication service is the external server using?

    A. Diameter

    B. RADIUS

    C. LDAP

    D. SAML

10. What type of encryption does the RADIUS protocol use?

    A. Symmetric

    B. Asymmetric

    C. MD5

    D. SHA

11. A security auditor discovered that several employees in the Accounting department can print and sign checks. In her final report, she recommended restricting the number of people who can print checks and the number of people who can sign them. She also recommended that no one should be authorized to print and sign checks. What policy is she recommending?

    A. Discretionary access control

    B. Rule-based access control

    C. Separation of duties

    D. Job rotation

12. You are logging on to your bank's web site using your email address and a password. What is the purpose of the email address in this example?

    A. Identification

    B. Authentication

    C. Authorization

    D. Availability

13. Your organization is planning to implement remote access capabilities. Management wants strong authentication and wants to ensure that passwords expire after a predefined time interval. Which of the following choices BEST meets this requirement?

    A. HOTP

    B. TOTP

    C. CAC

    D. Kerberos

14. Which type of authentication is a fingerprint scan?

    A. Something you have

    B. Biometric

    C. PAP

    D. One-time password

15. When users log on to their computers, they are required to enter a username, a password, and a PIN. Which of the following choices BEST describes this?

    A. Single-factor authentication

    B. Two-factor authentication

    C. Multifactor authentication

    D. Mutual authentication

16. The security manager at your company recently updated the security policy. One of the changes requires dual-factor authentication. Which of the following will meet this requirement?

    A. Hardware token and PIN

    B. Fingerprint scan and retina scan

    C. Password and PIN

    D. Smart card

17. When you log on to your online bank account, you are also able to access a partner's credit card site, check-ordering services, and a mortgage site without entering your credentials again. What does this describe?

    A. SSO

    B. Same sign-on

    C. SAML

    D. Kerberos

18. You maintain a training lab with 18 computers. You have enough rights and permissions on these machines so that you can configure them as needed for classes. However, you do not have the rights to add them to your organization's domain. Which of the following choices BEST describes this example?

A. Least privilege

B. Need to know

C. User-based privileges

D. Separation of duties

19. Members of a project team came in on the weekend to complete some work on a key project. However, they found that they were unable to access any of the project data. Which of the following choices is the MOST likely reason why they can't access this data?

   A. Discretionary access control

   B. Time-of-day access control

   C. Rule-based access control

   D. Role-based access control

20. An administrator needs to grant users access to different servers based on their job functions. Which access control model is the BEST choice to use?

   A. Discretionary access control

   B. Mandatory access control

   C. Role-based access control

   D. Rule-based access control

21. Bart has read access to an accounting database and Lisa has both read and write access to this database. A database application automatically triggers a change in permissions so that Bart has both read and write access when Lisa is absent. What type of access control system is in place?

   A. DAC

   B. MAC

   C. Role-BAC

   D. Rule-BAC

22. Your organization hosts several classified systems in the data center. Management wants to increase security with these systems by implementing two-factor authentication. Management also wants to restrict access to these systems to employees who a have need to know. Which of the following choices should management implement for authorization?

    A. USB token and PIN

    B. Username and password

    C. Mandatory access control

    D. Rule-based access control

23. Which type of authentication does a hardware token provide?

    A. Biometric

    B. PIN

    C. Strong password

    D. One-time password

24. Users are required to log on to their computers with a smart card and a PIN. Which of the following BEST describes this?

    A. Single-factor authentication

    B. Multifactor authentication

    C. Mutual authentication

    D. TOTP

25. Your organization has implemented a system that stores user credentials in a central database. Users log on once with their credentials. They can then access other systems in the organization without logging on again. What does this describe?

A. Same sign-on

B. SAML

C. Single sign-on

D. Biometrics

26. Developers are planning to develop an application using role-based access control. Which of the following would they MOST likely include in their planning?

A. A listing of labels reflecting classification levels

B. A requirements list identifying need to know

C. A listing of owners

D. A matrix of functions matched with their required privileges

27. An organization has implemented an access control model that enforces permissions based on data labels assigned at different levels. What type of model is this?

A. DAC

B. MAC

C. Role-BAC

D. Rule-BAC

28. Security personnel recently identified potential fraud committed by a network administrator. Investigators discovered this administrator performs several job functions within the organization, including database administration and application development. Which of the following is the BEST solution to reduce risk associated with this activity?

A. Mandatory vacations

B. Mandatory access control

C. Change management

D. Separation of duties

29. Users at your organization currently use a combination of smart cards and passwords, but an updated security policy requires multifactor security using three different factors. Which of the following can you add to meet the new requirement?

    A. Four-digit PIN

    B. Hardware tokens

    C. Fingerprint readers

    D. USB tokens

30. Your organization has a password policy with a password history value of 12. What does this indicate?

    A. Your password must be at least 12 characters long.

    B. Twelve different passwords must be used before reusing the same password.

    C. Passwords must be changed every 12 days.

    D. Passwords cannot be changed until 12 days have passed.

31. Developers in your organization have created an application designed for the sales team. Salespeople can log on to the application using a simple password of 1234. However, this password does not meet the organization's password policy. What is the BEST response by the security administrator after learning about this?

    A. Nothing. Strong passwords aren't required in applications.

    B. Modify the security policy to accept this password.

    C. Document this as an exception in the application's documentation.

    D. Direct the application team manager to ensure the application adheres to the organization's password policy.

32. A company's account management policy dictates that administrators should disable user accounts instead of deleting them when an employee leaves the company. What security benefit does this provide?

    A. Ensures that user keys are retained

    B. Ensures that user files are retained

    C. Makes it easier to enable the account if the employee returns

    D. Ensures that users cannot log on remotely

33. You're asked to identify who is accessing a spreadsheet containing employee salary data. Detailed logging is configured correctly on this file. However, you are unable to identify a specific person who is accessing the file. What is the MOST likely reason?

    A. Shared accounts are not prohibited.

    B. Guest accounts are disabled.

    C. Permissions for the file were assigned to a group.

    D. Account lockout has been enabled.

34. Interns from a local college frequently work at your company. Some interns work with the database developers, some interns work with the web application developers, and some interns work with both developers. Interns working with the database developers require specific privileges, and interns working with the web application developers require different privileges. What is the simplest method to meet these requirements?

    A. Use generic accounts.

    B. Create user-based privileges.

    C. Use group-based privileges.

    D. Grant the interns access to the Guest account.

35. Which of the following is the BEST method to protect against someone trying to guess the correct PIN to withdraw money from an ATM?

    A. Account lockout

    B. Rainbow table

    C. Salting

    D. Input validation

36. Your organization wants to ensure that security controls continue to function, helping to maintain an appropriate security posture. Which of the following is the BEST choice to meet this goal?

    A. Auditing logs

    B. Routine audits

    C. Continuous security monitoring

    D. Vulnerability scans

37. Homer called into the help desk and says he forgot his password. Which of the following choices is the BEST choice for what the help-desk professional should do?

    A. Verify the user's account exists.

    B. Look up the user's password and tell the user what it is.

    C. Disable the user's account.

    D. Reset the password and configure the password to expire after the first use.

38. You are redesigning your password policy. You want to ensure that users change their passwords regularly, but they are unable to reuse passwords. What settings should you configure? (Select THREE.)

A. Maximum password age

B. Password length

C. Password history

D. Password complexity

E. Minimum password age

39. An outside security auditor recently completed an in-depth security audit on your network. One of the issues he reported was related to passwords. Specifically, he found the following passwords used on the network: Pa$$, 1@W2, and G7bT3. What should be changed to avoid the problem shown with these passwords?

A. Password complexity

B. Password length

C. Password history

D. Password reuse

40. A recent security audit discovered several apparently dormant user accounts. Although users could log on to the accounts, no one had logged on to them for more than 60 days. You later discovered that these accounts are for contractors who work approximately one week every quarter. What is the BEST response to this situation?

A. Remove the account expiration from the accounts.

B. Delete the accounts.

C. Reset the accounts.

D. Disable the accounts.

41. Your organization routinely hires contractors to assist with different projects. Administrators are rarely notified when a project ends and

contractors leave. Which of the following is the BEST choice to ensure that contractors cannot log on with their account after they leave?

    A. Enable account expiration.

    B. Enable an account enablement policy.

    C. Enable an account recovery policy.

    D. Enable generic accounts.

42. Your organization includes the following statement in the security policy: "Security controls need to protect against both online and offline password brute force attacks."
Which of the following controls is the LEAST helpful to meet these goals?

    A. Account expiration

    B. Account lockout

    C. Password complexity

    D. Password length

43. Security personnel recently performed a security audit. They identified several employees who had permissions for previously held jobs within the company. What should the organization implement to prevent this in the future?

    A. Role-BAC model

    B. Account disablement policy

    C. Vulnerability assessment

    D. Account management controls

44. An e-commerce web site does not currently have an account recovery process for customers who have forgotten their passwords. Which of the following choices are the BEST items to include if web site designers add this process? (Select TWO.)

A. Create a web-based form that verifies customer identities using another method.

B. Set a temporary password that expires upon first use.

C. Implement biometric authentication.

D. Email the password to the user.

45. You have discovered that some users have been using the same passwords for months, even though the password policy requires users to change their password every 30 days. You want to ensure that users cannot reuse the same password. Which settings should you configure? (Select TWO.)

    A. Maximum password age

    B. Password length

    C. Password history

    D. Password complexity

    E. Minimum password age

46. You configure access control for users in your organization. Some departments have a high employee turnover, so you want to simplify account administration. Which of the following is the BEST choice?

    A. User-assigned privileges

    B. Group-based privileges

    C. Domain-assigned privileges

    D. Network-assigned privileges

√ **Get Certified**

√ **Get Ahead**

Practice Test Questions with Answers for Access Control and Identity Management Domain

1. Which of the following authentication services uses tickets for user credentials?

> A. RADIUS
>
> B. Diameter
>
> C. Kerberos
>
> D. LDAP

1. C is correct. Kerberos uses a ticket-granting ticket server to create tickets for users and these tickets include user credentials for authentication.

A is incorrect. Remote Authentication Dial-In User Service (RADIUS) provides authentication for remote users.

B is incorrect. Diameter is an alternative to RADIUS and it can utilize Extensible Authentication Protocol (EAP).

D is incorrect Lightweight Directory Access Protocol (LDAP) is an X.500-based authentication service.

2. Your network uses an authentication service based on the X.500 specification. When encrypted, it uses TLS. Which authentication service is your network using?

> A. SAML
>
> B. Diameter
>
> C. RADIUS
>
> D. LDAP

2. D is correct. Lightweight Directory Access Protocol (LDAP) uses X.500-based phrases to identify components and Secure LDAP can be encrypted with Transport Layer Security (TLS).

A is incorrect. Security Assertion Markup Language (SAML) is an Extensible Markup Language (XML) used for single sign-on (SSO), but it is not based on X.500.

B and C are incorrect. Diameter is an alternative to Remote Authentication Dial-In User Service (RADIUS), but neither of these are based on X.500.

3. A user calls into the help desk and asks the help-desk professional to reset his password. Which of the following choices is the BEST choice for what the help-desk professional should do before resetting the password?

    A. Verify the user's original password.

    B. Disable the user's account.

    C. Verify the user's identity.

    D. Enable the user's account.

3. C is correct. Before resetting a user's password, it's important to verify the user's identity.

A is incorrect. Users often need the password reset because they have forgotten their original password, so it's not possible to verify the user's original password.

B is incorrect. It's not necessary to disable a user account to reset the password.

D is incorrect. You would enable the account if it was disabled or locked out, but the scenario doesn't indicate this is the case.

4. Your organization recently made an agreement with third parties for the exchange of authentication and authorization information. The solution uses

an XML-based open standard. Which of the following is the MOST likely solution being implemented?

    A. RADIUS

    B. Diameter

    C. TACACS+

    D. SAML

4. D is correct. Security Assertion Markup Language (SAML) is an Extensible Markup Language (XML) used for single sign-on (SSO) solutions.

A is incorrect. Remote Authentication Dial-In User Service (RADIUS) is a remote access authentication service.

B is incorrect. Diameter is an alternative to RADIUS.

C is incorrect. Terminal Access Controller Access-Control System Plus (TACACS+) is an authentication service that replaces the older TACACS protocol. RADIUS, Diameter, and TACACS+ do not use XML.

5. The Retirement Castle uses groups for ease of administration and management. They recently hired Jasper as their new accountant. Jasper needs access to all the files and folders used by the Accounting department. What should the administrator do to give Jasper appropriate access?

    A. Create an account for Jasper and add the account to the Accounting group.

    B. Give Jasper the password for the Guest account.

    C. Create an account for Jasper and use rule-based access control for accounting.

    D. Create an account for Jasper and add the account to the Administrators group.

5. A is correct. The administrator should create an account for Jasper and add it to the Accounting group. Because the organization uses groups, it makes sense that they have an Accounting group.

B is incorrect. The Guest account should be disabled to prevent the use of generic accounts.

C is incorrect. This scenario describes role-based access control, not rule-based access control.

D is incorrect. Jasper does not require administrator privileges, so his account should not be added to the Administrators group.

6. Which of the following choices provide authentication services for remote users and devices? (Select TWO.)

    A. Kerberos

    B. RADIUS

    C. Secure LDAP

    D. Diameter

6. B and D are correct. Both Remote Authentication Dial-In User Service (RADIUS) and Diameter are authentication services for remote users and devices. Diameter is more secure than RADIUS.

A and C are incorrect. Kerberos is an authentication service used with a domain or realm and Secure Lightweight Directory Access Protocol (LDAP) uses Transport Layer Security (TLS) for encryption and is used to query directories.

7. Your company recently began allowing workers to telecommute from home one or more days a week. However, your company doesn't currently have a remote access solution. They want to implement an AAA solution that supports different vendors. Which of the following is the BEST choice?

    A. TACACS+

    B. RADIUS

    C. Circumference

    D. SAML

7. B is correct. Remote Authentication Dial-In User Service (RADIUS) is an authentication, authorization, and accounting (AAA) protocol and is the best choice.

A is incorrect. TACACS+ is proprietary to Cisco, so it won't support different vendor solutions.

C is incorrect. Diameter is preferable to RADIUS, but there is no such thing as a Circumference protocol.

D is incorrect. SAML is an SSO solution used with web-based applications.

8. A network includes a ticket-granting ticket server used for authentication. What authentication service does this network use?

    A. TACACS+

    B. SAML

    C. LDAP

    D. Kerberos

8. D is correct. Kerberos uses a ticket-granting ticket server, which creates tickets for authentication.

A is incorrect. Terminal Access Controller Access-Control System Plus (TACACS+) is an authentication service created by Cisco.

B is incorrect. Security Assertion Markup Language (SAML) is an Extensible Markup Language (XML) used for single sign-on (SSO) solutions.

C is incorrect. Lightweight Directory Access Protocol (LDAP) is an X.500-based authentication service that can be secured with Transport Layer Security (TLS)

9. You are modifying a configuration file used to authenticate Unix accounts against an external server. The file includes phrases such as DC=Server1 and DC=Com. Which authentication service is the external server using?

A. Diameter

B. RADIUS

C. LDAP

D. SAML

9. C is correct. Lightweight Directory Access Protocol (LDAP) uses X.500-based phrases to identify components such as the domain component (DC).

A and B are incorrect. Diameter is an alternative to Remote Authentication Dial-In User Service (RADIUS), but neither of these use X.500-based phrases.

D is incorrect. Security Assertion Markup Language (SAML) is an Extensible Markup Language (XML) used for web-based single sign-on (SSO) solutions.

10. What type of encryption does the RADIUS protocol use?

A. Symmetric

B. Asymmetric

C. MD5

D. SHA

10. A is correct. Remote Authentication Dial-In User Service (RADIUS) uses symmetric encryption.

B is incorrect. It does not use asymmetric encryption, which uses a public key and a private key.

C and D are incorrect. Message Digest 5 (MD5) and Secure Hash Algorithm (SHA) are hashing algorithms.

11. A security auditor discovered that several employees in the Accounting department can print and sign checks. In her final report, she recommended restricting the number of people who can print checks and the number of people who can sign them. She also recommended that no one should be authorized to print and sign checks. What policy is she recommending?

    A. Discretionary access control

    B. Rule-based access control

    C. Separation of duties

    D. Job rotation

11. C is correct. This recommendation is enforcing a separation of duties principle, which prevents any single person from performing multiple job functions that might allow the person to commit fraud.

A is incorrect. Discretionary access control specifies that every object has an owner, but doesn't separate duties.

B is incorrect. Devices such as routers use a rule-based access control model, but it doesn't separate duties.

D is incorrect. Job rotation policies rotate employees into different jobs, but they don't necessarily separate job functions.

12. You are logging on to your bank's web site using your email address and a password. What is the purpose of the email address in this example?

    A. Identification

    B. Authentication

    C. Authorization

    D. Availability

12. A is correct. The email address provides identification for you and your account.

B is incorrect. The password combined with the email address provides authentication, proving who you are.

C is incorrect. Based on your identity, you are granted authorization to view your account details.

D is incorrect. Availability is unrelated to identification, authentication, and authorization.

13. Your organization is planning to implement remote access capabilities. Management wants strong authentication and wants to ensure that passwords expire after a predefined time interval. Which of the following choices BEST meets this requirement?

    A. HOTP

    B. TOTP

    C. CAC

    D. Kerberos

13. B is correct. A Time-based One-Time Password (TOTP) meets this requirement. Passwords created with TOTP expire after 30 seconds.

A is incorrect. HMAC-based One-Time Password (HOTP) creates passwords that do not expire.

C is incorrect. A Common Access Card (CAC) is a type of smart card, but it does not create passwords.

D is incorrect. Kerberos uses tickets instead of passwords.

14. Which type of authentication is a fingerprint scan?

    A. Something you have

    B. Biometric

    C. PAP

    D. One-time password

14. B is correct. A fingerprint scan is a biometric method of authentication in the something you are factor of authentication.

A and D are incorrect. The something you have factor of authentication refers to something you can hold, such as a hardware token for a one-time password.

C is incorrect. Password Authentication Protocol (PAP) is an authentication method that sends passwords across the network in cleartext.

15. When users log on to their computers, they are required to enter a username, a password, and a PIN. Which of the following choices BEST describes this?

    A. Single-factor authentication

    B. Two-factor authentication

    C. Multifactor authentication

    D. Mutual authentication

15. A is correct. Both the password and the PIN are in the something you know factor of authentication, so this is single-factor authentication.

B is incorrect. Two-factor authentication requires the use of two different authentication factors.

C is incorrect. Multifactor authentication requires two or more factors of authentication.

D is incorrect. Mutual authentication is when both entities in the authentication process authenticate with each other and it doesn't apply in this situation.

16. The security manager at your company recently updated the security policy. One of the changes requires dual-factor authentication. Which of the following will meet this requirement?

    A. Hardware token and PIN

    B. Fingerprint scan and retina scan

    C. Password and PIN

    D. Smart card

16. A is correct. A hardware token (such as an RSA token or a USB token) is in the something you have factor of authentication and the PIN is in the something you know factor of authentication. Combined, they provide dual-factor authentication. The remaining answers only provide single-factor authentication.

B is incorrect. A fingerprint scan and a retina scan are both in the something you are factor of authentication.

C is incorrect. A password and a PIN are both in the something you know factor of authentication.

D is incorrect. A smart card is in the something you have factor of authentication.

17. When you log on to your online bank account, you are also able to access a partner's credit card site, check-ordering services, and a mortgage site without entering your credentials again. What does this describe?

    A. SSO

    B. Same sign-on

    C. SAML

    D. Kerberos

17. A is correct. This is an example of single sign-on (SSO) capabilities because you can log on once and access all the resources without entering your credentials again.

B is incorrect. Same sign-on requires you to reenter your credentials for each new site, but you use the same credentials.

C is incorrect. Security Assertion Markup Language (SAML) is an SSO solution used for web-based applications and the bank might be using SAML, but other SSO solutions are also available.

D is incorrect. Kerberos is used in an internal network.

18. You maintain a training lab with 18 computers. You have enough rights and permissions on these machines so that you can configure them as needed for classes. However, you do not have the rights to add them to your organization's domain. Which of the following choices BEST describes this example?

A. Least privilege

B. Need to know

C. User-based privileges

D. Separation of duties

18. A is correct. When following the principle of least privilege, individuals have only enough rights and permissions to perform their job, and this is exactly what is described in this scenario.

B is incorrect. Need to know typically refers to data and information rather than the privileges required to perform an action, such as adding computers to a domain.

C is incorrect. User-based privileges refer to giving permissions to individual users rather than groups, and this question doesn't address either user-based privileges or group-based privileges.

D is incorrect. Separation of duties is a principle that prevents any single person or entity from being able to complete all the functions of a critical or sensitive process, and it isn't addressed in this question either.

19. Members of a project team came in on the weekend to complete some work on a key project. However, they found that they were unable to access any of the project data. Which of the following choices is the MOST likely reason why they can't access this data?

A. Discretionary access control

B. Time-of-day access control

C. Rule-based access control

D. Role-based access control

19. B is correct. A time-of-day access control restricts access based on the time of day. It is sometimes used to prevent employees from logging on or accessing resources after normal work hours and during weekends.

A, C, and D are incorrect. None of the other options restrict access-based dates or times.

20. An administrator needs to grant users access to different servers based on their job functions. Which access control model is the BEST choice to use?

    A. Discretionary access control

    B. Mandatory access control

    C. Role-based access control

    D. Rule-based access control

20. C is correct. The role-based access control model is the best choice for assigning access based on job functions.

A is incorrect. A discretionary access control model specifies that every object has an owner and owners have full control over objects, but it isn't related to job functions.

B is incorrect. Mandatory access control uses labels and a lattice to grant access rather than job functions.

D is incorrect. A rule-based access control model uses rules that trigger in response to events.

21. Bart has read access to an accounting database and Lisa has both read and write access to this database. A database application automatically triggers a change in permissions so that Bart has both read and write access when Lisa is absent. What type of access control system is in place?

    A. DAC

    B. MAC

    C. Role-BAC

    D. Rule-BAC

21. D is correct. A rule-based access control system (rule-BAC) is in place in this scenario with a rule designed to trigger a change in permissions based on an event.

A is incorrect. A discretionary access control (DAC) model does not use triggers.

B is incorrect. The mandatory access control (MAC) model uses labels to identify users and data, and is used in systems requiring a need to know.

C is incorrect. A role-based access control (role-BAC) system uses group-based privileges.

22. Your organization hosts several classified systems in the data center. Management wants to increase security with these systems by implementing two-factor authentication. Management also wants to restrict access to these systems to employees who a have need to know. Which of the following choices should management implement for authorization?

    A. USB token and PIN

    B. Username and password

    C. Mandatory access control

    D. Rule-based access control

22. C is correct. Mandatory access control (MAC) is an access control model that can be used in systems requiring a need to know. It uses labels to identify users and data. If the user has the correct label needed to access the data, the user is authorized access.

A is incorrect. A USB token and a PIN provide two factors of authentication, but the question asks what is needed for authorization.

B is incorrect. A username provides identification and a password provides authentication.

D is incorrect. A rule-based access control system (rule-BAC) uses rules to trigger a change in permissions based on an event, or rules within an access control list (ACL) on hardware devices such as routers.

23. Which type of authentication does a hardware token provide?

    A. Biometric

    B. PIN

    C. Strong password

    D. One-time password

23. D is correct. A hardware token (such as an RSA token) uses a one-time password for authentication in the something you have factor of authentication.

A is incorrect. Biometric methods are in the something you are factor of authentication, such as a fingerprint.

B and C are incorrect. A PIN and a password are both in the something you know factor of authentication and do not require a hardware token.

24. Users are required to log on to their computers with a smart card and a PIN. Which of the following BEST describes this?

    A. Single-factor authentication

    B. Multifactor authentication

    C. Mutual authentication

    D. TOTP

24. B is correct. Users authenticate with two factors of authentication in this scenario, which is multifactor authentication or dual-factor authentication. The smart card is in the something you have factor of authentication, and the PIN is in the something you know factor of authentication.

A is incorrect. They are using more than a single factor.

C is incorrect. Mutual authentication is when both entities in the authentication process authenticate with each other, but it doesn't apply in this situation.

D is incorrect. A Time-based One-Time Password (TOTP) is a protocol used to create passwords that expire after 30 seconds.

25. Your organization has implemented a system that stores user credentials in a central database. Users log on once with their credentials. They can then access other systems in the organization without logging on again. What does this describe?

    A. Same sign-on

    B. SAML

    C. Single sign-on

    D. Biometrics

25. C is correct. This describes a single sign-on (SSO) solution in which users only have to log on once.

A is incorrect. Same sign-on indicates users can access multiple systems using the same credentials, but they still have to enter their credentials again each time they access a new resource.

B is incorrect. Security Assertion Markup Language (SAML) is an SSO solution used for web-based applications, but not all SSO solutions are using SAML.

D is incorrect. Biometrics is a method of authentication, such as a fingerprint, but it isn't an SSO solution.

26. Developers are planning to develop an application using role-based access control. Which of the following would they MOST likely include in their planning?

A. A listing of labels reflecting classification levels

B. A requirements list identifying need to know

C. A listing of owners

D. A matrix of functions matched with their required privileges

26. D is correct. A matrix of functions, roles, or job titles matched with the required access privileges for each of the functions, roles, or job titles is a common planning document for a role-based access control model.

A is incorrect. The mandatory access control (MAC) model uses sensitivity labels and classification levels.

B is incorrect. MAC is effective at restricting access based on a need to know.

C is incorrect. The discretionary access control model specifies that every object has an owner and it might identify owners in a list.

27. An organization has implemented an access control model that enforces permissions based on data labels assigned at different levels. What type of model is this?

A. DAC

B. MAC

C. Role-BAC

D. Rule-BAC

27. B is correct. The mandatory access control (MAC) model uses labels assigned at different levels to restrict access.

A is incorrect. The discretionary access control (DAC) model assigns permissions based on object ownership.

C is incorrect. The role-based access control (role-BAC) model uses group-based privileges.

D is incorrect. The rule-based access control (rule-BAC) model uses rules that trigger in response to events.

28. Security personnel recently identified potential fraud committed by a network administrator. Investigators discovered this administrator performs several job functions within the organization, including database administration and application development. Which of the following is the BEST solution to reduce risk associated with this activity?

> A. Mandatory vacations
>
> B. Mandatory access control
>
> C. Change management
>
> D. Separation of duties

28. D is correct. A separation of duties policy prevents any single person from performing multiple job functions that might allow the person to commit fraud.

A is incorrect. A mandatory vacation policy is useful to discover fraud committed by an individual, but this scenario clearly indicates this individual controls too many job functions.

B is incorrect. Although mandatory access control is the strongest access control method available, it doesn't separate job functions.

C is incorrect. Change management ensures changes are reviewed before being implemented.

29. Users at your organization currently use a combination of smart cards and passwords, but an updated security policy requires multifactor security using three different factors. Which of the following can you add to meet the new requirement?

> A. Four-digit PIN
>
> B. Hardware tokens
>
> C. Fingerprint readers
>
> D. USB tokens

29. C is correct. Fingerprint readers would add biometrics from the something you are factor of authentication as a third factor of authentication. The current system includes methods in the something you have factor (smart cards) and in the something you know factor (passwords), so any solution requires a method that isn't using one of these two factors.

A is incorrect. A PIN is in the something you know factor.

B and D are incorrect. Hardware tokens and USB tokens are in the something you have factor.

30. Your organization has a password policy with a password history value of 12. What does this indicate?

    A. Your password must be at least 12 characters long.

    B. Twelve different passwords must be used before reusing the same password.

    C. Passwords must be changed every 12 days.

    D. Passwords cannot be changed until 12 days have passed.

30. B is correct. The password history indicates how many passwords a system remembers and how many different passwords must be used before a password can be reused.

A is incorrect. Password length identifies the minimum number of characters.

C is incorrect. Password maximum age identifies when users must change passwords.

D is incorrect. Password minimum age identifies the length of time that must pass before users can change a password again.

31. Developers in your organization have created an application designed for the sales team. Salespeople can log on to the application using a simple password of 1234. However, this password does not meet the organization's

password policy. What is the BEST response by the security administrator after learning about this?

    A. Nothing. Strong passwords aren't required in applications.

    B. Modify the security policy to accept this password.

    C. Document this as an exception in the application's documentation.

    D. Direct the application team manager to ensure the application adheres to the organization's password policy.

31. D is correct. The application should be recoded to adhere to the company's password policy, so the best response is to direct the application team manager to do so.

A and B are incorrect. Application passwords should be strong and should adhere to an organization's security policy. It is not appropriate to weaken a security policy to match a weakness in an application.

C is incorrect. Nor is it appropriate to simply document that the application uses a weak password.

32. A company's account management policy dictates that administrators should disable user accounts instead of deleting them when an employee leaves the company. What security benefit does this provide?

    A. Ensures that user keys are retained

    B. Ensures that user files are retained

    C. Makes it easier to enable the account if the employee returns

    D. Ensures that users cannot log on remotely

32. A is correct. User accounts typically have security keys associated with them. These keys are retained when the account is disabled, but they are no longer accessible when the account is deleted.

B is incorrect. By disabling the account, it helps ensure that access to files is retained, but it does not directly retain user files.

C is incorrect. Employees who leave are not expected to return, so this policy has nothing to do with making it easier to enable an account when they return.

D is incorrect. Users will not be able to use the accounts locally or remotely if they are disabled or deleted, which is a primary reason to have an account management policy.

33. You're asked to identify who is accessing a spreadsheet containing employee salary data. Detailed logging is configured correctly on this file. However, you are unable to identify a specific person who is accessing the file. What is the MOST likely reason?

    A. Shared accounts are not prohibited.

    B. Guest accounts are disabled.

    C. Permissions for the file were assigned to a group.

    D. Account lockout has been enabled.

33. A is correct. The most likely reason of those given is that shared accounts are not prohibited, allowing multiple users to access the same file.

B is incorrect. If the Guest account is enabled and used as a shared account by all users, the logs will indicate the Guest account accessed the file, but it won't identify specific individuals.

C is incorrect. It doesn't matter how permissions are assigned in order for a log to identify who accessed the file.

D is incorrect. Account lockout stops someone from guessing a password, but it doesn't affect file access logs.

34. Interns from a local college frequently work at your company. Some interns work with the database developers, some interns work with the web application developers, and some interns work with both developers. Interns working with the database developers require specific privileges, and interns

working with the web application developers require different privileges. What is the simplest method to meet these requirements?

A. Use generic accounts.

B. Create user-based privileges.

C. Use group-based privileges.

D. Grant the interns access to the Guest account.

34. C is correct. Using group-based privileges is the best choice to meet the needs of this scenario. For example, you can create a DB_Group and a Web_Group, assign appropriate privileges to the groups, and add intern accounts to the groups based on their assignments.

A and D are incorrect. Generic accounts such as the Guest account should not be used.

C is incorrect. User-based privileges take too much time to manage because you'd have to implement them separately.

35. Which of the following is the BEST method to protect against someone trying to guess the correct PIN to withdraw money from an ATM?

A. Account lockout

B. Rainbow table

C. Salting

D. Input validation

35. A is correct. Account lockout policies help prevent brute force attacks by locking the account after an incorrect password or personal identification number (PIN) is entered too many times. This prevents someone from hacking into an account by guessing.

B is incorrect. A rainbow table is a type of attack.

C is incorrect. Salting passwords prevents some offline brute force attacks by adding characters to passwords before hashing them.

D is incorrect. Input validation prevents attacks such as buffer overflow and cross-site scripting, but wouldn't help here because an attacker guessing PINs is entering valid data.

36. Your organization wants to ensure that security controls continue to function, helping to maintain an appropriate security posture. Which of the following is the BEST choice to meet this goal?

    A. Auditing logs

    B. Routine audits

    C. Continuous security monitoring

    D. Vulnerability scans

36. C is correct. Continuous security monitoring helps an organization maintain its security posture, by verifying that security controls continue to function as intended.

A, B, and D are incorrect. Auditing logs, performing routine audits, and performing vulnerability scans are all part of a continuous monitoring plan. However, individually, they do not verify all security controls are operating properly.

37. Homer called into the help desk and says he forgot his password. Which of the following choices is the BEST choice for what the help-desk professional should do?

    A. Verify the user's account exists.

    B. Look up the user's password and tell the user what it is.

    C. Disable the user's account.

    D. Reset the password and configure the password to expire after the first use.

37. D is correct. In this scenario, it's best to create a temporary password that expires after first use, which forces the user to create a new password.

A is incorrect. It's not necessary to verify the user's account exists, but the help-desk professional should verify the identity of the user.

B is incorrect. Passwords should not be available in such a way that allows help-desk professionals to look them up.

C is incorrect. It is not necessary to disable a user account to reset the password.

38. You are redesigning your password policy. You want to ensure that users change their passwords regularly, but they are unable to reuse passwords. What settings should you configure? (Select THREE.)

      A. Maximum password age

      B. Password length

      C. Password history

      D. Password complexity

      E. Minimum password age

38. A, C, and E and correct. The maximum password age ensures users change their passwords regularly. The password history records previously used passwords (such as the last 24 passwords) to prevent users from reusing the same passwords. The minimum password age prevents users from changing their password repeatedly to get back to their original password and should be used with the password history setting.

B is incorrect. Password length requires a minimum number of characters in a password.

D is incorrect. Password complexity requires a mix of uppercase and lowercase letters, numbers, and special characters.

39. An outside security auditor recently completed an in-depth security audit on your network. One of the issues he reported was related to passwords. Specifically, he found the following passwords used on the network: Pa$$,

1@W2, and G7bT3. What should be changed to avoid the problem shown with these passwords?

    A. Password complexity

    B. Password length

    C. Password history

    D. Password reuse

39. B is correct. The password policy should be changed to increase the minimum password length of passwords. These passwords are only four and five characters long, which is too short to provide adequate security.

A is incorrect. They are complex because they include a mixture of at least three of the following character types: uppercase letters, lowercase letters, numbers, and special characters.

C and D are incorrect. Password history and password reuse should be addressed if users are reusing the same passwords, but the scenario doesn't indicate this is a problem.

40. A recent security audit discovered several apparently dormant user accounts. Although users could log on to the accounts, no one had logged on to them for more than 60 days. You later discovered that these accounts are for contractors who work approximately one week every quarter. What is the BEST response to this situation?

    A. Remove the account expiration from the accounts.

    B. Delete the accounts.

    C. Reset the accounts.

    D. Disable the accounts.

40. D is correct. The best response is to disable the accounts and then enable them when needed by the contractors.

A is incorrect. Ideally, the accounts would include an expiration date so that they would automatically expire when no longer needed, but the scenario doesn't indicate the accounts have an expiration date.

B is incorrect. Because the contractors need to access the accounts periodically, it's better to disable them rather than deleting them.

C is incorrect. Reset the accounts implies you are changing the password, but this isn't needed.

41. Your organization routinely hires contractors to assist with different projects. Administrators are rarely notified when a project ends and contractors leave. Which of the following is the BEST choice to ensure that contractors cannot log on with their account after they leave?

    A. Enable account expiration.

    B. Enable an account enablement policy.

    C. Enable an account recovery policy.

    D. Enable generic accounts.

41. A is correct. The best choice is to enable account expiration so that the contractor accounts are automatically disabled at the end of their projected contract time period. If contracts are extended, it's easy to enable the account and reset the account expiration date.

B is incorrect. Account disablement policies help ensure that any user accounts (not just contractors) are disabled when the user leaves the organization, but an account enablement policy isn't a valid term.

C is incorrect. An account recovery policy allows administrators to recover accounts and associated security keys for ex-employees.

D is incorrect. It's best to prohibit the use of generic accounts (such as the Guest account), so enabling generic accounts is not recommended.

42. Your organization includes the following statement in the security policy: "Security controls need to protect against both online and offline password brute force attacks."

Which of the following controls is the LEAST helpful to meet these goals?

> A. Account expiration
>
> B. Account lockout
>
> C. Password complexity
>
> D. Password length

42. A is correct. Account expiration is not an effective defense against brute force attacks.

B is incorrect. Account lockout helps protect against online brute force attacks.

C and D are incorrect. Password complexity and password length help protect against offline brute force attacks.

43. Security personnel recently performed a security audit. They identified several employees who had permissions for previously held jobs within the company. What should the organization implement to prevent this in the future?

> A. Role-BAC model
>
> B. Account disablement policy
>
> C. Vulnerability assessment
>
> D. Account management controls

43. D is correct. Account management controls ensure that accounts only have the permissions they need and no more, and would ensure that user permissions are removed when users no longer need them. User rights and permission reviews also help ensure the controls are effective.

A is incorrect. A role-based access control (role-BAC) model uses group-based permissions, but it doesn't force administrators to take a user out of a security group when the user moves to a different job.

B is incorrect. An account disablement policy ensures accounts are disabled when an employee leaves.

C is incorrect. A vulnerability assessment might detect this as it reviews the organization's security posture, but it won't prevent it.

44. An e-commerce web site does not currently have an account recovery process for customers who have forgotten their passwords. Which of the following choices are the BEST items to include if web site designers add this process? (Select TWO.)

    A. Create a web-based form that verifies customer identities using another method.

    B. Set a temporary password that expires upon first use.

    C. Implement biometric authentication.

    D. Email the password to the user.

44. A and B are correct. A web-based form using an identity-proofing method, such as requiring users to enter the name of their first pet, can verify their identity. Setting a password that expires upon first use ensures that the user changes the password.

C is incorrect. Biometric authentication is not reasonable for an online e-commerce web site.

D is incorrect. Emailing the password is a possibility, but not without configuring the password to expire upon first use.

45. You have discovered that some users have been using the same passwords for months, even though the password policy requires users to change their

password every 30 days. You want to ensure that users cannot reuse the same password. Which settings should you configure? (Select TWO.)

    A. Maximum password age

    B. Password length

    C. Password history

    D. Password complexity

    E. Minimum password age

45. C and E are correct. The password history setting records previously used passwords (such as the last 24 passwords) to prevent users from reusing the same passwords. Using password history setting combined with the minimum password age setting prevents users from changing their password repeatedly to get back to their original password.

A is incorrect. The maximum password age setting ensures users change their passwords regularly, but this is already set to 30 days in the scenario.

B is incorrect. Password length requires a minimum number of characters in a password.

D is incorrect. Password complexity requires a mix of uppercase and lowercase letters, numbers, and special characters.

46. You configure access control for users in your organization. Some departments have a high employee turnover, so you want to simplify account administration. Which of the following is the BEST choice?

    A. User-assigned privileges

    B. Group-based privileges

    C. Domain-assigned privileges

    D. Network-assigned privileges

46. B is correct. Group-based privileges is a form of role-based access control and it simplifies administration. Instead of assigning permissions to new employees individually, you can just add new employee user accounts into the

appropriate groups to grant them the rights and permissions they need for the job.

A is incorrect. User-assigned privileges require you to manage privileges for each user separately, and it increases the account administration burden.

C and D are incorrect. Domain-assigned and network-assigned privileges are not valid administration practices.

√ **Get Certified**

√ **Get Ahead**

Chapter 6 Cryptography

Cryptography topics are **12 percent** of the CompTIA Security+ exam. The objectives in this domain are:

6.1 Given a scenario, utilize general cryptography concepts.
- Symmetric vs. asymmetric
- Session keys
- In-band vs. out-of-band key exchange
- Fundamental differences and encryption methods
  - Block vs. stream
- Transport encryption
- Non-repudiation
- Hashing
- Key escrow
- Steganography
- Digital signatures
- Use of proven technologies
- Elliptic curve and quantum cryptography
- Ephemeral key
- Perfect forward secrecy

6.2 Given a scenario, use appropriate cryptographic methods.
- WEP vs. WPA/WPA2 and preshared key
- MD5
- SHA
- RIPEMD
- AES
- DES
- 3DES
- HMAC
- RSA
- Diffie-Hellman
- RC4
- One-time pads
- NTLM
- NTLMv2
- Blowfish

- PGP/GPG
- TwoFish
- DHE
- ECDHE
- CHAP
- PAP
- Comparative strengths and performance of algorithms
- Use of algorithms/protocols with transport encryption
  - SSL
  - TLS
  - IPSec
  - SSH
  - HTTPS
- Cipher suites
  - Strong vs. weak ciphers
- Key stretching
  - PBKDF2
  - Bcrypt

6.3 Given a scenario, use appropriate PKI, certificate management and associated components.
- Certificate authorities and digital certificates
  - CA
  - CRLs
  - OCSP
  - CSR
- PKI
- Recovery agent
- Public key
- Private key
- Registration
- Key escrow
- Trust models

The CompTIA Security+: Get Certified Get Ahead SY0-401 Study Guide (ISBN 1939136024) discusses these topics in much more depth.

√ **Get Certified**

√ **Get Ahead**

Practice Test Questions for Cryptography Domain

1. Your organization plans to issue some employees mobile devices such as smartphones and tablets. These devices don't have a lot of processing power. Which of the following cryptographic methods has the LEAST overhead and will work with these mobile devices?

    A. ECC

    B. 3DES

    C. Bcrypt

    D. PBKDF2

2. A manager is suspected of leaking trade secrets to a competitor. A security investigator is examining his laptop and notices a large volume of vacation pictures on the hard drive. Data on this laptop automatically uploads to a private cloud owned by the company once a week. The investigator noticed that the hashes of most of the pictures on the hard drive are different from the hashes of the pictures in the cloud location. Which of the following is the MOST likely explanation for this scenario?

    A. The manager is leaking data using hashing methods.

    B. The manager is leaking data using digital signatures.

    C. The manager is leaking data using steganography methods.

    D. The manager is not leaking data.

3. A software company occasionally provides application updates and patches via its web site. It also provides a checksum for each update and patch. Which of the following BEST describes the purpose of the checksum?

A. Availability of updates and patches

B. Integrity of updates and patches

C. Confidentiality of updates and patches

D. Integrity of the application

4. A function converts data into a string of characters and the string of characters cannot be reversed to re-create the original data. What type of function is this?

A. Symmetric encryption

B. Asymmetric encryption

C. Stream cipher

D. Hashing

5. An organization requested bids for a contract and asked companies to submit their bids via email. After winning the bid, Acme realized it couldn't meet the requirements of the contract. Acme instead stated that it never submitted the bid. Which of the following would provide proof to the organization that Acme did submit the bid?

A. Digital signature

B. Integrity

C. Repudiation

D. Encryption

6. Your organization is investigating possible methods of sharing encryption keys over a public network. Which of the following is the BEST choice?

A. CRL

B. PBKDF2

C. Hashing

D. ECDHE

7. You need to ensure data sent over an IP-based network remains confidential. Which of the following provides the BEST solution?

    A. Stream ciphers

    B. Block ciphers

    C. Transport encryption

    D. Hashing

8. Lenny and Carl work in an organization that includes a PKI. Carl needs to send a digitally signed file to Lenny. What does Carl use in this process?

    A. Carl's public key

    B. Carl's private key

    C. Lenny's public key

    D. Lenny's private key

9. Bart recently sent out confidential data via email to potential competitors. Management suspects he did so accidentally, but Bart denied sending the data. Management wants to implement a method that would prevent Bart from denying accountability in the future. What are they trying to enforce?

    A. Confidentiality

    B. Encryption

    C. Access control

    D. Non-repudiation

10. Of the following choices, what can you use to verify data integrity?

    A. AES

    B. DES

    C. RC4

    D. SHA

11. A security technician runs an automated script every night designed to detect changes in files. Of the following choices, what are the most likely protocols used in this script?

    A. PGP and MD5

    B. ECC and HMAC

    C. AES and Twofish

    D. MD5 and HMAC

12. Some encryption algorithms use stream ciphers and some use block ciphers. Which of the following are examples of block ciphers? (Choose THREE.)

    A. AES

    B. DES

    C. MD5

    D. SHA

    E. RC4

    F. Blowfish

13. Which of the following algorithms encrypts data in 64-bit blocks?

    A. AES

    B. DES

    C. Twofish

    D. RC4

14. An application developer needs to use an encryption protocol to encrypt credit card data within a database used by the application. Which of the following would be the FASTEST, while also providing strong confidentiality?

A. AES-256

B. DES

C. Blowfish

D. SHA-2

15. Your network requires a secure method of sharing encryption keys over a public network. Which of the following is the BEST choice?

A. Symmetric encryption

B. Bcrypt

C. Diffie-Hellman

D. Steganography

16. You are planning to encrypt data in transit. Which of the following protocols meets this need and encapsulates IP packets within an additional IP header?

A. TLS

B. SSL

C. HMAC

D. IPsec

17. An application requires users to log on with passwords. The application developers want to store the passwords in such a way that it will thwart rainbow table attacks. Which of the following is the BEST solution?

A. SHA

B. Blowfish

C. ECC

D. Bcrypt

18. Your organization's security policy requires that PII data at rest and PII data in transit be encrypted. Of the following choices, what would the organization use to achieve these objectives? (Select TWO.)

    A. FTP

    B. SSH

    C. SMTP

    D. PGP/GPG

    E. HTTP

19. Which of the following is a symmetric encryption algorithm that encrypts data one bit at a time?

    A. Block cipher

    B. Stream cipher

    C. AES

    D. DES

    E. MD5

20. You are planning to encrypt data in transit with IPsec. Which of the following is MOST likely to be used with IPsec?

    A. HMAC

    B. Blowfish

    C. Twofish

    D. MD5

21. Application developers are creating an application that requires users to log on with strong passwords. The developers want to store the passwords in such a way that it will thwart brute force attacks. Which of the following is the BEST solution?

A. 3DES

B. MD5

C. PBKDF2

D. Database fields

22. Your organization recently updated its security policy and indicated that Telnet should not be used within the network. Which of the following should be used instead of Telnet?

A. SCP

B. SFTP

C. SSL

D. SSH

23. An organization is implementing a PKI and plans on using public and private keys. Which of the following can be used to create strong key pairs?

A. MD5

B. RSA

C. AES

D. HMAC

24. Homer wants to send a secure email to Marge so he decides to encrypt it. Homer wants to ensure that Marge can verify that he sent it. Which of the following does Marge need to verify the certificate that Homer used in this process is valid?

A. The CA's private key

B. The CA's public key

C. Marge's public key

D. Marge's private key

25. Users in your organization sign their emails with digital signatures. What provides integrity for these digital signatures?

    A. Hashing

    B. Encryption

    C. Non-repudiation

    D. Private key

26. Homer wants to use digital signatures for his emails and realizes he needs a certificate. Which of the following will issue Homer a certificate?

    A. CRL

    B. CA

    C. OCSP

    D. Recovery agent

27. You need to submit a CSR to a CA. Which of the following would you do FIRST?

    A. Generate a new RSA-based session key.

    B. Generate a new RSA-based private key.

    C. Generate the CRL.

    D. Implement OCSP.

28. Your organization is planning to implement an internal PKI. What is required to ensure users can validate certificates?

    A. An intermediate CA

    B. CSR

    C. Wildcard certificates

    D. CRL

29. Your organization requires the use of a PKI and it wants to implement a protocol to validate trust with minimal traffic. Which of the following protocols validates trust by returning short responses, such as "good" or "revoked"?

> A. OCSP
>
> B. CRL
>
> C. CA
>
> D. CSR

30. A user's laptop developed a problem and can no longer boot. Help desk personnel tried to recover the data on the disk, but the disk is encrypted. Which of the following can be used to retrieve data from the hard drive?

> A. A trust relationship
>
> B. Public key
>
> C. Recovery agent
>
> D. CRL

31. A web site is using a certificate. Users have recently been receiving errors from the web site indicating that the web site's certificate is revoked. Which of the following includes a list of certificates that have been revoked?

> A. CRL
>
> B. CA
>
> C. OCSP
>
> D. CSR

32. An organization is planning to implement an internal PKI for smart cards. Which of the following should the organization do FIRST?

> A. Install a CA.
>
> B. Generate key pairs.
>
> C. Generate a certificate.
>
> D. Identify a recovery agent.

33. Which of the following is a valid reason to use a wildcard certificate?

    A. Reduce the administrative burden of managing certificates.

    B. Support multiple private keys.

    C. Support multiple public keys.

    D. Increase the lifetime of the certificate.

34. Homer works as a contractor at a company on a one-year renewing contract. After renewing his contract, the company issues him a new smart card. However, he is now having problems digitally signing email or opening encrypted email. What is the MOST likely solution?

    A. Copy the original certificate to the new smart card.

    B. Copy his original private key to the new smart card.

    C. Copy his original public key to the new smart card.

    D. Publish the certificate in his new smart card.

35. You need to request a certificate for a web server. Which of the following would you MOST likely use?

    A. CA

    B. CRL

    C. CSR

    D. OCSP

36. An organization is implementing a data policy and wants to designate a recovery agent. Which of the following indicates what a recovery agent can do?

    A. A recovery agent can retrieve a user's public key.

    B. A recovery agent can decrypt data if users lose their private key.

    C. A recovery agent can encrypt data if users lose their private key.

    D. A recovery agent can restore a system from backups.

√ Get Certified   √ Get Ahead

Practice Test Questions with Answers for Cryptography Domain

1. Your organization plans to issue some employees mobile devices such as smartphones and tablets. These devices don't have a lot of processing power. Which of the following cryptographic methods has the LEAST overhead and will work with these mobile devices?

    A. ECC

    B. 3DES

    C. Bcrypt

    D. PBKDF2

1. A is correct. Elliptic curve cryptography (ECC) has minimal overhead and is often used with mobile devices for encryption.

B is incorrect. Triple Data Encryption Standard (3DES) consumes a lot of processing time and isn't as efficient as ECC.

C and D are incorrect. Password-Based Key Derivation Function 2 (PBKDF2) and bcrypt are key stretching techniques that salt passwords with additional bits to protect against brute force attempts.

2. A manager is suspected of leaking trade secrets to a competitor. A security investigator is examining his laptop and notices a large volume of vacation pictures on the hard drive. Data on this laptop automatically uploads to a private cloud owned by the company once a week. The investigator noticed that the hashes of most of the pictures on the hard drive are different from the hashes of the pictures in the cloud location. Which of the following is the MOST likely explanation for this scenario?

A. The manager is leaking data using hashing methods.

B. The manager is leaking data using digital signatures.

C. The manager is leaking data using steganography methods.

D. The manager is not leaking data.

2. C is correct. The manager is most likely leaking data using steganography methods by embedding the data into the vacation pictures. If the file is the same, the hash of the file and the hash of a file copy should be the same. Because the hashes are different, it indicates the files are different and the most likely explanation is because some of the files have other data embedded within them.

A and B are incorrect. Hashing and digital signatures are not methods that would support leaking data.

D is incorrect. The scenario indicates the manager is suspected of leaking data, and the different hashes provide evidence to support this suspicion.

3. A software company occasionally provides application updates and patches via its web site. It also provides a checksum for each update and patch. Which of the following BEST describes the purpose of the checksum?

A. Availability of updates and patches

B. Integrity of updates and patches

C. Confidentiality of updates and patches

D. Integrity of the application

3. B is correct. The checksum (also known as a hash) provides integrity for the patches and updates so that users can verify they have not been modified.

A is incorrect. Installing patches and updates increases the availability of the application.

C is incorrect. Confidentiality is provided by encryption.

D is incorrect. The checksums are for the updates and patches, so they do not provide integrity for the application.

4. A function converts data into a string of characters and the string of characters cannot be reversed to re-create the original data. What type of function is this?

> A. Symmetric encryption
>
> B. Asymmetric encryption
>
> C. Stream cipher
>
> D. Hashing

4. D is correct. A hash function creates a string of characters (typically displayed in hexadecimal) when executed against a file or message, and hashing functions cannot be reversed to re-create the original data.

A, B, and C are incorrect. Encryption algorithms (including symmetric encryption, asymmetric encryption, and stream ciphers) create ciphertext from plaintext data, but they include decryption algorithms to re-create the original data.

5. An organization requested bids for a contract and asked companies to submit their bids via email. After winning the bid, Acme realized it couldn't meet the requirements of the contract. Acme instead stated that it never submitted the bid. Which of the following would provide proof to the organization that Acme did submit the bid?

> A. Digital signature
>
> B. Integrity
>
> C. Repudiation
>
> D. Encryption

5. A is correct. If Acme submitted the bid via email using a digital signature, it would provide proof that the bid was submitted by Acme. Digital signatures provide verification of who sent a message, non-repudiation preventing them from denying it, and integrity verifying the message wasn't modified.

B is incorrect. Integrity verifies the message wasn't modified.

C is incorrect. Repudiation isn't a valid security concept.

D is incorrect. Encryption protects the confidentiality of data, but it doesn't verify who sent it or provide non-repudiation.

6. Your organization is investigating possible methods of sharing encryption keys over a public network. Which of the following is the BEST choice?

  A. CRL

  B. PBKDF2

  C. Hashing

  D. ECDHE

6. D is correct. Elliptic Curve Diffie-Hellman Ephemeral (ECDHE) allows entities to negotiate encryption keys securely over a public network.

A is incorrect. A certificate revocation list (CRL) identifies revoked certificates and is unrelated to sharing encryption keys.

B is incorrect. Password-Based Key Derivation Function 2 (PBKDF2) is a key stretching technique designed to make password cracking more difficult.

C is incorrect. Hashing methods do not support sharing encryption keys over a public network.

7. You need to ensure data sent over an IP-based network remains confidential. Which of the following provides the BEST solution?

  A. Stream ciphers

  B. Block ciphers

  C. Transport encryption

  D. Hashing

7. C is correct. Transport encryption techniques such as Internet Protocol security (IPsec) provide confidentiality.

A and B are incorrect. Both stream ciphers and block ciphers can be used by different transport encryption protocols.

D is incorrect. Hashing provides integrity, but encryption is needed to provide confidentiality.

8. Lenny and Carl work in an organization that includes a PKI. Carl needs to send a digitally signed file to Lenny. What does Carl use in this process?

    A. Carl's public key

    B. Carl's private key

    C. Lenny's public key

    D. Lenny's private key

8. B is correct. Carl uses his private key to digitally sign the file.

A is incorrect. Lenny uses Carl's public key to decrypt the digital signature.

C and D are incorrect. Lenny's keys are not used in this scenario.

9. Bart recently sent out confidential data via email to potential competitors. Management suspects he did so accidentally, but Bart denied sending the data. Management wants to implement a method that would prevent Bart from denying accountability in the future. What are they trying to enforce?

    A. Confidentiality

    B. Encryption

    C. Access control

    D. Non-repudiation

9. D is correct. Non-repudiation methods such as digital signatures prevent users from denying they took an action.

A and B are incorrect. Encryption methods protect confidentiality.

C is incorrect. Access control methods protect access to data.

10. Of the following choices, what can you use to verify data integrity?

    A. AES

    B. DES

    C. RC4

    D. SHA

10. D is correct. Secure Hash Algorithm (SHA) is one of many available hashing algorithms used to verify data integrity. None of the other options are hashing algorithms.

A, B, and C are incorrect. Advanced Encryption Standard (AES), Data Encryption Standard (DES), and Rivest Cipher 4 (RC4) are symmetric encryption algorithms.

11. A security technician runs an automated script every night designed to detect changes in files. Of the following choices, what are the most likely protocols used in this script?

      A. PGP and MD5

      B. ECC and HMAC

      C. AES and Twofish

      D. MD5 and HMAC

11. D is correct. Hashing algorithms can detect changes in files (or verify the files have not lost integrity) and Message Digest 5 (MD5) and Hash-based Message Authentication Code (HMAC) are both hashing algorithms.

A is incorrect. Pretty Good Privacy (PGP) is a method used to secure email communication.

B and C are incorrect. Elliptic curve cryptography (ECC), Advanced Encryption Standard (AES), and TwoFish are all encryption algorithms.

12. Some encryption algorithms use stream ciphers and some use block ciphers. Which of the following are examples of block ciphers? (Choose THREE.)

      A. AES

      B. DES

      C. MD5

      D. SHA

E. RC4

F. Blowfish

12. A, B, and F are correct. Advanced Encryption Standard (AES), Data Encryption Standard (DES), and Blowfish are all block ciphers. Although it's not listed, Triple DES (3DES) is also a block cipher.

C and D are incorrect. Message Digest 5 (MD5) and Secure Hash Algorithm (SHA) are hashing algorithms.

E is incorrect. Rivest Cipher 4 (RC4) is a stream cipher.

13. Which of the following algorithms encrypts data in 64-bit blocks?

A. AES

B. DES

C. Twofish

D. RC4

13. B is correct. Data Encryption Standard (DES) encrypts data in 64-bit blocks similar to how 3DES and Blowfish encrypt data in 64-bit blocks.

A and C are incorrect. Advanced Encryption Standard (AES) and Twofish encrypt data in 12-bit blocks.

D is incorrect. Rivest Cipher 4 (RC4) is a stream cipher and it encrypts data one bit at a time.

14. An application developer needs to use an encryption protocol to encrypt credit card data within a database used by the application. Which of the following would be the FASTEST, while also providing strong confidentiality?

A. AES-256

B. DES

C. Blowfish

D. SHA-2

14. C is correct. Blowfish would be the fastest in this scenario. Blowfish provides strong encryption so would provide strong confidentiality.

A is incorrect. Advanced Encryption Standard-256 (AES-256) is a strong encryption protocol, but Blowfish is faster than AES in some situations such as when comparing it against AES-256.

B is incorrect. Data Encryption Standard (DES) is not secure and is not recommended today.

D is incorrect. Secure Hash Algorithm version 2 (SHA-2) is a hashing algorithm used for integrity.

15. Your network requires a secure method of sharing encryption keys over a public network. Which of the following is the BEST choice?

    A. Symmetric encryption

    B. Bcrypt

    C. Diffie-Hellman

    D. Steganography

15. C is correct. Diffie-Hellman allows entities to negotiate encryption keys securely over a public network.

A is incorrect. Once the entities negotiate the keys, they use symmetric encryption, but they can't share keys using symmetric encryption without first using a secure method such as Diffie-Hellman.

B is incorrect. Bcrypt is a key stretching technique used by some Unix systems to make password cracking more difficult.

D is incorrect. Steganography hides data within data, but it isn't the best method of sharing encryption keys over a public network.

16. You are planning to encrypt data in transit. Which of the following protocols meets this need and encapsulates IP packets within an additional IP header?

A. TLS

B. SSL

C. HMAC

D. IPsec

16. D is correct. Internet Protocol security (IPsec) can encrypt data in transit and encapsulates IP packets with an additional IP header.

A and B are incorrect. Transport Layer Security (TLS) and Secure Sockets Layer (SSL) are both transport encryption protocols that can protect the data while it is in transit. Although they both use certificates for security, they do not encapsulate IP packets within an additional IP header.

C is incorrect. Hash-based Message Authentication Code (HMAC) is often used with IPsec, but HMAC does not encrypt data.

17. An application requires users to log on with passwords. The application developers want to store the passwords in such a way that it will thwart rainbow table attacks. Which of the following is the BEST solution?

A. SHA

B. Blowfish

C. ECC

D. Bcrypt

17. D is correct. Bcrypt is a key stretching technique designed to protect against brute force attempts and is the best choice of the given answers. Another alternative is Password-Based Key Derivation Function 2 (PBKDF2). Both salt the password with additional bits.

A is incorrect. Passwords stored using Secure Hash Algorithm (SHA) are easier to crack because they don't use salts.

B is incorrect. PBKDF2 is based on Blowfish, but Blowfish itself isn't commonly used to encrypt passwords.

C is incorrect. Elliptic curve cryptography (ECC) is efficient and sometimes used with mobile devices, but not to encrypt passwords.

18. Your organization's security policy requires that PII data at rest and PII data in transit be encrypted. Of the following choices, what would the organization use to achieve these objectives? (Select TWO.)

    A. FTP

    B. SSH

    C. SMTP

    D. PGP/GPG

    E. HTTP

18. B are D are correct. You can use Secure Shell (SSH) to encrypt Personally Identifiable Information (PII) data when transmitting it over the network (data in transit). While Pretty Good Privacy (PGP)/GNU Privacy Guard (GPG) is primarily used to encrypt email, it can also be used to encrypt data at rest.

A, C and E are incorrect. File Transfer Protocol (FTP), Simple Mail Transfer Protocol (SMTP), and Hypertext Transfer Protocol (HTTP) transmit data in cleartext unless they are combined with an encryption protocol.

19. Which of the following is a symmetric encryption algorithm that encrypts data one bit at a time?

    A. Block cipher

    B. Stream cipher

    C. AES

    D. DES

    E. MD5

19. B is correct. A stream cipher encrypts data a single bit or a single byte at a time and is more efficient when the size of the data is unknown, such as streaming audio or video.

A is incorrect. A block cipher encrypts data in specific-sized blocks, such as 64-bit blocks or 128-bit blocks.

C, D, and E are incorrect. Advanced Encryption Standard (AES), Data Encryption Standard (DES), and Message Digest 5 (MD5) are all block ciphers.

20. You are planning to encrypt data in transit with IPsec. Which of the following is MOST likely to be used with IPsec?

    A. HMAC

    B. Blowfish

    C. Twofish

    D. MD5

20. A is correct. Hash-based Message Authentication Code (HMAC) is used with Internet Protocol security (IPsec) and is more likely to be used than any of the other choices. RFC 4835 mandates the use of HMAC for authentication and integrity. When encryption is used, it also mandates the use of either Advanced Encryption Standard (AES) or Triple Data Encryption Standard (3DES).

B and C are incorrect. RFC 4835 does not list Blowfish or Twofish.

D is incorrect. Message Digest 5 (MD5) is a hashing algorithm.

21. Application developers are creating an application that requires users to log on with strong passwords. The developers want to store the passwords in such a way that it will thwart brute force attacks. Which of the following is the BEST solution?

A. 3DES

B. MD5

C. PBKDF2

D. Database fields

21. C is correct. Password-Based Key Derivation Function 2 (PBKDF2) is a key stretching technique designed to protect against brute force attempts and is the best choice of the given answers. Another alternative is bcrypt. Both salt the password with additional bits.

A is incorrect. Triple DES (3DES) is an encryption protocol.

B is incorrect. Passwords stored using Message Digest 5 (MD5) are easier to crack because they don't use salts.

D is incorrect. Storing the passwords in encrypted database fields is a possible solution, but just storing them in unencrypted database fields does not protect them at all.

22. Your organization recently updated its security policy and indicated that Telnet should not be used within the network. Which of the following should be used instead of Telnet?

A. SCP

B. SFTP

C. SSL

D. SSH

22. D is correct. Secure Shell (SSH) is a good alternative to Telnet. SSH encrypts transmissions, whereas Telnet transmits data in cleartext.

A, B, and C are incorrect. Secure Copy (SCP) and Secure File Transfer Protocol (SFTP) use SSH to encrypt files sent over the network.

23. An organization is implementing a PKI and plans on using public and private keys. Which of the following can be used to create strong key pairs?

A. MD5

B. RSA

C. AES

D. HMAC

23. B is correct. Rivest, Shamir, Adleman (RSA) is used to create key pairs. A and D are incorrect. Message Digest 5 (MD5) and Hash-based Message Authentication Code (HMAC) are hashing algorithms.

C is incorrect. Advanced Encryption Standard (AES) is a symmetric encryption algorithm.

24. Homer wants to send a secure email to Marge so he decides to encrypt it. Homer wants to ensure that Marge can verify that he sent it. Which of the following does Marge need to verify the certificate that Homer used in this process is valid?

    A. The CA's private key

    B. The CA's public key

    C. Marge's public key

    D. Marge's private key

24. B is correct. Marge would verify Homer's certificate is valid by querying the Certificate Authority (CA) that issued Homer's certificate and the CA's public certificate includes the CA's public key. Homer would use a digital signature to provide verification that he sent the message. Homer would encrypt the digital signature with his private key and Marge would decrypt the digital signature with Homer's public key.

A is incorrect. The CA's private key remains private.

C and D are incorrect. Marge's keys are not used for Homer's digital signature, but might be used for the encryption of the email.

25. Users in your organization sign their emails with digital signatures. What provides integrity for these digital signatures?

    A. Hashing

    B. Encryption

    C. Non-repudiation

    D. Private key

25. A is correct. Hashing provides integrity for digital signatures and other data.

B is incorrect. A digital signature is a hash of the message encrypted with the sender's private key, but the encryption doesn't provide integrity.

C is incorrect. The digital signature provides non-repudiation, but non-repudiation does not provide integrity.

D is incorrect. The private key and public key are both needed, but the private key does not provide integrity.

26. Homer wants to use digital signatures for his emails and realizes he needs a certificate. Which of the following will issue Homer a certificate?

    A. CRL

    B. CA

    C. OCSP

    D. Recovery agent

26. B is correct. A Certificate Authority (CA) issues and manages certificates.

A is incorrect. A certificate revocation list (CRL) is a list of revoked certificates.

C is incorrect. Online Certificate Status Protocol (OCSP) is an alternative to a CRL and validates certificates with short responses such as good, unknown, or revoked.

D is incorrect. A recovery agent can retrieve a private key if the original private key is no longer accessible.

27. You need to submit a CSR to a CA. Which of the following would you do FIRST?

    A. Generate a new RSA-based session key.

    B. Generate a new RSA-based private key.

    C. Generate the CRL.

    D. Implement OCSP.

27. B is correct. You create the RSA-based private key first and then create the matching public key from it, which you include in the certificate signing request (CSR) that you send to the Certificate Authority (CA).

A is incorrect. The RSA algorithm technically creates the private key first, but most applications that create the key pair appear to create them at the same time. A session key is a symmetric key, but RSA is an asymmetric algorithm.

C and D are incorrect. The CA generates the certificate revocation list (CRL) to identify revoked certificates. Online Certificate Status Protocol (OCSP) is an alternative to using CRLs to validate certificates, but it is not required.

28. Your organization is planning to implement an internal PKI. What is required to ensure users can validate certificates?

    A. An intermediate CA

    B. CSR

    C. Wildcard certificates

    D. CRL

28. D is correct. A certificate revocation list (CRL) includes a list of revoked certificates and it allows users to validate certificates.

A is incorrect. Any CA can issue a CRL, so an intermediate CA is not needed.

B is incorrect. Users request certificates with a certificate signing request (CSR).

C is incorrect. Wildcard certificates reduce the administrative burden for certificates, but do not have anything to do with validating certificates.

29. Your organization requires the use of a PKI and it wants to implement a protocol to validate trust with minimal traffic. Which of the following protocols validates trust by returning short responses, such as "good" or "revoked"?

    A. OCSP

    B. CRL

    C. CA

    D. CSR

29. A is correct. Online Certificate Status Protocol (OCSP) validates trust with certificates. Clients send the serial number of the certificate to the Certificate Authority (CA) within the Public Key Infrastructure (PKI) and the CA returns short responses such as good, unknown, or revoked.

B is incorrect. A certificate revocation list (CRL) includes a list of revoked certificates listed by serial numbers and can become quite large after a while.

C is incorrect. The CA isn't a protocol.

D is incorrect. You request certificates with a certificate signing request (CSR).

30. A user's laptop developed a problem and can no longer boot. Help desk personnel tried to recover the data on the disk, but the disk is encrypted. Which of the following can be used to retrieve data from the hard drive?

    A. A trust relationship

    B. Public key

    C. Recovery agent

    D. CRL

30. C is correct. Recovery agents can decrypt data and messages if the user's private key is no longer available.

A is incorrect. Although certificate authorities use trust models, a trust relationship doesn't directly apply here.

B is incorrect. A user's public key is already publicly available, so it isn't useful here.

D is incorrect. A certificate revocation list (CRL) is a list of revoked certificates and doesn't apply in this scenario.

31. A web site is using a certificate. Users have recently been receiving errors from the web site indicating that the web site's certificate is revoked. Which of the following includes a list of certificates that have been revoked?

    A. CRL

    B. CA

    C. OCSP

    D. CSR

31. A is correct. A certificate revocation list (CRL) is a list of certificates that a Certificate Authority (CA) has revoked.

B is incorrect. The CA stores a database repository of revoked certificates and issues the CRL to anyone who requests it.

C is incorrect. The Online Certificate Status Protocol (OCSP) validates trust with certificates, but only returns short responses such as good, unknown, or revoked.

D is incorrect. A certificate signing request (CSR) is used to request certificates.

32. An organization is planning to implement an internal PKI for smart cards. Which of the following should the organization do FIRST?

    A. Install a CA.

    B. Generate key pairs.

    C. Generate a certificate.

    D. Identify a recovery agent.

32. A is correct. A Public Key Infrastructure (PKI) requires a certification authority (CA), so a CA should be installed first. Smart cards require certificates and would be issued by the CA.

B and C are incorrect. After installing the CA, you can generate key pairs to be used with certificates issued by the CA.

D is incorrect. A recovery agent can be identified, but it isn't required to be done as a first step for a CA.

33. Which of the following is a valid reason to use a wildcard certificate?

    A. Reduce the administrative burden of managing certificates.

    B. Support multiple private keys.

    C. Support multiple public keys.

    D. Increase the lifetime of the certificate.

33. A is correct. A wildcard certificate reduces the certificate management burden by using an asterisk (*) in place of child domain names.

B and C are incorrect. The certificate still has a single public and private key pair.

D is incorrect. The wildcard doesn't affect the lifetime of the certificate.

34. Homer works as a contractor at a company on a one-year renewing contract. After renewing his contract, the company issues him a new smart card. However, he is now having problems digitally signing email or opening encrypted email. What is the MOST likely solution?

    A. Copy the original certificate to the new smart card.

    B. Copy his original private key to the new smart card.

    C. Copy his original public key to the new smart card.

    D. Publish the certificate in his new smart card.

34. D is correct. He should publish the certificate in his new smart card in a global address list within the domain.

A, B, and C are incorrect. It is not possible for users to copy a certificate, a public key, or a private key to a smart card.

35. You need to request a certificate for a web server. Which of the following would you MOST likely use?

    A. CA

    B. CRL

    C. CSR

    D. OCSP

35. C is correct. A certificate signing request (CSR) uses a specific format to request a certificate.

A is incorrect. You submit the CSR to a Certificate Authority (CA), but the request needs to be in the CSR format.

B is incorrect. A certificate revocation list (CRL) is a list of revoked certificates.

D is incorrect. The Online Certificate Status Protocol (OCSP) is an alternate method of validating certificates and indicates if a certificate is good, revoked, or unknown.

36. An organization is implementing a data policy and wants to designate a recovery agent. Which of the following indicates what a recovery agent can do?

    A. A recovery agent can retrieve a user's public key.

    B. A recovery agent can decrypt data if users lose their private key.

    C. A recovery agent can encrypt data if users lose their private key.

    D. A recovery agent can restore a system from backups.

36. B is correct. Recovery agents can decrypt data and messages if users lose their private key.

A is incorrect. Public keys are publicly available, so recovery agents aren't needed to retrieve them.

C is incorrect. A recovery agent wouldn't encrypt a user's data.

D is incorrect. Although backups are important, this isn't the role of a recovery agent.

√ **Get Certified**

√ **Get Ahead**

Cryptography Extras

When preparing for the Security+ exam, make sure you know the hashing protocols listed in Table 6.1, and the important symmetric encryption algorithms listed in Table 6.2:

Algorithm	Type	Comments
MD5	Hashing - Integrity	Creates 128-bit hashes
SHA-1	Hashing - Integrity	Creates 160-bit hashes
SHA-2	Hashing - Integrity	Creates 224-, 256-, 384-, or 512-bit hashes
HMAC-MD5	Integrity/Authenticity	Creates 128-bit hashes
HMAC-SHA1	Integrity/Authenticity	Creates 160-bit hashes

Table 6.1: Hashing protocols

Algorithm	Type	Method	Key Size
AES	Symmetric encryption	128-bit block cipher	128-, 192-, or 256-bit key
DES	Symmetric encryption	64-bit block cipher	56-bit key
3DES	Symmetric encryption	64-bit block cipher	56-, 112-, or 168-bit key
Blowfish	Symmetric encryption	64-bit block cipher	32- to 448-bit key
Twofish	Symmetric encryption	128-bit block cipher	128-, 192-, or 256-bit key
RC4	Symmetric encryption	Stream cipher	40- to 2,048-bit key

Table 6.2: Symmetric encryption protocols

Acronym List

This acronym list provides you with a quick reminder of many of the different security-related terms along with a short explanation. Where appropriate, the concepts are explained in greater depth within the book. You can use the index to identify the specific pages where the topics are covered.

802.1x—A port-based authentication protocol. Wireless can use 802.1x. For example, WPA2 Enterprise mode uses an 802.1x server (implemented as a RADIUS server). Enterprise mode requires an 802.1x server. PEAP and EAP-TTLS require a certificate on the 802.1x server. EAP-TLS also uses TLS, but it requires certificates on both the 802.1x server and each of the clients.

3DES—Triple Digital Encryption Standard. A symmetric algorithm used to encrypt data and provide confidentiality. It is a block cipher that encrypts data in 64-bit blocks. It was originally designed as a replacement for DES, and is still used in some applications, such as when hardware doesn't support AES.

AAA—Authentication, Authorization, and Accounting. AAA protocols are used in remote access systems. For example, TACACS+ is an AAA protocol that uses multiple challenges and responses during a session. Authentication verifies a user's identification. Authorization determines if a user should have access. Accounting tracks a user's access with logs.

ACE—Access Control Entry. Identifies a user or group that is granted permission to a resource. ACEs are contained within a DACL in NTFS.

ACK—Acknowledge. A packet in a TCP handshake. In a SYN flood attack, attackers send the SYN packet, but don't complete the handshake after receiving the SYN/ACK packet.

ACL—Access control list. Routers and packet-filtering firewalls perform basic filtering using an ACL to control traffic based on networks, subnets, IP addresses, ports, and some protocols. In NTFS, a list of ACEs makes up the ACL for a resource.

AES—Advanced Encryption Standard. A symmetric algorithm used to encrypt data and provide confidentiality. AES is a block cipher and it encrypts data in 128-bit blocks. It is quick, highly secure, and used in a wide assortment of cryptography schemes. It includes key sizes of 128 bits, 192 bits, or 256 bits.

AES-256—Advanced Encryption Standard 256 bit. AES sometimes includes the number of bits used in the encryption keys and AES-256 uses 256-bit encryption keys. Interestingly, Blowfish is quicker than AES-256.

AH—Authentication Header. IPsec includes both AH and ESP. AH provides authentication and integrity using HMAC. ESP provides confidentiality, integrity, and authentication using HMAC, and AES or 3DES. AH is identified with protocol ID number 51.

ALE—Annual (or annualized) loss expectancy. The ALE identifies the expected annual loss and is used to measure risk with ARO and SLE in a quantitative risk assessment. The calculation is SLE × ARO = ALE.

AP—Access point, short for wireless access point (WAP). APs provide access to a wired network to wireless clients. Many APs support Isolation mode to segment wireless users from other wireless users.

API—Application Programming Interface. A software module or component that identifies inputs and outputs for an application.

APT—Advanced persistent threat. A group that has both the capability and intent to launch sophisticated and targeted attacks.

ARO—Annual (or annualized) rate of occurrence. The ARO identifies how many times a loss is expected to occur in a year and it is used to measure risk with ALE and SLE in a quantitative risk assessment. The calculation is SLE $\times$ ARO = ALE.

ARP—Address Resolution Protocol. Resolves IPv4 addresses to MAC addresses. ARP poisoning attacks can redirect traffic through an attacker's system by sending false MAC address updates. NDP is used with IPv6 instead of ARP.

ASCII—American Standard Code for Information Interchange. Code used to display characters.

ASP—Application Service Provider. Provides an application as a service over a network.

AUP—Acceptable use policy. An AUP defines proper system usage. It will often describe the purpose of computer systems and networks, how users can access them, and the responsibilities of users when accessing the systems.

BAC—Business Availability Center. An application that shows availability and performance of applications used or provided by a business.

BCP—Business continuity plan. A plan that helps an organization predict and plan for potential outages of critical services or functions. It includes disaster recovery elements that provide the steps used to return critical functions to operation after an outage. A BIA is a part of a BCP and the BIA drives decisions to create redundancies such as failover clusters or alternate sites.

BIA—Business impact analysis. The BIA identifies systems and components that are essential to the organization's success. It identifies various scenarios that can impact these systems and components, maximum downtime limits, and potential losses from an incident. The BIA helps identify RTOs and RPOs.

BIND—Berkeley Internet Name Domain. BIND is DNS software that runs on Linux and Unix servers. Most Internet-based DNS servers use BIND.

BIOS—Basic Input/Output System. A computer's firmware used to manipulate different settings such as the date and time, boot drive, and access password. UEFI is the designated replacement for BIOS.

BPA—Business partners agreement. A written agreement that details the relationship between business partners, including their obligations toward the partnership.

BYOD—Bring your own device. A policy allowing employees to connect personally owned devices, such as tablets and smartphones, to a company network. Data security is often a concern with BYOD policies and organizations often use VLANs to isolate mobile devices.

CA—Certificate Authority. An organization that manages, issues, and signs certificates and is part of a PKI. Certificates are an important part of asymmetric encryption. Certificates include public keys along with details on the owner of the certificate and on the CA that issued the certificate. Certificate owners share their public key by sharing a copy of their certificate.

CAC—Common Access Card. A specialized type of smart card used by the U.S. Department of Defense. It includes photo identification and provides confidentiality, integrity, authentication, and non-repudiation for the users. It is similar to a PIV.

CAN—Controller Area Network. A standard that allows microcontrollers and devices to communicate with each other without a host computer.

CAPTCHA—Completely Automated Public Turing Test to Tell Computers and Humans Apart. Technique used to prevent automated tools from interacting with a web site. Users must type in text, often from a slightly distorted image.

CAR—Corrective Action Report. A report used to document actions taken to correct an event, incident, or outage.

CCMP—Counter Mode with Cipher Block Chaining Message Authentication Code Protocol. An encryption protocol based on AES and used with WPA2 for wireless security. It is more secure than TKIP, which was used with the original release of WPA.

CCTV—Closed-circuit television. This is a detective control that provides video surveillance. Video surveillance provides reliable proof of a person's location and activity. It is also a physical security control and it can increase the safety of an organization's assets.

CERT—Computer Emergency Response Team. A group of experts who respond to security incidents. Also known as CIRT, SIRT, or IRT.

CHAP—Challenge Handshake Authentication Protocol. Authentication mechanism where a server challenges a client. More secure than PAP and uses PPP. MS-CHAPv2 is an improvement over CHAP and uses mutual authentication.

CIA—Confidentiality, integrity, and availability. These three form the security triad. Confidentiality helps prevent the unauthorized disclosure of data. Integrity provides assurances that data has not been modified, tampered with, or corrupted. Availability indicates that data and services are available when needed.

CIO—Chief Information Officer. A "C" level executive position in some organizations. A CIO focuses on using methods within the organization to answer relevant questions and solve problems.

CIRT—Computer Incident Response Team. A group of experts who respond to security incidents. Also known as CERT, SIRT, or IRT.

COOP—Continuity of operations planning. Continuity of operations planning (COOP) sites provide an alternate location for operations after a critical outage. A hot site includes personnel, equipment, software, and communication capabilities of the primary site with all the data up to date. A cold site will have power and connectivity needed for COOP activation, but little else. A warm site is a compromise between a hot site and a cold site.

Mobile sites do not have dedicated locations, but can provide temporary support during a disaster.

CP—Contingency planning. Plans for contingencies in the event of a disaster to keep an organization operational. BCPs include contingency planning.

CRC—Cyclical Redundancy Check. An error detection code used to detect accidental changes that can affect the integrity of data.

CRL—Certification revocation list. A list of certificates that a CA has revoked. Certificates are commonly revoked if they are compromised, or issued to an employee who has left the organization. The Certificate Authority (CA) that issued the certificate publishes a CRL, and a CRL is public.

CSR—Certificate signing request. A method of requesting a certificate from a CA. It starts by creating an RSA-based private/public key pair and then including the public key in the CSR.

CSR—Control Status Register. A register in a processor used for temporary storage of data.

CSU—Channel Service Unit. A line bridging device used with T1 and similar lines. It typically connects with a DSU as a CSU/DSU.

CTO—Chief Technology Officer. A "C" level executive position in some organizations. CTOs focus on technology and evaluate new technologies.

CVE—Common Vulnerabilities and Exposures (CVE). A dictionary of publicly known security vulnerabilities and exposures.

DAC—Discretionary access control. An access control model where all objects have owners and owners can modify permissions for the objects (files and folders). Microsoft NTFS uses the DAC model. Other access control models are MAC and RBAC.

DACL—Discretionary access control list. List of Access Control Entries (ACEs) in Microsoft NTFS. Each ACE includes a security identifier (SID) and a permission.

DBA—Database administrator. A DBA administers databases on database servers.

dBd—Decibels-dipole. Identifies the gain of an antenna compared with a type of dipole antenna. Higher dBd numbers indicate the antenna can transmit and receive over greater distances.

dBi—Decibels-isotropic. Identifies the gain of an antenna and is commonly used with omnidirectional antennas. It references an isotropic antenna that can theoretically transmit the signal equally in all directions. Higher numbers indicate the antenna can transmit and receive over greater distances.

dBm—Decibels-milliwatt. Identifies the power level of the WAP and refers to the power ratio in decibels referenced to one milliwatt. Higher numbers indicate the WAP transmits the signal over a greater distance.

DDoS—Distributed denial-of-service. An attack on a system launched from multiple sources intended to make a computer's resources or services unavailable to users. DDoS attacks typically include sustained, abnormally high network traffic. Compare to DoS.

DEP—Data Execution Prevention. A security feature in some operating systems. It helps prevent an application or service from executing code from a nonexecutable memory region.

DES—Digital Encryption Standard. An older symmetric encryption standard used to provide confidentiality. DES is a block cipher and it encrypts data in 64-bit blocks. DES uses 56 bits and is considered cracked. Use AES instead, or 3DES if the hardware doesn't support AES.

DHCP—Dynamic Host Configuration Protocol. A service used to dynamically assign TCP/IP configuration information to clients. DHCP is often used to assign IP addresses, subnet masks, default gateways, DNS server addresses, and much more.

DHE—Data-Handling Electronics. Term used at NASA indicating electronic systems that handle data.

DHE—Diffie-Hellman Ephemeral. An alternative to traditional Diffie-Hellman. Instead of using static keys that stay the same over a long period, DHE uses ephemeral keys, which change for each new session. Sometimes listed as EDH.

DLL—Dynamic Link Library. A compiled set of code that can be called from other programs.

DLP—Data loss prevention. A network-based DLP system can examine and analyze network traffic. It can detect if confidential company data or any PII data is included in email and reduce the risk of internal users emailing sensitive data outside the organization. End-point DLP systems can prevent users from copying or printing sensitive data.

DMZ—Demilitarized zone. A buffer zone between the Internet and an internal network. It allows access to services while segmenting access to the internal network. Internet clients can access the services hosted on servers in the DMZ, but the DMZ provides a layer of protection for the internal network.

DNAT—Destination Network Address Translation. A form of NAT that changes the destination IP address for incoming traffic. It is used for port forwarding.

DNAT—Dynamic Network Address Translation. A form of NAT that uses multiple public IP addresses. In contrast, PAT uses a single public IP address. It hides addresses on an internal network.

DNS—Domain Name System. Used to resolve host names to IP addresses. DNS zones include records such as A records for IPv4 addresses and AAAA records for IPv6 addresses. DNS uses UDP port 53 for DNS client queries and TCP port 53 for zone transfers. DNS poisoning attacks attempt to modify or corrupt DNS data. Secure zone transfers help prevent these attacks. A pharming attack is a type of DNS poisoning attack that redirects a web site's traffic to another web site.

DNSSEC—Domain Name System Security Extensions. A suite of specifications used to protect the integrity of DNS records and prevent DNS poisoning attacks.

DoS—Denial-of-service. An attack from a single source that attempts to disrupt the services provided by the attacked system. Compare to DDoS.

DRP—Disaster recovery plan. A document designed to help a company respond to disasters, such as hurricanes, floods, and fires. It includes a hierarchical list of critical systems and often prioritizes services to restore after an outage. Testing validates the plan. The final phase of disaster recovery includes a review to identify any lessons learned and may include an update of the plan.

DSA—Digital Signature Algorithm. A digital signature is an encrypted hash of a message. The sender's private key encrypts the hash of the message to create the digital signature. The recipient decrypts the hash with the sender's public key, and, if successful, it provides authentication, non-repudiation, and integrity. Authentication identifies the sender. Integrity verifies the message has not been modified. Non-repudiation is used with online transactions and prevents the sender from later denying he sent the email.

DSL—Digital subscriber line. Improvement over traditional dial-up to access the Internet.

DSU—Data Service Unit. An interface used to connect equipment to a T1 and similar lines. It typically connects with a CSU as a CSU/DSU.

EAP—Extensible Authentication Protocol. An authentication framework that provides general guidance for authentication methods. Variations include EAP-TLS, EAP-TTLS, LEAP, and PEAP.

EAP-TLS—Extensible Authentication Protocol-Transport Layer Security. An extension of EAP sometimes used with 802.1x. This is one of the most secure EAP standards and is widely implemented. The primary difference between PEAP and EAP-TLS is that EAP-TLS requires certificates on the 802.1x server and on each of the wireless clients.

EAP-TTLS—Extensible Authentication Protocol-Tunneled Transport Layer Security. An extension of EAP sometimes used with 802.1x. It allows systems to use some older authentication methods such as PAP within a TLS tunnel. It requires a certificate on the 802.1x server but not on the clients.

ECC—Elliptic curve cryptography. An asymmetric encryption algorithm commonly used with smaller wireless devices. It uses smaller key sizes and requires less processing power than many other encryption methods.

ECDHE—Elliptic Curve Diffie-Hellman Ephemeral. A version of Diffie-Hellman that uses ECC to generate encryption keys. Ephemeral keys are re-created for each session.

EFS—Encrypting File System. A feature within NTFS on Windows systems that supports encrypting individual files or folders for confidentiality.

EMI—Electromagnetic interference. Interference caused by motors, power lines, and fluorescent lights. EMI shielding prevents outside interference sources from corrupting data and prevents data from emanating outside the cable.

ESD—Electrostatic discharge. Release of static electricity. ESD can damage equipment and low humidity causes a higher incidence of electrostatic discharge (ESD). High humidity can cause condensation on the equipment, which causes water damage.

ESN—Electronic Serial Number. Numbers used to uniquely identify mobile devices.

ESP—Encapsulating Security Protocol. IPsec includes both AH and ESP. AH provides authentication and integrity using HMAC. ESP provides confidentiality, integrity, and authentication using HMAC and AES or 3DES. ESP is identified with protocol ID number 50.

FACL—File System Access Control List. An ACL used for file systems. As an example, NTFS uses the DAC model to protect files and folders.

FCoE—Fibre Channel over Ethernet. A lower-cost alternative to traditional SANs. It supports sending Fibre Channel commands over an IP network.

FDE—Full Disk Encryption. Method to encrypt an entire disk. TrueCrypt is an example.

FTP—File Transfer Protocol. Used to upload and download files to an FTP server. FTP uses TCP ports 20 and 21. Secure FTP (SFTP) uses SSH for encryption on TCP port 22. FTP Secure (FTPS) uses SSL or TLS for encryption.

FTPS—File Transfer Protocol Secure. An extension of FTP that uses SSL to encrypt FTP traffic. Some implementations of FTPS use TCP ports 989 and 990.

GPG—GNU Privacy Guard (GPG). Free software based on the OpenPGP standard and used to encrypt and decrypt files. It is similar to PGP but avoids any conflict with existing licensing by using open standards.

GPO—Group Policy Object. Group Policy is used within Microsoft Windows to manage users and computers. It is implemented on a domain controller within a domain. Administrators use it to create password policies, lock down the GUI, configure host-based firewalls, and much more.

GPS—Global Positioning System. GPS tracking can help locate lost mobile devices. Remote wipe, or remote sanitize, erases all data on lost devices. Full disk encryption protects the data on the device if it is lost.

GRE—Generic Routing Encapsulation. A tunneling protocol developed by Cisco Systems.

GUI—Graphical user interface. Users interact with the graphical elements instead of typing in commands from a text interface. Windows is an example of a GUI.

HDD—Hard disk drive. A disk drive that has one or more platters and a spindle. In contrast, USB flash drives and SSD drives use flash memory.

HIDS—Host-based intrusion detection system. An IDS used to monitor an individual server or workstation. It protects local resources on the host such as the operating system files, and in some cases, it can detect malicious activity missed by antivirus software.

HIPS—Host-based intrusion prevention system. An extension of a host-based IDS. Designed to react in real time to catch an attack in action.

HMAC—Hash-based Message Authentication Code. A hashing algorithm used to verify integrity and authenticity of a message with the use of a shared secret. When used with TLS and IPsec, HMAC is combined with MD5 and SHA-1 as HMAC-MD5 and HMAC-SHA1, respectively.

HOTP—HMAC-based One-Time Password (HOTP). An open standard used for creating one-time passwords, similar to those used in tokens or key fobs. It combines a secret key and an incrementing counter, and then uses HMAC to create a hash of the result. HOTP passwords do not expire until they are used.

HSM—Hardware security module. A removable or external device that can generate, store, and manage RSA keys used in asymmetric encryption. High-volume e-commerce sites use HSMs to increase the performance of SSL sessions. High-availability clusters needing encryption services can use clustered HSMs.

HTML—Hypertext Markup Language. Language used to create web pages. HTML documents are displayed by web browsers and delivered over the Internet using HTTP or HTTPS. It uses less-than and greater-than characters (< and >) to create tags. Many sites use input validation to block these tags and prevent cross-site scripting attacks.

HTTP—Hypertext Transfer Protocol. Used for web traffic on the Internet and in intranets. HTTP uses TCP port 80.

HTTPS—Hypertext Transfer Protocol Secure. Encrypts HTTP traffic with SSL or TLS using TCP port 443.

HVAC—Heating, ventilation, and air conditioning. HVAC systems increase availability by regulating airflow within data centers and server rooms. They use hot and cold aisles to regulate the cooling, thermostats to ensure a relatively constant temperature, and humidity controls to reduce the potential for static discharge, and damage from condensation. Higher-tonnage HVAC systems provide more cooling capacity to keep server rooms at operating temperatures, resulting in fewer failures and longer MTBF times. HVAC systems should be integrated with fire alarm systems and either have dampers or the ability to be turned off in the event of a fire.

IaaS—Infrastructure as a Service. A cloud-computing technology that allows an organization to rent access to hardware. It provides customers with access to hardware in a self-managed platform. Customers are responsible for keeping an IaaS system up to date. Compare to PaaS and SaaS.

ICMP—Internet Control Message Protocol. Used for diagnostics such as ping. Many DoS attacks use ICMP. It is common to block ICMP at firewalls and routers. If ping fails, but other connectivity to a server succeeds, it indicates that ICMP is blocked.

ID—Identification. For example, a protocol ID identifies a protocol based on a number. AH is identified with protocol ID number 51 and ESP is identified with protocol ID number 50.

IDS—Intrusion detection system. A detective control used to detect attacks after they occur. Monitors a network (NIDS) or host (HIDS) for intrusions and provides ongoing protection against various threats. IDSs include sniffing capabilities. Many IDSs use numbering systems to identify vulnerabilities.

IEEE—Institute of Electrical and Electronics Engineers. IEEE is an international organization with a focus on electrical, electronics, and information technology topics. IEEE standards are well respected and followed by vendors around the world.

IGMP—Internet Group Management Protocol. Used for multicasting. Computers belonging to a multicasting group have a multicasting IP address in addition to a standard unicast IP address.

IIS—Internet Information Services. A Microsoft Windows web server. IIS comes free with Microsoft Windows Server products. Linux systems use Apache as a web server.

IKE—Internet Key Exchange. Used with IPsec to create a secure channel over UDP port 500 in a VPN tunnel.

IM—Instant messaging. Real-time direct text-based communication between two or more people, often referred to as chat. Spim is a form of spam using IM.

IMAP4—Internet Message Access Protocol version 4. Used to store email on servers and allow clients to manage their email on the server. IMAP4 uses TCP port 143.

IP—Internet Protocol. Used for addressing. *See* IPv4 and IPv6.

IPS—Intrusion prevention system. A preventive control that will stop an attack in progress. It is similar to an active IDS except that it's placed in-line with traffic. An IPS can actively monitor data streams, detect malicious content, and stop attacks in progress. It can be used internally to protect private networks, such as those holding SCADA equipment.

IPsec—Internet Protocol security. Used to encrypt data in transit and can operate in both Tunnel mode and Transport mode. It uses Tunnel mode for VPN traffic. IPsec is built in to IPv6, but can also work with IPv4. Both versions support AH and ESP. AH provides authentication and integrity using HMAC. ESP provides confidentiality, integrity, and authentication using HMAC and AES or 3DES. IPsec creates secure tunnels for VPNs using UDP port 500 for IKE.

IPv4—Internet Protocol version 4. Identifies hosts using a 32-bit IP address. IPv4 is expressed in dotted decimal format with decimal numbers separated by dots or periods like this: 192.168.1.1.

IPv6—Internet Protocol version 6. Identifies hosts using a 128-bit address. IPv6 has a significantly larger address space than IPv4. IPsec is built in to IPv6 and can encrypt any type of IPv6 traffic.

IR—Incident response. Process of responding to a security incident. Organizations often create an incident response policy that outlines procedures and responsibilities of personnel on incident response teams.

IRC—Internet Relay Chat. A form of real-time Internet text messaging often used with chat sessions. Some botnets have used IRC channels to control zombie computers through a command-and-control server.

IRP—Incident Response Procedure. Procedures documented in an incident response policy.

IRT—Incident Response Team. A group of experts who respond to security incidents. Also known as CERT, CIRT, or SIRT.

ISA—Interconnection Security Agreement. Specifies technical and security requirements for connections between two or more entities. An ISA includes details on planning, establishing, maintaining, and disconnecting a secure connection between two or more entities.

iSCSI—Internet Small Computer System Interface. A lower-cost alternative to traditional SANs. It supports sending traditional SCSI commands over an IP network.

ISP—Internet Service Provider. A company that provides Internet access to customers.

ISSO—Information Systems Security Officer. A job role within an organization focused on information security.

IT—Information technology. Computer systems and networks used within organizations.

ITCP—IT contingency plan. Part of risk management. Plan to ensure that IT resources remain available after a security incident, outage, or disaster.

IV—Initialization vector. An IV provides randomization of encryption keys to help ensure that keys are not reused. WEP was susceptible to IV attacks because it used relatively small IVs. In an IV attack, the attacker uses packet injection, increasing the number of packets to analyze, and discovers the encryption key.

JBOD—Just a Bunch of Disks. Disks installed on a computer but not as a RAID.

KDC—Key Distribution Center. Also known as TGT server. Part of the Kerberos protocol used for network authentication. The KDC issues timestamped tickets that expire.

L2TP—Layer 2 Tunneling Protocol. Tunneling protocol used with VPNs. L2TP is commonly used with IPsec (L2TP/IPsec). L2TP uses UDP port 1701. Compare to PPTP, which uses TCP port 1723.

LAN—Local area network. Group of hosts connected within a network.

LANMAN—Local area network manager. Older authentication protocol used to provide backward compatibility to Windows 9x clients. LANMAN passwords are easily cracked due to how they are stored.

LDAP—Lightweight Directory Access Protocol. Language used to communicate with directories such as Microsoft Active Directory. Identifies objects with query strings using codes such as CN=Users and DC=GetCertifiedGetAhead. LDAP uses TCP port 389. Secure LDAP encrypts transmissions with SSL or TLS over TCP port 636. LDAP injection attacks attempt to access or modify data in directory service databases.

LEAP—Lightweight Extensible Authentication Protocol. A modified version of the Challenge Handshake Authentication Protocol (CHAP) created by Cisco. LEAP does not require a digital certificate and Cisco now recommends using stronger protocols such as EAP-TLS.

LSO—Local shared objects or locally shared objects. A Flash cookie created by Adobe Flash Player.

MaaS—Monitoring as a Service or Management as a Service. Allows an organization to outsource the management and monitoring of IT resources.

MAC—Mandatory access control. Access control model that uses sensitivity labels assigned to objects (files and folders) and subjects (users). MAC restricts access based on a need-to-know.

MAC—Media access control. A 48-bit address used to identify network interface cards. It is also called a hardware address or a physical address, and is commonly displayed as six pairs of hexadecimal characters. Port security on a switch or an AP can limit access using MAC filtering.

MAC—Message authentication code. Method used to provide integrity for messages. A MAC uses a secret key to encrypt the hash. HMAC is a commonly used version.

Malware—Malicious software. Includes viruses, Trojans, adware, spyware, rootkits, backdoors, logic bombs, and ransomware.

MAN—Metropolitan area network. A computer network that spans a metropolitan area such as a city or a large campus.

MBR—Master Boot Record. An area on a hard disk in its first sector. When the BIOS boots a system, it looks at the MBR for instructions and information on how to boot the disk and load the operating system. Some malware tries to hide here.

MD5—Message Digest 5. A hashing function used to provide integrity. MD5 creates 128-bit hashes, which are also referred to as MD5 checksums. A hash is simply a number created by applying the algorithm to a file or message at different times. Comparing the hashes verifies integrity.

MITM—Man in the middle. A MITM attack is a form of active interception allowing an attacker to intercept traffic and insert malicious code sent to other clients. Kerberos provides mutual authentication and helps prevent MITM attacks.

MOU—Memorandum of understanding. Defines responsibilities of each party, but it is not as strict as an SLA or an ISA. If the parties will be handling sensitive data, they should include an ISA to ensure strict guidelines are in place to protect the data while in transit.

MPLS—Multi-Protocol Layer Switch. A WAN topology provided by some telecommunications companies. Directs data to nodes using labels rather than IP addresses.

MS-CHAP—Microsoft Challenge Handshake Authentication Protocol. Microsoft implementation of CHAP. MS-CHAPv2 provides mutual authentication.

MTBF—Mean time between failures. Provides a measure of a system's reliability and is usually represented in hours. The MTBF identifies the average (the arithmetic mean) time between failures. Higher MTBF numbers indicate a higher reliability of a product or system.

MTTF—Mean time to failure. The length of time you can expect a device to remain in operation before it fails. It is similar to MTBF, but the primary difference is that the MTBF metric indicates you can repair the device after it fails. The MTTF metric indicates that you will not be able to repair a device after it fails.

MTTR—Mean time to recover. Identifies the average (the arithmetic mean) time it takes to restore a failed system. Organizations that have maintenance contracts often specify the MTTR as a part of the contract.

MTU—Maximum Transmission Unit. The MTU identifies the size of data that can be transferred.

NAC—Network access control. Inspects clients for health and can restrict network access to unhealthy clients to a remediation network. Clients run agents and these agents report status to a NAC server. NAC is used for VPN and internal clients. MAC filtering is a form of NAC.

NAT—Network Address Translation. A service that translates public IP addresses to private IP addresses and private IP addresses to public IP addresses. Compare to PAT and DNAT.

NDA—Non-disclosure agreement. Ensures that third parties understand their responsibilities. It is commonly embedded as a clause in a contract with the third party. Most NDAs prohibit sharing data unless you are the data owner.

NDP—Neighbor Discovery Protocol performs several functions on IPv6. For example, it performs functions similar to ARP, which is used on IPv4. It also performs autoconfiguration of device IPv6 addresses and discovers other devices on the network such as the IPv6 address of the default gateway.

NetBIOS—Network Basic Input/Output System (NetBIOS) is a name resolution service for NetBIOS names on internal networks. NetBIOS also includes session services for both TCP and UDP communication. NetBIOS uses UDP ports 137 and 138, and TCP port 139. It can use TCP port 137, but rarely does.

NFC—Near field communication. A group of standards used on mobile devices that allow them to communicate with other nearby mobile devices. Many credit card readers support payments using NFC technologies with a smartphone.

NIC—Network interface card. Provides connectivity to a network.

NIDS—Network-based intrusion detection system. A NIDS is installed on network devices, such as routers or firewalls and monitors network traffic. It can detect network-based attacks.

NIPS—Network-based intrusion prevention system. An IPS that monitors the network. An IPS can actively monitor data streams, detect malicious content, and stop attacks in progress.

NIST—National Institute of Standards and Technology. NIST is a part of the U.S. Department of Commerce, and it includes an Information Technology Laboratory (ITL). The ITL publishes special publications related to security that are freely available for download at *http://csrc.nist.gov/publications/PubsSPs.html*.

NOP—No operation, sometimes listed as NOOP. NOP instructions are often used in a buffer overflow attack. An attacker often writes a large number of NOP instructions as a NOP sled into memory, followed by malicious code. Some processors use hexadecimal code x90 for NOP so a string of x90 characters indicates a potential buffer overflow attack.

NOS—Network Operating System. Software that runs on a server and enables the server to manage resources on a network.

NoSQL—Not only Structured Query Language. An alternative to traditional SQL databases. NoSQL databases use unstructured query language queries instead of traditional SQL queries.

NTFS—NT File System. A file system used in Microsoft operating systems that provides security. NTFS uses the DAC model.

NTLM—New Technology LANMAN. Authentication protocol intended to improve LANMAN. The LANMAN protocol stores passwords using a hash of the password by first dividing the password into two 7-character blocks, and then converting all lowercase letters to uppercase. This makes LANMAN easy to crack. NTLM stores passwords in LANMAN format for backward compatibility, unless the passwords are greater than 15 characters. NTLMv1 is older and has known vulnerabilities. NTLMv2 is newer and secure.

NTP—Network Time Protocol. Protocol used to synchronize computer times.

OCSP—Online Certificate Status Protocol. An alternative to using a CRL. It allows entities to query a CA with the serial number of a certificate. The CA answers with good, revoked, or unknown.

OLA—Open License Agreement. A volume licensing agreement allowing an organization to install software on multiple systems.

OS—Operating system. Includes Windows, Linux, and Apple iOS systems. OSs are hardened to make them more secure from their default installation.

OSI—Open Systems Interconnection. The OSI reference model conceptually divides different networking requirements into seven separate layers.

OVAL—Open Vulnerability Assessment Language. International standard proposed for vulnerability assessment scanners to follow.

P2P—Peer-to-peer. P2P applications allow users to share files such as music, video, and data over the Internet. Data leakage occurs when users install P2P software and unintentionally share files. Organizations often block P2P software at the firewall.

PaaS—Platform as a Service. A cloud-computing technology that provides cloud customers with a preconfigured computing platform they can use as needed. PaaS is a fully managed platform, meaning that the vendor keeps the platform up to date with current patches. Compare to IaaS and SaaS.

PAC—Proxy Auto Configuration. Method used to automatically configure systems to use a proxy server.

PAM—Pluggable Authentication Modules. A library of APIs used for authentication-related services.

PAN—Personal area network. A network of devices close to a single person.

PAP—Password Authentication Protocol. An older authentication protocol where passwords or PINs are sent across the network in cleartext. CHAP is more secure. PAP uses PPP.

PAT—Port Address Translation. A form of NAT that translates public IP addresses to private IP addresses, and private IP addresses back to public IP addresses. PAT uses a single public IP address. Compare to DNAT.

PBKDF2—Password-Based Key Derivation Function 2. A key stretching technique that adds additional bits to a password as a salt. This method helps prevent brute force and rainbow table attacks. Bcrypt is a similar key stretching technique.

PBX—Private Branch Exchange. A telephone switch used with telephone calls.

PCAP—Packet Capture. A file that contains packets captured from a protocol analyzer or sniffer.

PDF—Portable Document Format. Type of file for documents. Attackers have embedded malware in PDFs.

PEAP—Protected Extensible Authentication Protocol. PEAP provides an extra layer of protection for EAP and it is sometimes used with 802.1x. PEAP requires a certificate on the 802.1x server. *See also* EAP-TTLS and EAP-TLS.

PED—Personal Electronic Device. Small devices such as cell phones, radios, CD players, DVD players, video cameras, and MP3 players.

PGP—Pretty Good Privacy. Commonly used to secure email communications between two private individuals but is also used in companies. It provides confidentiality, integrity, authentication, and non-repudiation. It can digitally sign and encrypt email. It uses both asymmetric and symmetric encryption.

PII—Personally Identifiable Information. Information about individuals that can be used to trace a person's identity, such as a full name, birth date, biometric data, and identifying numbers such as a Social Security number (SSN). Organizations have an obligation to protect PII and often identify procedures for handling and retaining PII in data policies such as encrypting it.

PIN—Personal identification number. A number known by a user and entered for authentication. PINs are often combined with smart cards to provide dual-factor authentication.

PIV—Personal Identity Verification card. A specialized type of smart card used by U.S. federal agencies. It includes photo identification and provides confidentiality, integrity, authentication, and non-repudiation for the users. It is similar to a CAC.

PKI—Public Key Infrastructure. Group of technologies used to request, create, manage, store, distribute, and revoke digital certificates. Certificates include public keys along with details on the owner of the certificate, and on the CA that issued the certificate. Certificate owners share their public key by sharing a copy of their certificate. A PKI requires a trust model between CAs and most trust models are hierarchical and centralized with a central root CA.

POP3—Post Office Protocol version 3. Used to transfer email from mail servers to clients. POP3 uses TCP port 110.

POTS—Plain old telephone service. Voice-grade telephone service using traditional telephone wires.

PPP—Point-to-Point Protocol. Used to create remote access connections. Used by PAP and CHAP.

PPTP—Point-to-Point Tunneling Protocol. Tunneling protocol used with VPNs. PPTP uses TCP port 1723.

PSK—Preshared key. A secret shared among different systems. Wireless networks support Personal mode, where each device uses the same PSK. In contrast, Enterprise mode uses an 802.1x or RADIUS server for authentication.

PTZ—Pan tilt zoom. Refers to cameras that can pan (move left and right), tilt (move up and down), and zoom to get a closer or a wider view.

RA—Recovery agent. A designated individual who can recover or restore cryptographic keys. In the context of a PKI, a recovery agent can recover private keys to access encrypted data, or in some situations, recover the data without recovering the private key. In some cases, recovery agents can recover the private key from a key escrow.

RADIUS—Remote Authentication Dial-In User Service. Provides central authentication for remote access clients. RADIUS uses symmetric encryption to encrypt the password packets and it uses UDP. In contrast, TACACS+ encrypts the entire authentication process and uses TCP. Diameter is an improvement over RADIUS.

RAID—Redundant array of inexpensive disks. Multiple disks added together to increase performance or provide protection against faults. RAID helps prevent disk subsystems from being a single point of failure.

RAID-0—Disk striping. RAID-0 improves performance, but does not provide fault tolerance.

RAID-1—Disk mirroring. RAID-1 uses two disks and provides fault tolerance.

RAID-5—Disk striping with parity. RAID-5 uses three or more disks and provides fault tolerance. It can survive the failure of a single drive.

RAID-6—Disk striping with parity. RAID-6 uses four or more disks and provides fault tolerance. It can survive the failure of two drives.

RAM—Random access memory. Volatile memory within a computer that holds active processes, data, and applications. Data in RAM is lost when the computer is turned off. Memory forensics analyzes data in RAM.

RAS—Remote Access Service. Provides access to an internal network from an outside source location using dial-up or a VPN.

RAT—Remote access tool. Commonly used by APTs and other attackers. A RAT gives an attacker full control over a user's system from a remote location over the Internet.

RC—Ron's Code or Rivest's Cipher. Symmetric encryption algorithm that includes versions RC2, RC4, RC5, and RC6. RC4 is a stream cipher, and RC5 and RC6 are block ciphers.

RC4—Rivest Cipher 4. A popular stream cipher. RC4 was implemented incorrectly in WEP, causing vulnerabilities. A rare spelling for RC4 is RSA Variable Key Size Encryption Algorithm.

RDP—Remote Desktop Protocol. Used to connect to remote systems. Microsoft uses RDP in different services such as Remote Desktop Services and Remote Assistance. RDP uses either port TCP 3389 or UDP 3389.

RFI—Radio frequency interference. Interference from RF sources such as AM or FM transmitters. RFI can be filtered to prevent data interference, and cables can be shielded to protect signals from RFI.

RFID—Radio-frequency identification. RFID methods are often used for inventory control.

RIPEMD—RACE Integrity Primitives Evaluation Message Digest. A hash function used for integrity. It creates fixed-length hashes of 128, 160, 256, or 320 bits.

ROI—Return of investment or return on investment. A performance measure used to identify when an investment provides a positive benefit to the investor. It is sometimes considered when evaluating the purchase of new security controls.

Role-BAC—Role-based access control. An access control model that uses roles based on jobs and functions to define access and it is often implemented with groups (providing group-based privileges). Often uses a matrix as a planning document to match roles with the required privileges.

RPO—Recovery point objective. The recovery point objective (RPO) refers to the amount of data you can afford to lose by identifying a point in time where data loss is acceptable. It is related to RTO and the BIA often includes both RTOs and RPOs.

RSA—Rivest, Shamir, and Adleman. An asymmetric algorithm used to encrypt data and digitally sign transmissions. It is named after its creators, Rivest, Shamir, and Adleman. RSA uses both a public key and a private key in a matched pair.

RSTP—Rapid Spanning Tree Protocol. An improvement over STP. STP and RSTP protocols are enabled on most switches and protect against switching loops, such as those caused when two ports of a switch are connected together.

RTO—Recovery time objective. An RTO identifies the maximum amount of time it should take to restore a system after an outage. It is derived from the maximum allowable outage time identified in the BIA.

RTP—Real-time Transport Protocol. A standard used for delivering audio and video over an IP network.

Rule-BAC—Rule-based access control. An access control model that uses rules to define access. Rule-based access control is based on a set of approved instructions, such as an access control list, or rules that trigger in response to an event such as modifying ACLs after detecting an attack.

S/MIME—Secure/Multipurpose Internet Mail Extensions. Used to secure email. S/MIME provides confidentiality, integrity, authentication, and non-repudiation. It can digitally sign and encrypt email, including the encryption of email at rest and in transit. It uses RSA, with public and private keys for encryption and decryption, and depends on a PKI for certificates.

SaaS—Software as a Service. A cloud-computing technology that provides applications over the Internet. Web mail is an example of a cloud-based technology. Compare to IaaS and PaaS.

SAML—Security Assertions Markup Language. An XML-based standard used to exchange authentication and authorization information between different parties. SAML provides SSO for web-based applications.

SAN—Storage Area Network. A specialized network of high-speed storage devices.

SCADA—Supervisory control and data acquisition. Typically industrial control systems within large facilities such as power plants or water treatment facilities. SCADA systems are often contained within isolated networks that do not have access to the Internet, but are still protected with redundant and diverse security controls. SCADA systems can be protected with NIPS systems and VLANs.

SCAP—Security Content Automation Protocol. A set of security specifications for various applications and operating systems. Compliance tools such as vulnerability scanners use these to check systems for compliance.

SCEP—Simple Certificate Enrollment Protocol. A method of requesting a certificate from a CA.

SCP—Secure Copy. Based on SSH, SCP allows users to copy encrypted files over a network. SCP uses TCP port 22.

SCSI—Small Computer System Interface. Set of standards used to connect peripherals to computers. Commonly used for SCSI hard disks and/or tape drives.

SDLC—Software Development Life Cycle. A software development process. Many different models are available.

SDLM—Software Development Life Cycle Methodology. The practice of using a SDLC when developing applications.

SEH—Structured Exception Handler. Module within an application that handles errors or exceptions. It prevents applications from crashing or responding to events that can be exploited by attackers.

SELinux—Security-Enhanced Linux. An operating system platform that prevents malicious or suspicious code from executing on both Linux and Unix systems. It is one of the few operating systems that use the MAC model.

SFTP—Secure File Transfer Protocol. An extension of Secure Shell (SSH) using SSH to transmit the files in an encrypted format. SFTP transmits data using TCP port 22.

SHA—Secure Hash Algorithm. A hashing function used to provide integrity. SHA-1 uses 160 bits, and SHA-256 uses 256 bits. As with other hashing algorithms, SHA verifies integrity.

SHTTP—Secure Hypertext Transfer Protocol. An alternative to HTTPS. Rarely used.

SID—Security identifier. Unique set of numbers and letters used to identify each user and each group in Microsoft environments.

SIEM—Security Information and Event Management. A security system that attempts to look at security events throughout the organization.

SIM—Subscriber Identity Module. A small smart card that contains programming and information for small devices such as cell phones.

SIRT—Security Incident Response Team. A group of experts who respond to security incidents. Also known as CERT, CIRT, or IRT.

SLA—Service level agreement. An agreement between a company and a vendor that stipulates performance expectations, such as minimum uptime and maximum downtime levels. Organizations use SLAs when contracting services from service providers such as Internet Service Providers (ISPs).

SLE—Single loss expectancy. The SLE identifies the amount of each loss and is used to measure risk with ALE and ARO in a quantitative risk assessment. The calculation is SLE × ARO = ALE.

SMTP—Simple Mail Transfer Protocol. Used to transfer email between clients and servers and between email servers and other email servers. SMTP uses TCP port 25.

SNMP—Simple Network Management Protocol. Used to manage and monitor network devices such as routers or switches. SNMP agents report information via notifications known as SNMP traps, or SNMP device traps. SNMP uses UDP ports 161 and 162.

SONET—Synchronous Optical Network Technologies. A multiplexing protocol used to transfer data over fiber-optic cable.

SPIM—Spam over Internet Messaging. A form of spam using instant messaging that targets instant messaging users.

SPOF—Single point of failure. An SPOF is any component whose failure results in the failure of an entire system. Elements such as RAID, failover clustering, UPS, and generators remove many single points of failure.

SQL—Structured Query Language. Used by SQL-based databases, such as Microsoft SQL Server. Web sites integrated with a SQL database are subject to SQL injection attacks. Input validation with forms and stored procedures help prevent SQL injection attacks. Microsoft SQL Server uses TCP port 1433 by default.

SSD—Solid State Drive. A drive used in place of a traditional hard drive. An SSD has no moving parts, but instead stores the contents as nonvolatile memory. SSDs are much quicker than traditional drives.

SSH—Secure Shell. SSH encrypts a wide variety of traffic such as SCP, SFTP, Telnet, and TCP Wrappers. SSH uses TCP port 22. SSH is a more secure alternative than Telnet.

SSID—Service set identifier. Identifies the name of a wireless network. Disabling SSID broadcast can hide the network from casual users, but an attacker can easily discover it with a wireless sniffer. It's recommended to change the SSID from the default name.

SSL—Secure Sockets Layer. Used to encrypt data in transit with the use of certificates. SSL is used with HTTPS to encrypt HTTP traffic and can also encrypt SMTP and LDAP traffic.

SSO—Single sign-on. Authentication method where users can access multiple resources on a network using a single account. SSO can provide central authentication against a federated database for different operating systems.

SSTP—Secure Socket Tunneling Protocol. A tunneling protocol that encrypts VPN traffic using SSL over TCP port 443.

STP—Shielded twisted-pair. Cable type used in networks that includes shielding to prevent interference from EMI and RFI. It can also prevent data from emanating outside the cable.

STP—Spanning Tree Protocol. Protocol enabled on most switches that protects against switching loops. A switching loop can be caused if two ports of a switch are connected together.

SYN—Synchronize. The first packet in a TCP handshake. In a SYN flood attack, attackers send this packet, but don't complete the handshake after receiving the SYN/ACK packet. A flood guard is a logical control that protects against SYN flood attacks.

TACACS+—Terminal Access Controller Access-Control System+. Provides central authentication for remote access clients and used as an alternative to RADIUS. TACACS+ uses TCP port 49. It encrypts the entire authentication process, compared with RADIUS, which only encrypts the password. It uses multiple challenges and responses.

TCO—Total cost of ownership. A factor considered when purchasing new products and services. TCO attempts to identify the cost of a product or service over its lifetime.

TCP—Transmission Control Protocol. Provides guaranteed delivery of IP traffic using a three-way handshake.

TCP/IP—Transmission Control Protocol/Internet Protocol. Represents the full suite of protocols used on the Internet and most internal networks.

TFTP—Trivial File Transfer Protocol. Used to transfer small amounts of data with UDP port 69. In contrast, FTP is used to transfer larger files using TCP ports 20 and 21.

TGT—Ticket granting ticket. Used with Kerberos. A KDC (or TGT server) issues timestamped tickets that expire after a certain time period.

TKIP—Temporal Key Integrity Protocol. Wireless security protocol introduced to address the problems with WEP. TKIP was used with WPA but has been deprecated. WPA2 with CCMP is recommended instead.

TLS—Transport Layer Security. Used to encrypt data in transit. TLS is the replacement for SSL and like SSL, it uses certificates issued by CAs. PEAP-

TLS uses TLS to encrypt the authentication process and PEAP-TLS requires a CA to issue certificates.

TOTP—Time-based One-Time Password. Similar to HOTP, but it uses a timestamp instead of a counter. One-time passwords created with TOTP expire after 30 seconds.

TPM—Trusted Platform Module. A hardware chip on the motherboard included on many newer laptops. A TPM includes a unique RSA asymmetric key, and when first used, creates a storage root key. TPMs generate and store other keys used for encryption, decryption, and authentication. TPM provides full disk encryption.

TSIG—Transaction Signature. A method of securely providing updates to DNS with the use of authentication.

UAT—User Acceptance Testing. One of the last phases of testing an application before its release.

UDP—User Datagram Protocol. Used instead of TCP when guaranteed delivery of each packet is not necessary. UDP uses a best-effort delivery mechanism.

UEFI—Unified Extensible Firmware Interface. A method used to boot some systems and intended to replace Basic Input/Output System (BIOS) firmware.

UPS—Uninterruptible power supply. A battery backup system that provides fault tolerance for power and can protect against power fluctuations. A UPS provides short-term power giving the system enough time to shut down smoothly, or to transfer to generator power. Generators provide long-term power in extended outages.

URI—Uniform Resource Identifier. Used to identify the name of a resource and always includes the protocol such as *http://GetCertifiedGetAhead.com*.

URL—Uniform Resource Locator. A type of URI. Address used to access web resources, such as *http://GetCertifiedGetAhead.com*. Pop-up blockers can include URLs of sites where pop-ups are allowed.

USB—Universal Serial Bus. A serial connection used to connect peripherals such as printers, flash drives, and external hard disk drives. Data on USB drives can be protected against loss of confidentiality with encryption. Attackers have spread malware through Trojans.

UTM—Unified threat management. A security appliance that combined multiple security controls into a single solution. UTM appliances can inspect data streams for malicious content and often include URL filtering, malware inspection, and content inspection components.

UTP—Unshielded twisted-pair. Cable type used in networks that do not have any concerns over EMI, RFI, or cross talk. If these are a concern, STP is used.

VDI—Virtualization Desktop Infrastructure. Virtualization software designed to reproduce a desktop operating system as a virtual machine on a remote server.

VLAN—Virtual local area network. A VLAN separates or segments traffic. A VLAN can logically group several different computers together, or logically separate computers, without regard to their physical location. It is possible to create multiple VLANs with a single switch. You can also create VLANs with virtual switches.

VM—Virtual machine. A virtual system hosted on a physical system. A physical server can host multiple VMs as servers. Virtualization helps reduce the amount of physical equipment required, reducing overall physical security requirements such as HVAC and power.

VoIP—Voice over IP. A group of technologies used to transmit voice over IP networks. Vishing is a form of phishing that sometimes uses VoIP.

VPN—Virtual private network. Provides access to a private network over a public network such as the Internet. VPN concentrators provide VPN access to large groups of users.

VSAN—Virtual Storage Area Network. A lower-cost alternative to traditional SANs.

VTC—Video teleconferencing. A group of interactive telecommunication technologies that allow people in two or more locations to interact with two-way video and audio transmissions.

WAF—Web application firewall. A firewall specifically designed to protect a web application, such as a web server. A WAF inspects the contents of traffic to a web server, can detect malicious content such as code used in a cross-scripting attack, and block it.

WAP—Wireless access point, sometimes called an access point (AP). Provides wireless clients connectivity to a wired network. Most WAPs use an omnidirectional antenna. You can connect two WLANs together using high-gain directional Yagi antennas. Increasing the power level of a WAP increases the wireless coverage of the WAP. Decreasing the power levels decreases the coverage.

WEP—Wired Equivalent Privacy. Original wireless security protocol. Had significant security flaws and was replaced with WPA, and ultimately WPA2. WEP used RC4 incorrectly making it susceptible to IV attacks, especially when the attacker used packet injection techniques.

WIDS—Wireless intrusion detection system. An IDS used for wireless networks.

WIPS—Wireless intrusion prevention system. An IPS used for wireless networks.

WLAN—Wireless local area network. Network connected wirelessly.

WPA—Wi-Fi Protected Access. Replaced WEP as a wireless security protocol without replacing hardware. Originally used TKIP with RC4 and later implementations support AES. Superseded by WPA2. In WPA cracking attacks, attackers capture the four-way authentication handshake and then use a brute force attack to discover the passphrase.

WPA2—Wi-Fi Protected Access II. Security protocol used to protect wireless transmissions. It supports CCMP for encryption, which is based on AES and is stronger than TKIP, which was originally released with WPA. It uses an 802.1x server for authentication in WPA2 Enterprise mode and a preshared key for WPA2 Personal mode, also called WPA2-PSK.

WPS—Wi-Fi Protected Setup. Allowed users to easily configure a wireless network, often by using only a PIN. WPS brute force attacks can discover the PIN.

WTLS—Wireless Transport Layer Security. Used to encrypt traffic for smaller wireless devices.

XML—Extensible Markup Language. Used by many databases for inputting or exporting data. XML uses formatting rules to describe the data.

XSRF—Cross-site request forgery. Attackers use XSRF attacks to trick users into performing actions on web sites, such as making purchases, without their knowledge. In some cases, it allows an attacker to steal cookies and harvest passwords.

XSS—Cross-site scripting. Attackers use XSS to capture user information such as cookies. Input validation techniques on the server-side help prevent XSS attacks by blocking HTML and JavaScript tags. Many sites prevent the use of < and > characters to block cross-site scripting.

XTACACS—Extended Terminal Access Controller Access-Control System. An improvement over TACACS developed by Cisco Systems and proprietary to Cisco systems. TACACS+ is used more commonly.

√ **Get Certified**

√ **Get Ahead**

Made in the USA
San Bernardino, CA
07 March 2016